Praise for *The Finish*

"Where the book shines is in Bowden's reconstruction and refined analysis of the intelligence operations that turned up bin Laden's location. . . . The book also succeeds in its artful portrait of Obama as commander in chief. . . . Compelling drama, and Bowden has captured it with skill and style."   —*The Seattle Times*

"*The Finish* leverages access to key White House, military, intelligence, and foreign-policy officials—including President Obama himself—to get behind the intricate story of how SEAL Team Six was sent to Abbottabad, Pakistan, to kill Osama bin Laden. . . . Bowden reviews the evolutionary progress made in intelligence processing and military capabilities that led to the raid on Abbottabad. . . . close to a textbook example of complex national security decision-making."—*The Atlantic*

"The death of the man responsible for the 9/11 attacks is a fantastic story. It has goodies and baddies, a long, slow build to the climax, exotic locations and lots of hardware. . . . Bowden [shows] how success in the raid last May was the culmination not just of a decade of often tedious data-crunching by the CIA and other analysts, but of a vast and ongoing effort within the American security establishment and government to develop a new range of capabilities. . . . How the Americans finally got their man is an extraordinary tale and Bowden does it justice."
—*The Guardian*

"[A] dramatic narrative . . . the actual champion of the bin Laden hunt is a collective of mostly nameless hands within the intelligence bureaucracy. . . . *The Finish* is at its best when Mr. Bowden goes deep into mission planning, gameboarding the choice of means of attack—air strike? sniper drone? ground-force raid?"   —*The Wall Street Journal*

"Bowden's new book outlines the changes in warfare since the Sept. 11, 2011, terrorist attacks, and the way our increasing computational power has helped capture terrorists like Osama bin Laden."   —NPR

"*The Finish* seems ripe for cinematic adaptation."

—*The New York Observer*

"Bowden would seem like the perfect person to tell the bin Laden story. . . . There is an excellent setting-the-record-straight section at the end that has been missing in other volumes." —*The Washington Post*

"A superb storyteller, Bowden captures the tense drama accompanying the final months of the bin Laden hunt, even as he underscores the quiet, essential work of years." —*Kirkus Reviews* (starred review)

"A page-turner . . . an informative, on-the-ground account of the mission. Adept at maintaining suspense even when the outcome is widely known, Bowden also makes judicious assessments of how much credit Obama deserves—and the impact of the assassination on al Qaeda."

—*StarTribune* (Minneapolis)

"Bowden tells the story of the CIA's two-decade hunt for bin Laden . . . with a veteran journalist's ability to organize loads of factual information into a propulsive narrative. *The Finish* is a masterful piece of long-form journalism and, for the military buffs ... a refreshingly mature rejoinder to the dumb, jingoistic Navy SEAL fever that's been ebbing and flowing since bin Laden's violent death. . . . If you were one of the many who picked up a newspaper on May 1, 2011, to find out we'd finally, and somewhat unbelievably, taken down our main target, and if you felt a subsequent surge of national pride that day, then *The Finish* will pretty much be the book for you." —*Spectrum Culture*

"To chart the tale of the hunt for the world's most notorious terrorist, Bowden assembled an extensive history of the modern warfare and intelligence tactics that led to the raid, execution and deep-sea burial."

—*Philadelphia Weekly*

"In *The Finish*, Mark Bowden does a good job of piecing together this Washington drama. . . . The strength of Bowden's book, though, is that he got Obama to talk, which adds rich detail."

—*The Sunday Times* (UK)

"Bowden . . . offers new insights from the first-person perspective of the officer who commanded [the raid] on the ground."

—*The Daily Telegraph*

"Bowden, a journalist and author of the 1999 prize winner *Black Hawk Down*, benefited from exclusive access to President Barack Obama to tell this story . . . it is interesting to learn about the president's deliberations that led to his decision to go ahead with the raid."

—*Winnipeg Free Press*

"Bowden . . . reveals the details of the planning, but knows when to pull back from a close focus to give the wider view of what was at stake for President Obama, military planners and the Navy SEALS team. . . . [His] experience as a reporter and author shows."

—*The Fayetteville Observer*

"Bowden's book draws back to look at the raid in strategic context. I suspect that readers who choose Bowden's wide-angle approach will find themselves better informed."

—*St. Louis Today*

"Mr. Bowden . . . uses his hard-earned access to focus on the decade of intelligence-gathering and decision-making that led up to the Abbottabad raid."

—*National Post* (Canada)

"*The Finish* paints the U.S. government's relationship to technology and social media as integral in the capture of bin Laden. . . . Many see Bowden as one of the most respected writers covering the U.S. military and Special Forces today."

—*Books & Review*

The Finish

Also by Mark Bowden

Doctor Dealer

Bringing the Heat

Black Hawk Down

Killing Pablo

Finders Keepers

Road Work

Guests of the Ayatollah

The Best Game Ever

Worm

The Finish

The Killing of
Osama bin Laden

Mark Bowden

Grove Press
New York

Published simultaneously in Canada
Printed in the United States of America

ISBN-13: 978-0-8021-2152-3
eBook ISBN: 978-0-8021-9410-7

Grove Press
an imprint of Grove/Atlantic, Inc.
841 Broadway
New York, NY 10003

Distributed by Publishers Group West

www.groveatlantic.com

13 14 15 16   10 9 8 7 6 5 4 3 2 1

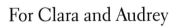

For Clara and Audrey

Human groupings have one main purpose: to assert everyone's right to be different, to be special, to think, to feel and live in his or her own way. People join together in order to win or defend this right. But this is where a terrible, fateful error is born: the belief that these groupings in the name of a race, a God, a party, or a state are the very purpose of life and not simply a means to an end. No! The only true and lasting meaning of the struggle for life lies in the individual, in his modest peculiarities and in his right to these peculiarities.

—Vasily Grossman, *Life and Fate*

The properties of a movement are spontaneity, impulsiveness, dynamic expansiveness—and a short life. The properties of a structure are inertia, resilience, and an amazing, almost instinctive, ability to survive.

—Ryszard Kapuściński, *Shah of Shahs*

Contents

Prologue

2007–2008

One fall night in western Iraq, as a unit from the U.S. Joint Special Operations Command (JSOC) was executing one of its nightly raids on suspected al Qaeda terrorists, this one a suspected regional commander who called himself "Muthanna," the raiders inadvertently discovered the mother lode.

In another war in a different time, the "mother lode" might have been a huge cache of valuable weapons or a collection of battlefield maps showing enemy troop movements and positions. In the twenty-first century, the raiders of JSOC had discovered something of equivalent value: a Rolodex.

Muthanna was killed in the raid. It was clear from material seized at his residence that he was responsible for coordinating the movement of foreign al Qaeda fighters and potential suicide bombers across the nearby border with Syria and into Iraq, where American and Iraqi forces, and Iraqi civilians, were enduring a mounting campaign of mass slaughter. What they found was not an actual Rolodex; it was something better: a collection of names and numbers that referenced computer files containing names, photos, travel documents, expense reports for phone cards, clothing, vehicles, fuel, money transfers, and many other detailed documents for about five hundred current al Qaeda recruits—just about every *mujahidin* who had made the trek in recent years through Syria and into Iraq.

For centuries, the basic tactics of infantry warfare were "fire and maneuver." A skilled officer could defeat a larger force by mastering the art of moving his men and effectively focusing their firepower. Those kinds of skills are still essential on a conventional battlefield, but the battles being fought today rarely boil down to armies maneuvering on the ground. "Information and intelligence is the fire and maneuver of the twenty-first century," says Lt. Gen. Michael Flynn, who now heads the U.S. Defense Intelligence Agency.

What does he mean?

The mother lode of documents seized in what became known as the Sinjar raid illustrates the point nicely. It played a big part in decapitating al Qaeda in Iraq. In the six years after the 9/11 attacks, the U.S. military and intelligence communities, representing a wide variety of agencies large and small, those notorious and those secret, had been collaborating on an unprecedented capability for crushing furtive terrorist networks. In addition to the skills of JSOC's talented special operators, the effort used supercomputers and custom software, the forward deployment of skilled analysts, and the ability to turn just about every kind of intel into searchable data, whether tips or documents from old-fashioned human spy networks, transcripts of detainee interrogations, logs of electronic surveillance monitoring communications between cell phones and computers, or the images and sensory readings gathered by drones hovering high and silent over potential targets for days, weeks, months, and even years. With an enormous database consisting of these fragments, few of them clearly related, computers are capable of finding links that would previously remain hidden—a bank account shared by a Hezbollah official and an al Qaeda recruit, a street address in Najaf visited by two known suicide bombers on two separate occasions, a snapshot from the wallet of a slain American soldier on the hard drive of a suspected terrorist paymaster. The computer instantly draws bloody threads between data points that would otherwise remain random and disconnected. Webs are drawn from these bloody threads, illuminating secret networks. Once such connections are made, the special operators know where and whom to hit next.

In the case of the Sinjar haul, JSOC Commander Stanley McChrystal took the surprising step of declassifying all of the material and turning it over to West Point's Combating Terrorism Center, so that analysts from a variety of disciplines could take a crack at it. And what did they uncover? For one thing, the data exploded the propaganda claim that al Qaeda in Iraq was a homegrown resistance movement. The recruits in the Sinjar data came from Libya, Morocco, Syria, Algeria, Oman, Yemen, Tunisia, Egypt, Jordan, Saudi Arabia, Belgium, France, and the UK. American Treasury agents mapping the data's financial transactions were able to identify the entire Syrian-based leadership of al Qaeda in Iraq's foreign-support network, all of it under the direction of a man who called himself Abu Ghadiya. His real name was Badran Turki Hashim al-Mazidih.

Just over one year after the Sinjar raid, the entire senior leadership of this Syrian-based support network for al Qaeda had been destroyed. A single October 2008 raid inside Syria killed Abu Ghadiya, one of his brothers, and two cousins, all members of the top leadership. The database would also provide a road map for JSOC operations throughout Iraq, tracking down and capturing or killing those foreign recruits who had not already sacrificed themselves in suicide attacks.

By the end of 2008, the overall level of violence in Iraq had declined by 80 percent, according to the U.S. Department of Defense. This sharp trend has continued through the withdrawal of U.S. forces from that country in 2011, and remains lower today than at any time since before the American invasion in 2003.

There are multiple reasons for this striking turnabout. The Sunni Awakening in 2008 turned many Iraqi insurgents against al Qaeda — abetted at least to some extent by the Sinjar data analysis, reported in the summer of 2008, which revealed the foreign-born nature of the organization. The dramatic shift in strategy orchestrated by Gen. David Petraeus toward counterinsurgency tactics during the same period deserves much of the credit. But a large part of Petraeus's own approach included ramping up the pressure on "irreconcilable" elements. As he put it, "I like to go to bed every night with more friends and with fewer enemies."

JSOC provided the "fewer enemies," and McChrystal has cited the Sinjar raid as one of his unit's most important breakthroughs.

Prevailing in war often demands new tactics, methods, and tools. The attacks on America on September 11, 2001, challenged a long-standing premise of its national defense. Osama bin Laden and his extremist movement, al Qaeda, posed a new kind of threat, a global network of well-funded, clever, suicidal killers with no fixed address. The nation's vast arsenal, its nuclear stockpiles, its incomparable air force, its army and navy, even its bureaucratic structure for global surveillance, spying, and intel analysis, was designed primarily to *deter* attack. Who would dare when the response would be swift, fatal, and unstoppable?

But what if attacks came from nowhere? What then?

This was the problem posed by 9/11. The answer was information. Finding the enemy has long been one of the most basic challenges of war. All al Qaeda did was up the level of difficulty. They lived and worked scattered all over the world, using global telecommunications to stay linked. Given the complexity and international nature of those links, the use of pseudonyms and all the tricks of spy craft, how was this new enemy ever to be found?

The seizure of the Sinjar Rolodex and the subsequent takedown shows how. Six years after the 9/11 attacks, deep into two wars, still haunted by the defiant image of a free Osama bin Laden, the United States of America had one strong consolation.

It had figured out exactly how to fight back.

The Finish

1

A Definition of Evil

September 11, 2001

Just before eight o'clock on a brilliant sunny Chicago morning, Barack Obama was driving up Lake Shore Drive when the music on his radio was interrupted by a news bulletin. A plane had crashed into one of the World Trade Center towers in New York City. He thought little of it. He assumed it meant some poor Cessna pilot had screwed up badly.

The Loop was a familiar fifteen-minute commute from Illinois State Senator Obama's house in Hyde Park. To his right stretched the flat expanse of Lake Michigan and ahead, on his left, was the soaring skyline, anchored by the black monolith of the Sears Tower, spiked with antennae. Surrounded by so much lake and Illinois sky, the drive can feel like free falling into a world of blue.

Obama was bound for the Thompson Center, the city's seventeen-story government building, a monumental shiny structure of curved reflective glass that looks like a grounded spaceship.

The setting was remarkable but the business he had there was strictly routine, a hearing of the Joint Committee on Administrative Rules. Today's agenda promised hours of bureaucratic minutiae—rules changes for thirty-nine separate boards, programs, commissions, and departments.

Obama represented District 13 at the northern edge of the South Side. He had two other jobs, one practicing law for a prominent Chicago firm and another as a senior lecturer in constitutional law at Chicago University's Law School. He was a moderately prominent man in his adoptive city, seen locally as a young man of great promise, but for all that his career seemed stalled. He had been soundly beaten in a run for Congress two years earlier—a rebuke, really. He had lost by a margin of two-to-one. His intellect was obvious, maybe too obvious, given his Harvard Law degree and his tenure as the first African-American president of that school's prestigious *Law Review*. Ivy credentials play well in big city politics only when they come with a smothering dose of *street*, which Obama did not have. He looked and sounded like a law professor. What he *did* have was "cool," a word people applied to him in both a good and a bad way. He was cool in that he had style and *presence*; he was tall and lean, poised and charming. But he was cool in the other way, too. He often seemed distant, aloof, even superior. He had turned forty a month before, too old to be considered a prodigy. His black Jeep Cherokee was the car of a family man. He and his wife, Michelle, had two daughters: infant Sasha, and Malia, who was three.

He parked, ascended in one of the exposed shafts inside the center's vast atrium, and was in his chair listening to a witness read a prepared statement when digital phones began chirping and dinging from every corner of the room. Obama looked down to see messages stacking up on his BlackBerry. Murmuring quickly overtook the testimony. The witness plowed on but soon no one was paying attention to him. The news from lower Manhattan flowed in from a thousand points at once. The second tower had been hit. Both planes were commercial airliners. The towers were on fire. This was no accident. This was a coordinated attack.

At that point the Thompson Center was evacuated and Obama left with everyone else. On the sidewalk outside with the thousands of other Chicagoans evacuated from tall buildings in the Loop, his eyes moved involuntarily up to the Sears Tower. Suddenly the city's landmark skyscraper appeared in a different light. It was no longer just a symbol of the lakeside city's identity. It loomed now like a giant target.

In Sarasota, Michael Morell wondered if a plane was bearing down on *him*. He was President George W. Bush's CIA briefer and was part of the president's entourage that morning. The visit was big news in the west Florida city. Anyone targeting Bush would know right where to find him, and a commercial airliner would do the job nicely.

Morell had been in the backseat of a van in the president's motorcade when the first plane hit. They were racing down Gulf of Mexico Drive on Longboat Key when Ari Fleischer, Bush's press secretary, took a call and then turned to him.

"Michael, do you know anything about a plane hitting the World Trade Center?"

As the in-house intelligence officer, Morell was the man they looked to for the scoop when something startling happened. The plane had hit while they were en route, so he had heard nothing. He was thinking it was probably a small plane that had gotten disoriented in bad weather, something like that, but he called headquarters in Langley, Virginia. The CIA operations center told him that a crash had occurred, the building was the North Tower, and that it wasn't a small plane but a commercial jet.

The veteran CIA analyst had been up before dawn that day, as he usually was, and had spent some time alone in his hotel room prepping for his regular morning session with the president. Each day at eight o'clock, Morell delivered the President's Daily Briefing (PDB), a summary of the most current intelligence reports from around the world. He had flown south on Air Force One the previous afternoon, the start of a weeklong cross-country trip to promote Bush's education initiatives. They had stopped first in Jacksonville, for a round-table discussion, and then driven down to Sarasota, where they had spent the night at the Colony Beach and Tennis Resort, on the barrier island that parallels the city shoreline.

Morell's presence had nothing to do with the week's education theme. Like the military officer who carried the president's "football"—the coding device needed to authorize a nuclear attack—the CIA briefer went wherever Bush went. America had not been directly attacked in any significant way since Pearl Harbor, so the morning briefing usually concerned things more abstract: "national security concerns" was more like it. There were always terror threats, but there had been nothing in the brief that morning about anything specific or imminent.

Bush was not given to poring over written reports. He preferred for Morell to "tee up" highlights in the morning briefing, and would then read the most pertinent parts and ask questions. For Morell this made the morning half hour something of a daily command performance. The president enjoyed it. He would later call it "one of the most fascinating parts of my day." It was a heady role, albeit a virtually invisible one. Morell is a slight, precise man with glasses and neatly combed sandy brown hair, a man who seems ordinary by design. His suit is often rumpled and he moves in a distinctly civilian, loose-limbed slouch; he is the kind of man who tends to fold up on a chair, all knees and elbows. That and his indoor pallor made him look almost frail alongside the president's robust security detail and phalanx of ruddy military advisers. In conversation, Morell was intense. He spoke with a crisp Ohio accent, and bore down on ideas bodily, frowning, chin first. For most of his career at the spy agency he had been an Asian specialist.

By the time the president saw him that morning, Bush had already taken a few minutes to read from his Bible, had jogged in the darkness around the Colony golf course, and had dressed and eaten his breakfast. That day's briefing had mostly concerned China. The briefing is still classified, but months earlier a U.S. Navy EP-3, a propeller-driven intelligence-gathering aircraft, had collided with a Chinese jet fighter off the island of Hainan, killing the fighter pilot and triggering a small international crisis, the first of the Bush presidency. Morell also had fresh intel from Russia, again still classified, but fallout there from the then recent Robert Hanssen spy scandal had prompted both countries to expel some of each other's diplomats. Morell then presented new information about the ongoing Palestinian uprising, an increasingly violent affair at the center of the world's news. One item on the agenda prompted the president to call his national security adviser, Condoleezza Rice, who had stayed behind at the White House, but in later years no one would remember what the call was about. In light of what was coming—all four of the doomed commercial airliners were already in the air— the items on that day's agenda would soon seem small.

When the briefing was done, Bush left for his scheduled visit to Emma E. Booker Elementary School, where at nine a.m. he was supposed to visit a second grade classroom before an array of television cameras and reporters. They were at the school when news of the second plane came. Morell was waiting with the rest of the president's staff in a classroom next door. It had a TV set, which was soon showing video of the crash into the South Tower. Both towers were now aflame.

Andrew Card, Bush's chief of staff, went next door to whisper the news to the president, who was seated in a chair before the classroom, listening to the students read a book about a pet goat.

"A second plane hit the second tower," said Card. "America is under attack."

Cameras caught the stunned look on the president's face. Some would later ridicule him for it, but what is the correct facial expression for news like that? Bush resolved to stay calm. He remained before the class until the story was finished, but his demeanor had dramatically changed. He had been cheerful, enjoying the children's performance. Now he was grim, his mind clearly elsewhere. When the story was done he complimented the class and then walked briskly into the adjacent classroom. On the TV was video of United Airlines Flight 175 plowing straight into the South Tower in slow motion and erupting into a fireball. Fleischer consulted with the president, who hastily scribbled remarks in longhand before walking back into the crowded classroom to face the cameras and reporters again.

"Ladies and gentlemen, this is a difficult moment for America," he began.

Planes were falling from the sky, suicide hijackers guiding them into the nation's iconic public buildings, incinerating themselves and the planes' passengers and killing thousands. And no one knew how many airplanes there were.

Morell thought they ought to move Bush immediately. He started toward a Secret Service agent, but saw that the protection detail was ahead of him. They pointed him out of the building toward the motorcade. When the president's short statement was finished they were off at once to the airport.

Bad news kept on coming. A third plane, American Airlines Flight 77, hit the Pentagon while they were still speeding north on Route 41. Suddenly every tall building, every monument, every American landmark seemed in jeopardy. Where would the next one hit? There was nothing fanciful about the breadth of alarm in those first hours. But along with the fear, the attacks provoked something primal and self-protective. Just seventy-one minutes after the North Tower was hit, hundreds of miles west of New York City and high over Pennsylvania, the passengers aboard United Airlines Flight 93 hastily organized and attacked the men who had hijacked their plane. It crashed in a field just east of Pittsburgh, in Shanksville, Pennsylvania.

The reaction was sudden and national. The military scrambled fighters and secured its bases. Airports were closed, streets blocked, buildings vacated.

In Chicago, when Obama realized that no one was going back into the Thompson Center anytime soon he walked to his car and made the short drive to his law office. The firm of Davis, Miner, Barnhill, and Galland was housed in a brick town house. They had a small conference room in the basement with a TV where the office staff gathered to watch the unfolding tragedy. Along with millions around the world, they saw men and women stranded on the upper floors of the Twin Towers, still alive, crowding at windowsills with flames behind them, waving desperately for help that could not reach them, trying to figure out what to do, some of them jumping to their deaths.

Obama watched with the others as the towers fell, imagining the thousands trapped inside. They saw the smoke and flames rising from a demolished wall of the Pentagon.

In San Diego, Bill McRaven watched from a hospital bed in his home, where it was still very early in the morning. Even flat on his back, the Navy SEAL captain had a distinct military bearing. His tall body was lean and muscular. His buzz cut drew defiant attention to his jug ears, and the upper and lower halves of his face were slightly askew, which set his long jaw at a slight jutting angle that asserted resolve. Lately, Captain McRaven hadn't been doing much of anything beyond easing himself from hospital bed to wheelchair and back again. It was a humbling debility for someone so physical. He had been a track star at his high school in San Antonio, Texas, and had then joined the military. Like anyone in an elite special ops unit, he had spent his life pushing himself mentally and physically . . . which catches up to most people. Two months earlier he'd had a terrifying parachute accident, free-falling 10,000 feet before colliding with the opened chute of another jumper. Violently spinning and only half-conscious, he had managed to pull his rip cord, saving his life, but with one leg tangled in the chute's cords and the other in its risers, the force of the opening chute had nearly torn him in two, cracking his pelvis, breaking his back, and tearing away muscle from his stomach wall. There weren't going to be any daring missions in his near future, and even if he managed to rehab out of the chair he would always be held together by plates and pins.

He'd escaped the hospital by having his bed moved to his home, so that's where he watched the attacks unfold that morning.

He wasn't bitter. McRaven accepted the rough sorting of his profession. He figured that if he'd actually been good enough to free-fall with a SEAL team into combat, he would never have had the accident. He had been dealt out. He wasn't concerned about losing the chance to advance in rank. If he had been ambitious for rank, he would never have joined a SEAL team. It was the same in the army; special ops were a path to small-team action, not command, which traditionally involved assuming responsibility for more and more men. The regular force saw the "irregulars," the special ops teams, as . . . well, irregular. You went that direction to jump out of airplanes and blow things up and maybe get to test yourself on a real mission even when the nation wasn't officially at war. He was forty-five years old and had served most recently as commodore of the Naval Special Warfare Group in Coronado, which he figured was the best job he would ever have. What he was going to miss was the action.

McRaven had fought in the Persian Gulf War, and had trained for daring missions his entire adult life. There was no way to know exactly how the United States would respond to these attacks, but it was clear that the country was at war and the war was going to pass him by.

Whoever did this, it was not likely to be a nation-state. It was probably a small group of dedicated fanatics working out of a variety of places that were hard to find and hard to reach. War always poses new challenges. A nation, stirred to action by a novel threat, has to feel its way in, has to invent the strategy and tactics that will prevail. It would take time—in this case most of a decade—but McRaven was uniquely positioned to see where it would end. He had made a study of Special Operations. He was already convinced—the first inklings were beginning to appear on

TV—that this had been the work of a small terrorist group that called itself al Qaeda. Men like McRaven had heard a lot more about al Qaeda than most of the country. If not that group, then one like it. How would you fight a stealthy, stateless organization that plotted sneak attacks? You fought it with intelligence and with highly trained special units like his SEALs, men who could strike with speed and precision anywhere in the world. He could see it clearly. His squadron would be going to war without him.

But better than most, he also knew this war was going to take time. With time he would heal. With time there might just be a way for him to work himself back into it.

In Washington, Michèle Flournoy saw the smoke rising from the Pentagon across the Potomac River. She had a lot of friends who worked there.

A Harvard- and Oxford-educated scholar, she was, at forty, an influential thinker in defense circles, and one of the few women in Washington who had made national security her career. Everyone who knew her knew that it was only a matter of time before she would assume another top-level position at the Pentagon, but for now, as with many who owed their government jobs to the ascendance of one political party or the other, her background as a senior Pentagon planner during the Clinton administration meant that she was one of many policy experts who were effectively in exile during the first White House term of a Republican administration.

Flournoy was known for advocating an internationalist approach to national defense, one based more on partnerships and pragmatism than ideology. President Bush had filled many of the defense-related posts in his administration with those more inclined to use American military power unilaterally, to seek international partners but not to be bound by them. With the nation at peace, these philosophical differences were primarily of interest to subject matter experts and played out in forums related to military planning and development. Earlier that morning Flournoy had been interviewed on National Public Radio about some of the initiatives planned by Defense Secretary Donald Rumsfeld. She was working for the Center for Strategic and International Studies (CSIS), a bipartisan think tank, and was a professor at the National Defense University, helping the Pentagon prepare its Quadrennial Defense Review, a broad strategic plan for the massive department that afforded the most practical outline for national defense priorities. When the planes started to hit, she was attending a defense forecasts international briefing in a building across the street from the White House.

All of the buildings in the vicinity were evacuated. As she stood on Pennsylvania Avenue eyeing the ominous smoke column from across the river, she knew whatever they had been discussing at that briefing was suddenly moot, as if someone had taken an eraser to the whole board. America's defense priorities were being radically and violently reset.

She walked a few blocks to the CSIS's offices, called home to check on her children, and then began trying to get through to friends at the Pentagon on the phone, without success. So she took some calls from colleagues and from reporters, including the reporter from NPR she had just spoken with hours earlier. She shared the growing suspicion that the attacks were the work of al Qaeda, but at that point it was just a hypothesis.

*　　*　　*

11

Another Democrat in exile, Thomas Donilon, was also in downtown D.C., undergoing his annual physical in a suite on M Street. He was forty-six, an age when years of long hours sitting behind a desk begin to take their toll, especially for a big man like him. A lawyer with a long background in government, he was known for doing the work of three and had the slackening frame to show for it. In a world capital of the work-addicted, he was considered exceptional. Donilon had been the youngest aide on the staff of President Jimmy Carter in 1977 and had served as chief of staff for the State Department during the Clinton administration. He had joined the Clinton campaign in 1992 as a stand-in for President G. H. W. Bush and for Ross Perot in debate preparation. Hours of prep armed him with telling facts and examples. He was tenacious: unfailingly pleasant but tough. He had a way of displaying his teeth as he spoke, top and bottom, so that the words seemed chewed. Clinton liked to spar with him verbally before a big match. Now, less than a year into the new Republican administration, he was getting used to life as an outlier, putting his law degree and experience inside government to work as a lobbyist for Fannie Mae.

When his doctor was finished with him, he drove his car from the garage under the building and into gridlock. Office buildings throughout the District had emptied. It seemed as if the entire government workforce was making its way home. Donilon tried to call his wife, but cell phone service was so overwhelmed that his call could not go through. He turned on the radio and listened in horror as he inched his way northeast toward home. The drive took a long time. When he got there he found that his wife had also come home from work, after picking up their daughter early from her Bethesda preschool. They turned on the TV and watched with the rest of the country.

*   *   *

Michael Vickers was just a few blocks away at his own small think tank offices, the Center for Strategic and Budgetary Assessments. He had founded it after leaving intelligence and military work. Twenty years earlier, as a brainy CIA officer, he had put together the clandestine U.S. mission to help a loosely connected group of tribal leaders and Islamist extremists fight the Soviet Union in Afghanistan, an effort that was considered the largest covert mission in the intelligence agency's history. The former army special forces officer was legendary in his own world. He was an expert in the Near East, had extensive contacts in that region, and with a career that had straddled intelligence and special ops would prove to be uniquely credentialed for this new war. The next day he would be back at work at the Pentagon as a consultant, summoned by Rumsfeld to help figure out how the United States should respond.

In Bosnia, Brigadier General David Petraeus was at a Nordic-Polish brigade headquarters in the early evening when the news came. A small and wiry man who walked with a slight stoop from his own jump accident years earlier, he sat with a group of international officers watching as the towers collapsed and realized that his mission, and that of every American soldier, was about to change. His suspicions immediately fell to al Qaeda and its founder, a man named Osama bin Laden.

This was no wild guess. Petraeus had been executive officer for the Joint Chiefs of Staff at the Pentagon from 1997–1999, during the period when the Clinton administration frequently debated whether and how to go after the radical Islamist leader. The decisions then had been to launch cruise missiles at al Qaeda targets in the Sudan and Afghanistan, a noisy gesture that hadn't accomplished much. Bin Laden was slippery. The response now would be a lot bigger—world changing. One of Petraeus's jobs in Bosnia was commanding a clandestine joint task force, one made up of elite representatives from all the service branches, that had been finding and targeting fugitive Serbian and Croatian war criminals, gathering intelligence, and then swooping in on targets swiftly, often from helicopters at night.

Before he left to fly back to his own headquarters, Petraeus was already thinking about adapting his mission.

In New York, graduate student Ben Rhodes saw the tragedy unfold from Brooklyn. He was working toward a master's degree in creative writing at NYU but he also dabbled in hometown politics and, that day, had been pressed into service handing out flyers for City Council candidate Diana Reyna—it was an election day in New York. Rhodes had been pushed into political work after confronting borderline socialists at his upper west side prep school and then Texas-style Republicans at Rice University. He feared doing nothing would concede the field to dogmatism. So now he was on the Brooklyn Heights waterfront handing out flyers.

The flames and smoke rising from the North Tower were shocking enough. Rhodes assumed there had been a bad accident. Seventeen minutes later, across the East River he saw a bright flash high on the South Tower, and then both were aflame high up, sending two great black plumes across the Manhattan skyline. He couldn't believe his eyes. The radio of a cop standing near him squawked with a call for *all hands* to respond, and the air erupted with sirens. Rhodes turned to see the Brooklyn-Queens Express-way below him filled with flashing ambulances and police cars racing north toward the Brooklyn Bridge and across to Manhattan.

The flames and the smoke trails did not diminish. The magnitude of the event was hard to comprehend. He was still watching when the South Tower fell. No sound reached him across the river. No rumble or crash. The skyscraper just abruptly pancaked down, folding in on itself as if it were something it had been designed to do, vanishing into a great white billowing cloud of debris.

He started walking. It seemed clear that the North Tower was also doomed, and he was not eager to see it. The towers had been landmarks of his childhood in New York. There was nothing in his twenty-three-year-old worldview to accommodate what he had just seen. Rhodes admired Ernest Hemingway—he had carried a paperback copy of *The Sun Also Rises* in his back pocket for years as an undergrad. At his core, Hemingway believed in facing hard truths head on. Rhodes the would-be novelist walked away from fiction that day, too. Whatever this was he had just seen, it was a thing that needed to be met head on. Like many Americans who witnessed those events, his life would never be the same.

President Bush was airborne when the towers fell. He and his inner circle watched from the staff room at the front of Air Force One, where they could pick up local TV feeds from below. The signals faded in and out. It alarmed Bush that the plane had no satellite TV feed—something he would correct. One commentator said that responsibility for the attacks had been claimed by the Democratic Front for the Liberation of Palestine.

This made no sense to Morell. That organization was an old splinter group of the Palestine Liberation Organization and all but defunct.

"What do you know about this group?" Bush asked him.

"They don't have the capacity to carry out an attack like this," Morell answered.

Within minutes the report was retracted.

The transition to war footing was striking. When the motorcade had reached the tarmac at Sarasota Bradenton International Airport, Air Force One had been ringed with Secret Service armed with automatic rifles. No one had seen an attack like this before, so no one knew what to expect next, who was behind it, or how extensive it would prove to be. Everything and everyone was under suspicion. Agents checked every bag before the president's traveling party climbed the stairs to the plane, including Card's and Morell's, including even those of the military officer carrying the nuclear codes.

As the CIA man stepped on the plane, he had asked one of the agents, "Where are we going?"

"We're just going to be flying around," he said.

With the sky raining planes, perhaps the safest place for the president would just be . . . up.

They flew to Barksdale Air Force Base in Louisiana, to refuel and take on supplies. The taxiway was lined with bombers. Reports of further attacks kept coming in: bombs, more aircraft-turned-missiles, a threat on Air Force One, a report of an attack aimed at Bush's ranch in Crawford, Texas. All would prove false, but in light of how audacious and terrible the known attacks were, every new alarm sounded plausible.

When the president got off the plane to tape a message to the American people, Morell stayed in his seat with most of the staff.

The plane's crew hastily loaded water and food; no one was certain how long the president would continue flying around. When a military aide came down the aisle with a flight manifest, selectively ordering people off, the CIA man asked what was going on.

"We're having a bunch of people deplane here," he said.

"What about me?" Morell inquired.

"Andy Card says you stay."

They took off with the load lightened, bound for a Strategic Air Command base in Omaha, Nebraska. When they were back in the air, Morell was summoned once more to Bush's cabin.

"Who do you think did this?" the president asked him.

Morell had been on the phone to Langley, but so far no one had been able to give him a definite answer.

"There are two terror states capable, Iran and Iraq," Morell told the president, "but both have everything to lose and nothing to gain. If I had to guess I'd put a lot of money on the table that it was al Qaeda."

"So, when will we know?" Bush asked.

Morell couldn't say. He explained how long it had taken the agency to affix blame with certainty in earlier attacks—the Khobar Towers bombing in 1996 in Saudi Arabia, the U.S. embassy bombings in Tanzania and Kenya in 1998, the bombing of the USS *Cole* in waters off Yemen in 2000. In the first case it had taken ten days; in the latter ones, a few months.

"We could know it soon, or it could take a while," he said.

In fact, the news came fast. An analyst at Langley had checked the flight manifests of the doomed aircrafts and linked some of the hijackers directly to al Qaeda. The information had been known for about an hour, but it had not been passed to Morell. Instead, Bush got the news by videophone from CIA Director George Tenet after they had landed in Omaha. The president at that point overruled his own security team, directing them to fly him back to Washington. He was going to address the nation that night, and he wanted to do it from the White House.

On the way back to Washington, Morell briefed Bush again, this time on a foreign intelligence report that there were sleeper cells in the United States prepared to launch a second wave of attacks. One of Morell's briefings had warned Bush in August about al Qaeda's desire to attack, but it had been very low key. No special sense of urgency was felt or had been conveyed, despite the alarming title of the actual report: "Bin Laden Determined to Strike in the U.S." Certainly nothing on the scale of what had just happened. With much of the workforce vacationing, Morell had often scrambled for material to present to the president in August. He called them "summer doldrums pieces." They tended to be broadly strategic, discussions of potential threats with more of a shelf life than most items on the morning agenda, looming problems about which the agency was concerned, but with few details. Bin Laden had been talking about doing something big in the United States, something he said that his followers would "rejoice about," but this was from a man who had been making such threats for years. The report had noted that the FBI had "seventy full field investigations" under way on bin Laden–related threats. The thrust of the report was that al Qaeda was planning something and that the U.S. government had no idea what, but was nevertheless doing all it could to prevent it.

Air Force One descended to Andrews Air Force Base at dusk. Many of the people aboard were dozing, having worked a long and difficult day already and knowing that there was a long night ahead. Morell roused himself to look out the window. Two F-16s had maneuvered to escort them down, flying in precise formation off each wingtip so close that on his side he could see the pilot's face inside the cockpit. In the distance he could see smoke still rising from the Pentagon.

He was at home later that night to watch the president address the nation on TV. Before Morell went to bed, he checked in on his children, sleeping in piles of stuffed animals. He thought: *The world they live in has completely changed, and they have no idea.*

That night, President Bush spoke from the Oval Office.

"Today our fellow citizens, our way of life, our very freedom, came under attack in a series of deliberate and deadly terrorist acts," he said. He described the events of the day in detail and lauded those who had responded, at great peril, to the emergencies. He vowed "to find those responsible and bring them to justice."

The man ultimately responsible, Osama bin Laden, had not been well known outside national security circles prior to that day, but he would soon be the most famous terrorist in the world. In the coming weeks and months he would acknowledge responsibility for the attacks, praise the murderous hijackers as martyrs to his cause, and be caught on videotape chuckling with delight and praising Allah for their success.

"There is America, hit by God in one of its softest spots," he would say in a videotape released a few weeks later, wearing a camouflage coat, seated alongside the AK-47 he still carried from his days of jihad against the Soviet Union, his long beard showing streaks of gray. "Its great buildings were destroyed, thank God for that. There is America, full of fear from its north to its south, from its west to its east. Thank God for that. What America tastes now is something insignificant compared to what we have tasted for scores of years. Our Nation [he meant Muslims everywhere] has tasted this humiliation and this degradation for more than eighty years [since the demise of the Ottoman Empire during World War I]."

From 9/11 onward, every day that bin Laden eluded America's grasp was a victory for him. It would be hard to overstate the significance of that. No matter what else the country did to avenge 9/11, no matter how many regimes it overturned, no matter how much it hammered and crippled al Qaeda, every day that man remained at large was an affront. It meant he had done this and gotten away with it, and might well do something like it again.

The two men who would lead the United States in the next decade of warfare had markedly different immediate responses to the attacks. Bush would record his feelings in his book *Decision Points*. Obama would describe his in speeches and writings in coming years, and he spoke to me about it in the Oval Office.

Bush felt outrage and an urgent desire for revenge. "Someone had dared attack America," he wrote. "They were going to pay."

When they had landed at Barksdale Air Force Base that day, the row upon row of parked bombers had reminded Bush of the frightening power at his command. Another man witnessing this display might have reflected on the pointlessness of a Cold War–era arsenal against a stateless enemy with no fixed address, but Bush would later write, "I knew it was only a matter of time before I put that power to use against whoever ordered this attack."

In his remarks on the night of the attacks he expanded the range of this anticipated retribution: "We will make no distinction between those who committed these acts and those who harbor them." The president's eagerness to hit back would continue to pick up speed. It would result in the mobilization of vast armies, the invasion and occupation of two nations, and the launching of smaller military and intelligence missions all over the globe. These missions would consume the next seven and a half years of Bush's presidency, kill and maim untold thousands, and do more than anything else to shape America's first decade of the twenty-first century. The war in Afghanistan, the first country attacked, would prove to be the longest in American history. In Iraq, an even bloodier and costlier war would be launched in the mistaken belief that dictator Saddam Hussein bore some tangential responsibility for the attacks and was harboring weapons that could do worse. However misguided much of this would prove to be, Bush's response accurately reflected the public mood, and satisfied, to some extent, the nation's need to flex its muscles and lash back at its enemies.

If Bush's response on 9/11 was to start looking for somebody to bomb, Barack Obama sounded ready to launch some kind of global antipoverty campaign.

Few people were all that interested in the thoughts of the Illinois state senator, but in the days after the attacks his local newspaper, the *Hyde Park Herald*, solicited his reaction along with that of other local representatives. Obama gave an answer you might expect from a former community organizer with a distinctly international background—his father was Kenyan, and Obama had spent the early years of his childhood living with his mother in Indonesia (he could still speak some Bahasa Indonesia, a language he learned as a child). At Columbia University, living in uptown Manhattan, he had devoted much of his studies to international relations, and he had traveled widely. Certainly more so than any previous president, Obama had grown up globally, a fact that, along with his mixed race and African name, would fuel stubborn suspicions that he was not *authentically* American. He had firsthand experience with the resentment and anger directed at the United States by many of those living in less fortunate parts of the world, as well as by many blacks growing up in this country. Anti-Americanism was not just an abstraction for him. He had consciously wrestled throughout his life with his own multicultural, multiracial identity, a process he had described movingly in his 1995 memoir, *Dreams from My Father*. In his response for the *Hyde Park Herald*, he called for an examination of the root causes of terrorism. "It grows from a climate of poverty and ignorance, helplessness and despair," he said. He called for America "to devote far more attention to the monumental task of raising the hopes and prospects of embittered children across the globe — children not just in the Middle East, but also in Africa, Asia, Latin America, Eastern Europe, and within our own shores." It read like left-wing boilerplate and, right or wrong, was clearly out of step with the nation's anger.

In fairness, the might of America's armed forces was not yet his to command, and he was not yet responsible for protecting the nation. Nor were his political instincts that good. Obama had a hard time fitting in politically anywhere. In that run for Congress, he was trounced by former sixties activist Bobby Rush, who had co-founded the Black Panther party in Chicago and had once served six months in prison on a firearms charge. Rush's First Congressional District was one of the few in America where a résumé like his would lead to Congress. It was home to Louis Farrakhan's Nation of Islam. Obama's mixed race and international background, along with his Harvard credentials, had worked against him. In the coming years, his message would broaden with his horizons. He had already begun aggressively laying the foundation for his next campaign, a successful effort to unseat Republican Senator Peter

Fitzgerald in 2005. But for the moment his response to 9/11 was strictly mundane.

It was from a template that went back to Vietnam. Most liberal Democrats, and many black Americans, had never gotten over that conflict. A quarter century later they still tended to be antiwar and even antimilitary—another of Rush's curious countercredentials was that he had gone AWOL from the army. But the broad political pattern set in the 1960s and early 1970s—hawkish Republicans vs. dovish Democrats—had begun to show cracks. The old hawk vs. dove dynamic had grown a lot more complex, with liberals pushing for humanitarian interventions in Somalia, Bosnia, and elsewhere over the objections of conservatives, who inveighed against the folly of "nation building," and "becoming the world's policeman," and cooperating with the UN.

Obama is a cautious man, and in the days after the attacks his caution showed. He seemed more *interested* than provoked. He said he hoped America would "draw some measure of wisdom from this tragedy." He sounded more inclined to *study* the attack than to avenge it. Here was a man whose blood had a higher boiling point than most. He saw himself as someone skilled at navigating between implacable extremes, be they cultural or, as with his work with the *Harvard Law Review*, intellectual. But in this instance, the forces he imagined had shaped the 9/11 attackers, ignorance and poverty, did not apply. The suicidal killers would turn out to be neither embittered sons of poverty nor especially hopeless or ignorant. Most were well-to-do young Saudis whose families had shipped them overseas for expensive college educations. They were religious fanatics, led by a man who had inherited a fortune. Their grievances were not economic—they were political and religious.

Obama did call for some martial response, but even in that he was careful. "We must be resolute in identifying the perpetrators of these heinous acts and dismantling their organizations of destruction," he said. Not "find them and arrest or kill them," but *dismantle their organizations.* If Bush's response to the attacks started big and would keep getting bigger, his eventual successor's response was at the opposite end of the spectrum. Any thoughts about war for Obama were deeply couched in restraint. He would eventually wage war fiercely, but the restraint would remain. He was not a pacifist. He saw violence as a necessary resort, albeit a last one. But as long as he was not bearing the responsibility of defending the nation, he could afford to let the shocking events of the day sink in more slowly.

The events were unprecedented. America has had its share of bloodshed, invasion, and surprise attack. Pearl Harbor was a living memory for millions. But because of television, nothing in American history compared with the impact of 9/11. Pearl Harbor was over two thousand miles from the mainland, at a time when the Hawaiian islands were just an American territory. Reports of the Japanese attack arrived via radio and newspaper stories. The attacks on 9/11 happened on live TV and were broadcast worldwide, the key moments replayed in slow motion and in a constant loop. There was nothing indirect about this. Here was heedless slaughter of fellow citizens right before our eyes.

The debates over conflicts in Obama's lifetime—Panama, El Salvador, Kuwait, Somalia, Rwanda, Bosnia, etc.—had all involved abstract questions about the use of American power. What was the country's moral obligation? How broadly should "national interest" be defined? What were the costs of intervention? Would it make things better or worse? How would the rest of the world perceive the decision? There was nothing abstract about 9/11.

Some persistent critics of the United States would argue that the country had brought this on itself. They would blame, among other things, self-serving Middle East policies, attitudes of cultural supremacy, and a steadfast disregard for growing global disparities in wealth and opportunity. Obama's own statements hinted at this. But it was apparent to most that the attacks were rooted in something darker. Washington's global strategies, intrigues, and alliances stirred anger in many parts of the world, particularly the Middle East. Anti-Americanism was real and dangerous. But this . . . this went to some deep well of hatred. The death of innocents has always been a tragic consequence of war, but this was random murder as *strategy*. It was something new, or, perhaps, something very old.

Obama sat up late on the night of 9/11 watching TV while he cared for infant Sasha, changing her and then giving her a bottle. By then the links with al Qaeda were being widely reported, and screens flashed pictures of bin Laden, a tall, thin, lordly man with a prophet's beard and flowing robes. His picture conjured up wrathful images of the fanatical abolitionist John Brown, or even Jehovah. Obama already knew more about this Saudi Arabian renegade and his extremist movement than did most Americans. The explosions at U.S. embassies in Kenya and Tanzania in 1998 had killed 223 people, mostly Africans. Thousands more had been wounded. Obama had family in Kenya. He had visited that Nairobi embassy. His tendency to search for answers through mutual understanding would be sorely tested here.

It would end up mattering a great deal how the events of this day affected Barack Obama. Few of us are asked to make life and death decisions, or to order someone killed. It is doubtful that Obama, on that night, imagined that he ever would. His personal and intellectual inclination was to bridge the gaps between people, to empathize. He tended to see conflict as something that arose exclusively out of injustice and misunderstanding. He was the son of a Luo tribesman from Kenya and a white girl from Kansas. He was different wherever he went, as a boy making the transition to life and school in Jakarta, as a young interracial man with black skin in a primarily white world. Even internally, negotiating differences was his life story. As he would tell biographer David Maraniss years later, "The only way my life makes sense is if, regardless of culture, race, religion, tribe, there is this commonality, precepts that are universal. And that we can reach out beyond our differences. If that is not the case, then it is pretty hard for me to make sense of my life. So that's the core of who I am." Empathy was his milieu. It's a generous worldview, and often the correct one.

But on September 11 he confronted something that challenged that hopeful insight. Search as he might for some logic to justify or mitigate these attacks, no reach of empathy or reason got him there. Bin Laden's hateful beliefs could not be reconciled. Despite the soft tone of his remarks to the Hyde Park newspaper, Obama also spoke of "a fundamental absence of empathy on the part of the attackers: an inability to imagine, or connect with, the humanity and suffering of others."

There is little evidence that George W. Bush was given to this sort of reflection, at least not openly, about himself or his responsibility. He had been born into a family that wielded power as if it were part of its birthright, and when the attacks came he was more than ready to play his role. Obama came from an opposite place. His roots were among the powerless. But even in his wide experience there was no way to comprehend Osama bin Laden.

Four years after the attacks, after his election to the U.S. Senate sparked a wave of electoral enthusiasm that would eventually carry him to the White House, Obama wrote a new prologue to his memoir. In it, he returned briefly to 9/11: "It's beyond my skill as a writer to capture that day and the days that would follow. The planes like specters vanishing into steel and glass, the slow-motion cascade of towers crumbling into themselves. The ash-covered figures wandering the streets. The anguish and fear. Nor do I pretend to understand the stark nihilism that drove terrorists that day and drives their brethren still. My powers of empathy, my ability to reach into another's heart cannot penetrate the blank stares of those who would murder innocents with abstract, serene satisfaction."

He noted that the murderous swath of al Qaeda in the previous decade hewed oddly close to his own life path—Nairobi, Bali, Manhattan. He spoke more harshly of the attackers than he had years earlier. He condemned anyone "who would seek under whatever flag or slogan or sacred text, a certainty and simplification that justifies cruelty toward those not like us."

Obama had spent a lifetime, no matter where he looked, being *not like others*. The attacks had crystallized something for him.

When Sasha emptied her bottle that night in 2001 he lifted her to his shoulder and patted her back gently. The terrible images of the day replayed before him on the screen. He wondered what the future would hold for her and her older sister Malia. He felt the attacks personally, as a civilized man, as an American, and as a father. He was working his way toward a personal definition of evil.

2

The Path of Jihad

Summer 2010

In hiding, his hair and beard had grown white. The Sheik, as he liked to be called, was just fifty-three years old, but the long white whiskers made him look like an old man. In a sense, he had been playing an elder his entire adult life, having been severe and serenely self-important since he was old enough to sprout a beard. Wealthy, well connected, and male in a culture that excessively prized those things, he had known deference and esteem from those closest to him all his life.

Despite the hammering his movement had taken in recent years, bin Laden kept an upbeat tone in his letters. His faith did not allow for doubt, or even questions. His perambulations around the Middle and Near East aside, bin Laden's world was exceedingly narrow. If the man in the White House, Barack Obama, the man charged with defending the United States of America, was a surprising confluence of race and nationality, a man of international upbringing and broad liberal education, bin Laden was his opposite.

The Sheik had walked a relatively narrow path in life. He had found the truth at a young age and ever since had labored to resist any challenge or contradiction. Even before he became the world's most wanted fugitive, his daily habits and those he imposed on his family were calculated to reduce traffic with those outside his small circle of belief. The rituals he observed—the fasting, the avoidance of women other than his wives, the extra sessions of daily prayer—all of it was designed to stave off outside influence. It was designed to strengthen his devotion to the cause and his faith in ultimate victory.

He saw hopeful signs everywhere.

"Anyone who looks at the enemies in NATO, especially America, will know that they are in big trouble," he wrote. "This year has been the worst for them in Afghanistan since they invaded it. The number of their dead has never been this high, according to their own reports. Their financial crisis continues. Britain has lowered its defense budget and America is reducing the budget at the Pentagon. Anyone who knows the world and who understands politics realizes that it is impossible for them to continue with the war. There is no difference between them and the Soviet Union before it withdrew from Afghanistan."

At heart, the Sheik was a fantasist, and here was the nub of his fantasy. He had left home at age twenty-two to join a seemingly hopeless cause, a pan-Muslim jihad to drive the Soviet Union from Afghanistan. The *mujahidin* who took up this fight were little more than an untrained, poorly armed rabble going up against one of the richest, best-trained and -equipped, and most powerful military forces in the world. In later years bin Laden would be described as a murderous nihilist, someone who believed in nothing. He was murderous all right, but the opposite of a nihilist. He was a true believer. He had a complete vision of the world as he wanted it to be—indeed, as he was convinced it would be, as he was convinced God Almighty intended it to be. He believed in miracles and signs. He collected them throughout his life as proof of God's favor. His determination to join the jihad in Afghanistan was an act of faith, and the defeat of the Soviets vindicated his commitment. It was the first great miracle on this path, the one that convinced him more than anything else that he was right.

As a boy, growing up one of fifty-four children of a Saudi billionaire construction magnate, bin Laden had gone mostly to Islamist schools, and in religion he found an antidote to the worldliness of his family. He was one of the few bin Laden children who received all of his education in Saudi Arabia. The schools he had attended as a boy included religious studies, but also taught mathematics, science, history, geography, and English. He learned as a boy to speak passable English. Growing up in the 1960s he was among the best educated of his Saudi generation. He had also worked for his father, first as a simple laborer. The bin Laden company was renowned for building roads and parts of the mosques in Mecca and Medina. Young Osama worked his way up to foreman of a labor gang, and finally headed up construction projects himself. One of his specialties was tunneling. This kind of work put him shoulder to shoulder with Muslim workers from all over the region and the world: Egyptians, Yemenis, Moroccans, and even Malaysians. So his ideas about the Muslim world expanded well beyond those of most sheltered young Saudis, who viewed their own Wahhabi brand of the faith as superior to all others. At the same time, bin Laden became exceedingly devout, shunning all contact with women other than his wives (the first of whom, Najwa, he had married at age seventeen). He renounced the affluent lifestyles of his vast family and discovered the work of Egyptian scholar Sayyid Qutb, a small, mean, sickly man with a Hitler mustache who had been hanged by authorities in Egypt in 1966. In death, Qutb's angry words gained fiery eloquence for those who thought as he did.

Qutb had railed against the rapid Westernization of traditional Arab societies. He championed divine revelation in a fallen modern world, penning biting critiques of both capitalist democracy and communism. A fervent Jew hater, he saw secret Zionist plots behind most of what he disliked, embracing every cockeyed forgery and myth in the canon of anti-Semitism. The Koran, he argued, was the one true path. All the wisdom mankind needed was in that book, which he spent a lifetime interpreting and explaining to suit his own vision. Muslims held the truth, the only truth, and had a duty to confront un-believers, violently if necessary. Regimes and states that stood in the way of religious rule were *jahiliyya*—ignorant pre-Islamic societies—and as such were legitimate targets for violence. The forces of God must combat the forces of Satan, beginning with the secular regimes of modern Arab states. Qutb urged the faithful to carve out one coun-try in which to base a pure society founded on shariah, Islamist law, a foothold for the faithful in a fallen world, and from that base radiate righteousness outward, by the sword if necessary. The new caliphate thus created would bend all of civilization to God's will. At a time when well-to-do Arabs were becoming increasingly secular and West-ern, sending their children to Europe and the United States for ad-vanced degrees and adopting lifestyles antithetical to Arab tradition, Qutb urged them to go in the opposite direction.

He had lived for a time in the United States—briefly in Col-orado and in California—and seemingly everything he saw clari-fied his hatred not just for America, but also for the humanism that formed the intellectual undergirding of the Western world. A fas-tidious man who never married and seemed repelled by sex, Qutb denounced the licentiousness, materialism, and personal freedom of capitalist democracy. He saw clearly that for all its so-called respect for religion, Western society had become primarily secular, that faith, which for him was the dynamic principle of life, had been reduced in capitalist societies to something more akin to a commodity, as though there were different *flavors* of divine truth arrayed like items on a supermarket shelf for shoppers to pick through. What could it possibly matter to God what sort of truth a man preferred? There was only one truth, and man's job was to accept it reverently and try to live in accordance with it. The very idea of tolerance, of respect for a variety of beliefs, was anathema. One either embraced the truth or was lost. As for Marxism, the Western world's great rival notion, he saw it as simple idolatry, elevating human reason— "Rational Idealism"—above revelation. Lurking behind both Marxism and capitalism, he argued, was world Jewry.

"Islam is a system given by God and it aims to establish a fundamental principle of God's sovereignty and people's servitude to Him alone," Qutb wrote. "As such, Islam has the right to remove all obstacles from its way and address people freely without any impediments such as a political system or social customs and traditions . . . it is the right of Islam to take the initiative. It is not the creed of a particular people or the system of a particular country. It is a system given by God for the entire world. As such, it has the right to take action to remove all obstacles that fetter man's freedom of choice. It is a faith that does not force itself on any individual, it only attacks situations and regimes in order to free individuals from deviant influences that corrupt human nature and restrict man's freedom."

Young Osama bin Laden was not the first youth to be swept up by a pure, simple ideology that promised to create freedom of choice by abolishing everything that disagreed with it. The Koran stood like a rock in the shifting waters of human history. Progress for human beings meant one thing: living more closely to the teachings of the book.

"The Islamic concept of Divinity is utterly distinct from man's . . . and therefore it does not need to develop or change," Qutb wrote. "The One who established this concept can envision without limits of time or space. His knowledge is immune to the obstacles of ignorance and deficiency; and He chooses without being influenced by passion or emotion. Therefore, He has established for the entirety of humanity, in all places and at all times, a firm principle within the framework of which human life freely advances and develops."

Accused of participating in a Muslim Brotherhood plot to assassinate Egyptian strongman Gamal Abdel Nasser, Qutb went to the gallows with his beliefs unshaken. "The Muslim Brotherhood is not a party of preachers and missionaries but rather of divine enforcers," he wrote. "Its mission is to blot out, by force if necessary, oppression, moral anarchy, social disorder, and exploitation so as to finish the so-called divine role of self-styled gods and replace evil with good. 'Fight them,' the Koran says, 'until there is no more oppression, and all submission is made to God alone.'"

Bin Laden became a "divine enforcer." As a young man, he was not a scholar or much of a thinker, and he lacked Qutb's eloquence. Those who knew him found him tongue-tied and unimpressive. But he was ambitious, and rich. His billionaire father was killed in a plane crash in 1967, leaving behind enough of a fortune to make all of his offspring at least multimillionaires. Bin Laden's inheritance at age ten was estimated in the tens of millions. He had no interest in using his wealth to build a fine home or adopt a luxurious lifestyle, though, as many of his siblings did. His inclinations ran the opposite way. He had been educated in a private secular school, but by the time he attended King Abdulazzi University, where he studied economics and business management, he was already preaching simplicity and seemed primarily interested in religion and charitable work. He continued to pursue these interests until the Soviet Union invaded Afghanistan and launched him on the path toward his life's work.

Huthaifa Azzam was just fourteen years old when he answered a bell on the gate outside his father's house in Jordan. He found a very tall, very thin, swarthy and bearded young man wearing Arab robes and a simple white turban, not the typical red-and-white-checked headdress, or *shemagh*, worn by most Saudi men. The visitor asked, shyly, "Is this the house of Dr. Abdullah Azzam?"

Azzam was a prominent Palestinian Islamist and scholar whose fatwa, "Defense of the Muslim Lands: The First Obligation After Faith," had caused a stir in the Arab world, summoning the faithful to Afghanistan to resist the infidel Soviets. Azzam had done more than preach. He had relocated to Pakistan to take part in the holy war himself. Based in Peshawar, close to the Afghan border, he had established what he called the "Services Office," to recruit and train young Arab volunteers to join the fight. Magazines, photos, and videos prepared by the office spread news of the heroic religious resistance throughout the Arab world . . . and had found their way to young bin Laden. Azzam was taking a short holiday break with his family in Jordan when the young Saudi made the four-hour trip to ring his bell. This volunteer was different from most, of course, because of his fortune. Azzam must have been delighted. The two men spoke for hours that day, and by evening bin Laden was a recruit. He pledged himself to the cause. He was still enough of a loyal Saudi subject, however, that he delayed traveling back with Azzam in order to seek permission from King Fahd. He arrived in Peshawar several weeks later.

At that point, bin Laden's money was more valuable to the cause than his leadership or even his life, and so during those first years with Azzam he stayed safely behind the lines, working at the Services Office and helping to attract other young fighters to the cause. This was not destined to last. Bin Laden was a romantic, and a zealot, and he had not made his jihad to live safely behind the lines. He grew apart from Azzam, increasingly falling in with Ayman al-Zawahiri, the radical Egyptian physician who had left his home country after serving three years in prison. Zawahiri worked at a Red Crescent hospital in Peshawar. Although only six years older than bin Laden, he was a man of wider experience and education, and had been deeply embittered by the torture he had undergone at the hands of Egyptian police. His angry radicalism stirred bin Laden to play a more active role in the holy war—to become a full-fledged *mujahid* himself.

Bin Laden's growing extremism began to trouble his Palestinian mentor. Azzam, a college professor, balked at bin Laden's refusal to send his children to school. The younger man wanted Arab recruits to form separate, religiously pure fighting units, while Azzam believed the Arabs would be better employed if mixed with the savvier, more experienced Afghan militia. He also resisted his protégé's growing carelessness about human life. Bin Laden had embraced a broad definition of "infidel." Until that point, the enemy had been understood to be Russian soldiers and Afghans who fought with them. They were at war, after all. Bin Laden had expanded the definition. It now applied to any Russian, even any non-Muslim. He was fighting a bigger war than the one being promoted by Azzam. The older man's wife, Samira, remembers her husband arguing with bin Laden about the younger man's plan to place a bomb on a bus full of Russians visiting Pakistan.

"You entered Pakistan on a visa," Azzam reminded him. "The visa is a contract. You signed when you obtained the visa that you would not be a troublemaker nor break the laws. A Muslim should not break a contract."

"Pakistan is a Muslim country," bin Laden told him, by which he meant that non-Muslims had no business coming there.

It was one thing, Azzam argued, to kill Russians who invaded Afghanistan and held it by force, quite another to target innocent civilians on a holiday to a country that welcomed them.

"So what will happen if Russia loses a bus full of people?" bin Laden said dismissively. "It is not going to matter."

He had moved beyond the conflict in Afghanistan. His faith empowered him. God had touched him. This gave him the right to decide, to kill.

Bin Laden also felt that jihad demanded that he actually fight as well, not just take part in recruiting, training, and paying others to do so. The older man argued with him for months, no doubt convinced that a multimillionaire Saudi was worth more to the cause alive than dead. But bin Laden had made up his mind. He was going to cross the border and join the battle. In 1987, he split with Azzam. He recruited his own band of about two dozen Arab fighters, creating the kind of fighting unit he preferred—a pure, all-Arab force of men who fought for religious reasons alone, not just for the principle of Afghan nationalism. Equipped with weapons and bulldozers, they drove ten miles or so into Afghanistan, joined up with some like-minded Afghan fighters, and set about building a mountain outpost near the village of Jaji. Bin Laden fortified a series of ridges and began building roads and other structures—he said a school and a hospital—that advertised their presence. It was in easternmost Afghanistan, in rugged country, and was not a strategically important spot, at least not in any conventional sense. Bin Laden called it al-Masada, the Lion's Den. It was near a much larger Soviet garrison and its primary purpose was to provoke an attack. To a practical man like Azzam (who would be assassinated two years later) this probably appeared foolhardy, but bin Laden lived in a world of romantic fantasy, and in that realm, al-Masada made perfect sense. The battle was not just for Afghanistan, but for the whole world. It was the beginning of a new caliphate, the dawn of a new Muslim age. He was a holy warrior, and warriors did not win battles by writing checks and making videos and leading from the rear. In his view, the idea wasn't to defeat the Soviets in battle, or even to survive, but to display such heroism and resolve that it would inflame the fighting spirit of the greater Muslim Nation.

"God willing, we want the Lion's Den to be the first thing that the enemy faces," bin Laden told a Syrian journalist. "Its place as the first camp visible to the enemy means that they will focus their bombardments on us in an extreme manner."

And the Soviets obliged, dropping napalm and so many tons of conventional explosives that the outpost and the area around it were denuded of trees and vegetation. Then they attacked directly, encircling the outpost. The siege lasted for twenty-two days, with a heavy toll on both sides. Some of bin Laden's men were more skilled fighters than he was. Abu Hafs (Mohammed Atef, an Egyptian policeman who would be killed in 2001) and Abu Ubaidah (Ali Amin al-Rashidi, also a former Egyptian policeman, killed in

1996) led punishing counterattacks. The Soviets eventually gave up and retreated, handing the Arab fighters an inspirational victory. It had unfolded for bin Laden miraculously, a clear sign from heaven.

He would later tell the Syrian journalist, "At seven on the twenty-seventh morning of Ramadan 1407 [April of 1987], most of the people were sleeping in the camp because it was Ramadan. Then I saw things that, by God, I have never seen before. A Soviet airplane, a MIG, I believe, passed by in front of us, when a group of our Afghan *mujahidin* brothers grouped together [and attacked]. The plane then broke into pieces and fell right in front of our eyes. This battle is what gave me the strong will to continue with this war."

By all accounts bin Laden fought bravely, exposing himself to danger and the extremes of deprivation and cold like everyone else in the camp. He was injured during the fighting and, at one point, he later told an interviewer, he lay unconscious and bleeding in a trench, surrounded by his dead comrades. He was ultimately rescued, but only after losing a lot of blood, an incident that he would later say had given him chronically low blood pressure. Bin Laden's willingness to place himself at risk greatly enlarged his reputation. It mattered little in the end that the battle had been meaningless in practical terms. The Battle of Jaji was proclaimed a great victory, and bin Laden, having conceived it, was its hero. Reporters trekked out to al-Masada to meet this Saudi multimillionaire who fought with suicidal conviction. One of them, Ahmad Zaidan, a Pakistani newspaper reporter working for a group of Arab newspapers, found an extraordinarily pious young man in complete command, who had supplanted the role once played by the far more famous Azzam, and who was surrounded by devoted followers. Bin Laden had transformed himself from a rich-kid backer on the sidelines into a frontline *mujahidin* leader.

It brought him more than new recruits. It affirmed his sense of destiny. By then he had become the Sheik. He was thirty years old, tall and thin, with long full features and a long dark beard that further elongated his face. He preferred traditional Arab robes and cultivated a lofty, saintly mien, affecting abject humility. He was theatrically holy. From time to time he would receive audiences of reporters, and after each question he would sit silently for a few moments, mouthing prayers, as if waiting for the Almighty to formulate the response for him, and only then would he speak, in a voice so soft that everyone had to lean close to hear him. He fasted once or twice a week and rejected the simple comforts and conveniences of modern life that he could easily afford. He shunned electricity, doing without air-conditioning and refrigeration in even the warmest climates, as when he and his family lived in the Sudan. All the better to harden himself and his family for the privation of war, for life as a fugitive. Followers were now drawn to his renown, to his sincerity, to his daring and his conviction, but also to his money. His fortune was still key. For those who had experienced the heady days of jihad in Afghanistan and preferred to make a career of it, bin Laden could provide the means, and possessed the reckless vision. For most Arabs the caliphate was ancient history, but to the Sheik it was destiny. God had chosen him. Surviving the bitter Russian siege at Jaji reinforced those beliefs. Qutb had called for a pure Muslim state, a base from which to spread the cause. Afghanistan seemed to be the place. It had been called Khorasan when it was converted to Islam in the seventh century and had stood as one of the great pillars of the caliphate for centuries. Defeating the Soviets there would have deep resonance among believers. It was, perhaps, the right place. And in bin Laden's mind, it had started at al-Masada, where the pure of heart, outnumbered and outgunned, had righteously defied Soviet MIGs and bombs and weeks of determined assault.

Then the impossible happened. Just as they had backed away from al-Masada, in 1989 Russian armies retreated in frustration from Afghanistan. Within three years, the Soviet empire itself collapsed, closely followed by the regime it had left behind in Kabul. Bin Laden returned to Saudi Arabia with an outsized reputation as author of this titanic accomplishment, and he gained even more disciples. He and the men who had fought with him at Jaji saw themselves as the fulcrum of this triumph and named themselves "the Base," or al Qaeda. They were the soul of what bin Laden saw as the emerging caliphate, a true Muslim Nation.

It was, of course, absurd. If anything, the source of the *mujahidin*'s triumph had been the billions of dollars of U.S. aid and arms that Michael Vickers had helped steer to Afghanistan after the Soviet invasion. But bin Laden was less interested in the truth than in appearances, and in the latter, he and his followers excelled. Their style spoke volumes. Their long beards and hair and prayer caps and robes made them seem like men from an ancient, holier time. They adopted bin Laden's asceticism. They embraced struggle and death, bragging that their desire for martyrdom trumped their attachment to life itself. They pitted themselves against power. They were natural men, real men. Their very shabbiness advertised their authenticity. They were pious. They believed that happiness and justice were not things civilization was evolving toward, but things that had been lost.

The fall of the Soviet Union had many causes, of course, and the drawn-out humiliation in Afghanistan was certainly among them, but for the devout there was only one cause: the hand of God had once more moved clearly in human history, just as it had in the legends of old. No serious scholar would credit bin Laden with a critical role in the effort, much less a role in the collapse of the Soviet state, but in the Sheik's mind that was how it had gone. It made for a great story, the powerless but pure of heart overcoming impossible odds. The Sheik loved stories like these. He was a poet himself, a fantastical one, given to cosmic sweep and romantic cliché. He celebrated violence and death in the struggle to defend the faith, with centuries-old imagery of swords and steeds, soaring mountains, and fearless warriors.

> *He hunches forth,*
> *Staining the blades of lances red.*
> *May God not let my eye stray*
> *From the most eminent humans,*
> *Should they fall.*
> *As the stallion bears my witness*
> *That I hold them back,*
> *My stabbing is like the cinders of fire*
> *That explode into flame.*

He used his poems to explain, excite, and recruit in parts of the world where traditions were still tribal and oral, but the poems were also an expression of how he saw himself, how he believed the world to be. As a younger man he had composed and recited his poems at weddings and other occasions. He was stitching his own life and his modern struggle into images of a glorious past. The Sheik often enclosed verses in his letters, and instructed that they be read on important occasions—published or broadcast. The

Afghanistan victory brought the ages of heroes and mighty deeds to life in modern times. In his poetry, he was arguing that we, too, live in an age of miracles.

After the collapse of the Soviet state, even the wildest reach of his ambition seemed possible. When Saddam Hussein invaded Kuwait, the Sheik, then living in his home country, wrote a series of letters to King Fahd demanding that American forces not be allowed to enter Saudi Arabia and offering to put together a force of *mujahidin* to expel the Iraqi forces himself. His pleas were ignored. Huthaifa Azzam, who had remained friends with bin Laden for years after the Afghan conflict, remembers this as the only time he ever saw the studiously mild-mannered Sheik ever lose his temper. Bin Laden's outrage and sense of betrayal were complete. He was considered dangerous enough in his home country that he was placed under house arrest.

After the kingdom's refusal to adopt his plan for a renewed holy war, instead opting for the more practical option of inviting the United States and other apostate countries to assemble military forces to confront Saddam, bin Laden's brothers used their influence to get his passport back, and he left Saudi Arabia permanently, first traveling to Pakistan, then to Afghanistan, then the Sudan, and then back to Afghanistan.

The younger Azzam was attending a conference in the Sudan in 1995 when he dropped in to see bin Laden. During his visit, he recalls, he met Khalid Sheik Mohammed, who had brought his notorious nephew, Ramzi Yousef, a Sunni extremist who was at that time a fugitive sought by the United States for the first attack on the World Trade Center, two years earlier. Azzam described Yousef as a scrawny man whose bearded face had been scarred in a bomb-making accident. Both he and his uncle would later be characterized in *The 9/11 Commission Report* as "rootless but experienced operatives." Yousef would be captured in Pakistan later that year. According to Azzam, the Sheik listened as Yousef outlined a plan to attack targets in the United States again, including the World Trade Center towers, this time by hijacking commercial airliners and flying them into buildings. He wanted al Qaeda to help with recruiting martyrs and raise money for them to travel to the United States for flight training. As Azzam recalls it, the Sheik said, "We have nothing to do with the United States, why should we attack them?"

This may have been for Azzam's benefit, since bin Laden had been preaching a duty to attack America for years. Ever since he had broken with Azzam's father, the Sheik had steered a far more radical course. Huthaifa Azzam was not the radical bin Laden had become, and would have been seen as suspect, perhaps even as a spy. It might explain why bin Laden would have made a show of rejecting Yousef's idea in this meeting. Already al Qaeda had been implicated in attacks and plots on Americans, including sending military advisers to Somalia in 1993 to help tribal militiamen target American helicopters, and a car bomb explosion in Saudi Arabia that killed five American and two Indian soldiers. If the account is true, the meeting Azzam described is significant because it would be the first known mention of what became the 9/11 plot to bin Laden. The idea for the attacks is customarily attributed to Khalid Sheik Mohammed, but Yousef's fixation on the towers is well documented. He later confessed that he had hopes that the 1993 bombing would collapse the towers and kill 250,000 people. Whatever bin Laden said at this session, al Qaeda would endorse the plan soon enough.

Bin Laden left the Sudan when terrorists linked to al Qaeda and the Egyptian group Islamic Jihad were linked to an attempted assassination of the Egyptian President Hosni Mubarak. Pressure mounted on the Sudanese government after that, and the Sheik was expelled. He had other reasons to go. There had been one known attempt on his life there, and Saudi authorities had cut off payments to the al Qaeda leader from his family inheritance. With funding for his ambitious projects in the Sudan dried up, he left for Afghanistan in May 1996.

Three months later, back in the dusty, rugged homeland of the first great miracle, the Sheik held a press conference to declare war on "the head of the snake." He cited a list of grievances against America and demanded that its forces be withdrawn from "the land of the two Holy Places"—Saudi Arabia. It was time for the next great struggle, he preached, which would topple the world's other superpower, the United States. That would mean the end of Israel, America's client state, and the dawn of a new Islamist age. There was nothing stealthy about his plan, just as there had been no disguising his intentions when he built al-Masada near the Soviet garrison at Jaji. The whole idea was to confront the enemy openly, to make a show of inspired defiance. Indeed, making the show was more important than succeeding. Audacity was the point.

In 1998, he told ABC News correspondent John Miller, to whom he gave an interview in order to directly reach American audiences: "I'm declaring war on the United States. I am going to attack your country."

Few Americans took the threat seriously. Some crackpot Arab in the middle of nowhere had declared war on the United States. The country had more important things on its mind . . . like sex. Former White House intern Monica Lewinsky said it had transpired between her and President Clinton, and he was still denying it. Hillary Clinton was conjuring up "a vast right-wing conspiracy." House

Speaker Newt Gingrich, who was then secretly carrying on his own extramarital affair with a staffer twenty-three years his junior, was leading the charge to impeach the president. Basketball star Michael Jordan clinched the Chicago Bulls' sixth NBA title with a fade-away jumper in the final seconds of his last game with the team. Bin Laden was of interest to those whose job it was to protect the United States from foreign threats but, as we have seen, even in those circles he did not merit urgent concern.

But the Sheik had big plans, and the means to carry them out. The bombings of American embassies in Nairobi and Dar es Salaam in 1998 and the attack on the USS *Cole* two years later, got America's attention, but al Qaeda was still considered by most in the intelligence and military communities to be a nuisance—a deadly and growing nuisance, perhaps, but a nuisance. Bin Laden's own life grew more difficult, as the Clinton administration devoted more effort to finding and killing him. Two of bin Laden's wives left him during this period, choosing to abandon the path of jihad. But the Sheik persevered through the next decade, training recruits, plotting, and laying the groundwork for the next miracle.

The fall of the World Trade Center towers was his vindication. What greater proof of God's purpose could the world wish to see? Bin Laden placed great stock in signs. He had long sought to deliver a decapitating strike, hitting the American centers of finance, government, and military. It had seemed an impossible goal. One had to be crazy, or inspired, to think he could pull it off.

The collapse of the World Trade Center had been the second great miracle in his life. The fall of the iconic towers in Manhattan, symbols of the wealth and power of the world's remaining infidel superpower, seemed to presage the imminent collapse of America, too. It was further proof that the path he followed was divinely inspired.

In his wildest hopes he had not imagined that the planes might bring down the towers completely. God's hand had surely been in it. The physical force of the colliding planes, the exploding fuel, and the resulting infernos were themselves, he believed, inadequate to explain it. On a video found by American soldiers in Kandahar weeks after the attacks, bin Laden is seen conversing happily with a group of sympathetic Saudi visitors, alternately praising God and celebrating the remarkable outcome, painting the attacks in magical terms. It was a practice familiar in religious communities. You decorated the truth with dreams and portents, weaving magic into the facts, coloring them with divine favor.

In the footage, bin Laden knelt on a large pillow, wearing his military-style camouflage jacket, his head wrapped in a white turban, speaking so softly that his words were barely audible. When he spoke, the others in the room would fall silent. Bin Laden seemed stiff, perhaps because he knew he was being videotaped, and he elevated his long slender left hand and two fingers like Christ or a saint in an old icon. In older photographs, before he became so notorious, he appears more relaxed and human, even graceful, his long, thin features animated with a frequent smile. Now he was important. He assumed the pose of the important. He said he had received notice about the precise day of the attacks the week before, so he had been ready for the news. In Jalalabad it had been early evening. He described how he and his fellow *mujahidin* had gathered around a radio to listen to the BBC's Arabic-language radio broadcast.

"We calculated in advance the number of casualties from the enemy who would be killed based on the position of the tower," he explained. "We calculated that the floors that would be hit would [be at most] three or four floors. I was the most optimistic of them all due to my experience in this field [construction]. I was thinking that the fire from the gas in the plane would melt the iron structure of the building and collapse the area where the plane hit and all the floors above it only. This was all that we had hoped for."

When the others began celebrating after the first plane hit, bin Laden said he told them, "Be patient." There was more news to come. The difference between the first and second plane hitting the towers was twenty minutes, and the difference between the first plane and the plane that hit the Pentagon was one hour.

As much as the first miracle, this one seemed to mark a profound milestone in his struggle. But he was cautious at first about claiming credit.

He sought out Hamid Mir, a well-known Pakistani journalist who had met and interviewed him years earlier. As Mir explained it, he was in his Islamabad office when the 9/11 attacks occurred. Within hours a messenger came to him with a written statement from the Sheik. Mir recognized the messenger. He had seen him when he had first met with bin Laden years earlier in Kandahar. The statement read, "I praise all those who conducted that operation. But I am not directly involved."

Mir told the messenger: "You contacted me immediately after the attacks and you reached my office within a few hours and that means that you were not in Afghanistan at that time. That means that bin Laden gave you this statement before the attacks. And that means that you people were aware of the attacks."

The messenger pleaded ignorance.

"The Sheik just gave me this letter. He said, 'You will contact Mr. Mir at six o'clock and you will reach his office at seven o'clock and then you will come back.' So that was my job and I have done my job, okay? Bye."

The messenger left.

Mir's own reporting reputation in Pakistan is controversial. He has often angered the government there, and he has been accused of being sympathetic to extremists, but his reports have been recognized worldwide as credible and often extraordinary. His many run-ins with Pakistani officialdom had burnished his reputation for independence among Western reporters, so in the days immediately after the attacks he was interviewed by many who were searching for some insight into al Qaeda. After he appeared on Larry King's interview program on CNN, Mir was again contacted by one of bin Laden's messengers, who said the Sheik wanted to talk to him. So Mir traveled to Jalalabad in November of 2001 in search of the scoop of a lifetime. Bin Laden was now the most wanted fugitive in the world.

He said that when he arrived in Jalalabad he waited a full day before being contacted by a group of low-level al Qaeda figures, who said they knew nothing of bin Laden's summons.

"We are not aware of why you are here or who wanted you here," one said. "We are not aware, just wait."

More hours passed. Eventually, Mir was contacted and instructed to travel to Kabul. He spent several days in the Afghan capital, being shuttled first to one safe house, then another. It was now weeks into the American invasion, and just days before the Taliban fell. The capital was braced for tumultuous change. He could hear bombs falling on the city day and night, explosions that shook the earth. The Islamist kingdom under construction was coming apart all around him. Mir feared he would never get out alive. If an American bomb didn't kill him, these al Qaeda fighters would. On the morning of November 8, six days before the Taliban fled the city, he was escorted into the presence of bin Laden and al-Zawahiri. Both men said they had come to Kabul to attend funeral services for a comrade.

Bin Laden seemed serenely untroubled by the unfolding disaster around him, and in high spirits. Sitting with the two most wanted men in the world, surrounded by other members of their group, Mir began nervously. He asked, "Are you responsible for 9/11?"

Bin Laden reached over with one long finger and shut off Mir's tape recorder.

He asked, "Can you ask this question to George W. Bush: Are you responsible for the killing of many Muslims in Palestine and Iraq?"

"No, I cannot ask him this question because I'll not get any chance to interview him," said Mir.

"Okay, but if you do get a chance and if you ask this question, will he answer?"

"No," said Mir.

"Then why are you asking this question of me?"

"Because he is a politician and you are a fighter," said Mir, thinking fast, and then, falling back on any journalist's most trusted tactic, he resorted to flattery. "You said that you are a *mujahid*, so there must be a difference between a politician and a *mujahid*. *Mujahid* always speak the truth. You have to answer my question."

"Off the record, yes," said bin Laden. Then he turned the recorder back on. "I cannot answer your question because my answer will create problems for the Taliban."

Clearly the Taliban had problems enough. Bombs were exploding outside so close that the journalist was shaken. His fright amused bin Laden.

"Oh, Mr. Mir, maybe today you will be killed with me at this place," he said, lightly mocking him. "You are here to interview me and maybe you will not be able to report that interview back to your newspaper. What will happen with you?"

Bin Laden and the others laughed. They spoke for hours. Mir worked through a list of questions he had prepared. They discussed the various attempts that had been made on bin Laden's life, and after shutting off Mir's recorder again the Sheik spoke at length about his disdain for Iraqi dictator Saddam Hussein and Libyan strongman Muammar Gaddafi, neither of whom had joined the struggle against the Soviet Union years before. Mir asked him about widespread reports that he suffered a kidney disease and needed dialysis treatments. Again, the Sheik laughed. He promised to address the question in more detail when they had finished the interview. So when Mir finished asking his questions, breakfast was brought in for them—olives, cheese, bread and butter, beef. Bin Laden began eating vigorously.

"A kidney patient cannot eat a lot," he told Mir. "You see this is beef? I am eating beef. You see this is cheese? I am eating cheese."

Mir looked to al-Zawahiri, who agreed. "Yes, I am a doctor, I can confirm, kidney patients cannot eat a lot."

"I can ride my horse seventy kilometers without any stop," said bin Laden.

He kept Mir far longer than the reporter had expected, or desired. The Pakistani, having asked his questions, was eager to leave and get out of the city. He knew that bin Laden might well be a target for the Americans. After this exchange about the Sheik's health, Mir asked, "Can I leave now?"

"No," said his host. "You spend some more time with us and have some tea and you can ask some other questions, off the record questions."

Bin Laden told Mir that the day after the attacks in America, his youngest wife had given birth to a daughter, whom he named Safiyah.

"Why Safiyah?" Mir asked.

Bin Laden explained that Safiyah had been an aunt of the Prophet and an early convert to Islam. She had given up all her possessions to join the faith, and had taken part in battles and slain unbelievers in defense of the faith.

"Are you now planning to involve the females of your family in your fight against the Americans?" Mir asked, mindful of the Sheik's strictly traditional views on the role of women. Bin Laden laughed.

"Maybe Safiyah will follow the footsteps of her father," he said, and resisted when Mir seemed to be taking the comment too seriously.

"Just forget, forget," he said.

"No, no, it's very important for me."

"Okay, rest assured Safiyah will not become a *mujahid*, don't worry," bin Laden said, and laughed again. And at last he said, "Okay, now you can go back."

Despite the relentless American attacks and the imminent defeat of the Taliban, the Sheik was filled with confidence from the impact of 9/11. All was unfolding as he foretold.

He did not see any of his attacks as wanton terror, as his horrified enemies did. They were retribution. They were not simply just, but divinely inspired. They were his duty.

"We kill civilian infidels in exchange for those of our children they kill," he told an interviewer from Al Jazeera five months after the 9/11 attacks, citing an estimate he often used, that a "million children" had died in Iraq owing to UN–imposed sanctions on that country, a number most serious analysts considered absurdly inflated. Asked about the children killed who had been attending a school inside the World Trade Center, he reasoned: "[Retribution] is permissible in law and intellectually. The men that God helped [on September 11] did not intend to kill babies, they intended to destroy the strongest military power in the world, to attack the Pentagon that houses more than 64,000 employees, a military center that houses military intelligence. The twin towers are an economic power and not a children's school."

It is worth noting here, and for most it goes without saying, that Osama bin Laden's ideas were neither new nor compelling outside his relatively small circle of followers. They belonged to an ugly cul-de-sac of history, an era where witches and heretics were burned in town squares. They were adolescent ideas, in that they remained willfully ignorant of all that had come before. There are many who choose to believe that certain ancient texts are literally the word of one God or the other, but not many who would go so far as to regard as a sacred duty the slaughter of those who disagree with them, or to kill in order to advance their aims. This was a philosophy that would never appeal to more than a few dedicated fanatics. But one of the peculiarities of the modern world is that, because of telecommunications, small groups of like-minded people, even if widely scattered, can form a community of belief. They can feed off of each other, and can come to wield influence far beyond their actual numbers or appeal. Bin Laden's was the first to use these tools to build his network into a deadly force. The idea of turning fully fueled commercial airliners into guided bombs effectively gave al Qaeda the destructive power of a small air force or small arsenal of missiles. The suicide attackers who pulled it off had been recruited and trained internationally, financed by global money transfers, and steered by telephone and e-mail. The attacks themselves were designed to create a horrible spectacle for the entire world, television providing the audience, complete with replays and analyses for those who came late. It was a backward-looking movement with forward-looking tactics.

3

Taking Up Arms

Late Summer 2010

"Mr. President, Leon and the guys at Langley think they may have come up with something."

Tom Donilon brought this up at the end of President Obama's morning briefing one day in August. Instead of being briefed on sensitive national security issues by a CIA analyst, as President Bush had been, Obama preferred to be briefed by Donilon, his deputy national security adviser. Donilon would continue this practice even after he stepped into the top National Security Council job a few months later. It was that time of year when not much was going on in Washington. Heat and humidity drove everyone from the capital except the most determined tourists and those who had to stay.

"Something related to bin Laden," Donilon said. "We don't know yet what this is, but I think you need to have them in here for a briefing."

Donilon had been with Obama ever since the final stages of the 2008 campaign, when he was summoned to reprise a role he had played for President Clinton, coaching the candidate for a series of formal debates with his Republican rival. The Bush years had been a long break from government service for Donilon, who had continued with his work as a lobbyist for Fannie Mae for several years and had then moved on to become a partner in the D.C. law firm O'Melveny & Myers. But his heart was still in politics and governance, and when he was invited to help prep Obama for his face-off against Republican candidate Senator John McCain he leapt at it. He believed in the importance of presidential debates. They not only gave the public a better sense of the candidates, but they forced those running to examine the weaknesses in their own thinking and policy prescriptions, and to confront them, before an audience of millions. One of the first recommendations he made to Obama, which was adopted, was that he debate McCain on foreign policy issues first, precisely because it was an arena in which the veteran senator and war hero was thought to have a strong advantage. McCain's storied military service in Vietnam, where he was held prisoner for five years after his A-4E Skyhawk was shot down over Hanoi, and his twenty-six years in Congress, weighed impressively against Obama, who, twenty-five years younger than McCain, had never served in the military and had yet to complete his first Senate term. On paper, McCain had stronger qualifications for the job. But presidents were not hired, they were elected, and even the most distinguished résumé counted for little next to the impression the candidates made on the public. Donilon felt that if Obama could be seen on national television holding his own in a national security debate with McCain, voters could better begin to imagine him as their president. And better for that to happen sooner than later. He believed this is what Obama accomplished.

His role in prepping the candidate meant confronting him with the cracks in his thinking *before* he stepped onstage. In that sense, Donilon was one of the only people around Obama whose job it was to kick him, so to speak—to ruffle the candidate's famous cool. He worked at tripping Obama, poking holes in his reasoning, challenging his facts, pushing him beyond his stump-tested applause lines and polished talking points.

"All right, that's what you say on the campaign trail," he would say, "but if you are pressed on it, what do you really mean?"

Or, "I've heard you say that, but are you willing to live with it as president?"

Or, sniffing disagreeably at one of the candidate's typically long-winded responses, "And how do you explain *that* in ninety seconds?"

The candidate must have liked this sort of thing, because he had kept his tormentor close ever since. Donilon found him to possess a fine mind and a deep knowledge of American history and the law. It was hard to get the better of him in argument. To engage him fully meant being fully prepared; otherwise you were likely to come away humiliated. A physically expressive man, Obama had a way of shooing away an ill-founded argument with an amused smile or a more subtle expression like a raised eyebrow and dismissive tilt of his head. Donilon worked hard to avoid that look. He was rarely seen outside the corridors of the White House, a rumpled creature of the cramped warren of offices occupied by the National Security Council leadership downstairs. He was rarely interviewed by the press and seemed egoless. Obama drove his inner staff hard, but Donilon, if anything, drove himself harder. He graded his performance every day—*high* or *low*. After the election, Obama asked him to chair his State Department transition team, and had then placed him under General James Jones on the NSC staff. Jones, a former Marine Corps commandant, had been recruited in part as a bridge to the U.S. military, with which Obama had virtually no firsthand experience, and he had agreed from the start to stay in the job for only a year or two. From the beginning of the term Donilon was seen as Jones's likely successor.

It particularly pleased him to have something new for the president about bin Laden. There had been no scent of the world's most infamous terrorist for more than seven years, ever since he had slipped away from the mountain outpost of Tora Bora during a botched siege by allied troops. The Bush administration had said for years that he was somewhere in the mountainous regions of northwest Pakistan but, in truth, they had no idea. There had not been a lead or a sighting in years. Obama had taken office determined to resurrect the hunt.

On May 26, 2009, four months into his presidency, he had ended a routine national security briefing in the Situation Room by pointing to Donilon, Leon Panetta, his newly appointed CIA director, Mike Leiter, director of the National Counter Terrorism Center, and Rahm Emanuel, his chief of staff.

"You, you, you, and you," he said. "Come upstairs. I want to talk to you guys about something."

The four followed Obama up a short flight of stairs and through the warren of narrow West Wing hallways to the Oval Office. Afternoon sun poured through the windows from the Rose Garden. They didn't sit down. This was something quick that the president had been thinking about and wanted to impress on them personally. They had been on the job now long enough to have taken hold of

America's vast intelligence apparatus . . . time enough to have eased fully into their new roles.

As Donilon would tell me, Obama said: "Here's the deal. I want this hunt for Osama bin Laden and al-Zawahiri to come to the front of the line. I worry that the trail has gone cold. This has to be our top priority and it needs leadership in the tops of your organizations. You need to ensure that we have expended every effort to take down the top leadership of al Qaeda, especially these two individuals. And I want regular reports on this *to me*, and I want them starting in thirty days."

Donilon followed up and drove the point home with a memo, which the president signed. He sent it to each of those present. It read: "In order to ensure that we have extended every effort— directly provide to me a detailed operational plan for locating and bringing to justice Osama bin Laden."

That brief huddle in the Oval Office had not been scheduled, as virtually every minute of the president's day was, and Obama had not discussed it beforehand with Donilon. The president had plenty of other things to think about. He was beginning to withdraw U.S. troops from Iraq and was reevaluating the future of the ongoing conflict in Afghanistan. He had authorized a covert cyberwar on Iran's efforts to enrich uranium to weapons grade, and he was trying to assemble a coalition to apply economic pressure on that country to end its pursuit of nuclear weapons. He had vigorously expanded the secret program to target al Qaeda leaders inside Pakistan and other countries with drones, putting unrelenting daily pressure on the organization. He was trying to counter a Chinese military buildup by reorienting the nation's military forces toward the Pacific Rim. So there was plenty on the agenda every time his national security team sat down with him. But as the president would later tell me, he wasn't hearing enough about bin Laden to convince him that *everything* was being done, that *every effort* was being made. He wanted to make sure the right people knew what a big priority this was for him. And in the months that had followed, in between those monthly reports, he brought the matter up again and again. It was one of several things he raised at nearly every security meeting. He would always ask about cybersecurity efforts and he would always ask about Osama bin Laden.

Obama's leadership style was to enumerate clear, consistent priorities, and stay focused on them until they were accomplished. About twice a year he would meet with the national security team for several hours with nothing else on the agenda. He would bring in a legal pad on which he had listed his priorities in handwriting so small and meticulous that from across the room it looked like type.

"Hey guys, these are the three most important things we're working on right now," he'd say. "And this is where I want your efforts."

He'd go through his list item by item and they would discuss and critique their performance: where they had made progress and where they had not. Often he would move things up or down on his list or add things, but when he was done everyone had a clear understanding of where they should be spending their time and re-sources. Always, from the first such session, finding bin Laden had been at the top of that list.

As far as Obama was concerned, getting him was more than just symbolic. He had long been critical of Bush's "War on Terror." The way he saw it, America was not at war with something amor-phous, like a concept or a tactic. It was at war with specific indi-viduals who had attacked the country and continued to threaten it. When he took office in 2009 al Qaeda and its affiliate organizations remained the first clear and present danger, even after two long, bloody wars and the unceasing efforts of America's intelligence and special ops soldiers.

Obama had been sternly warned about this by Bruce Riedel, a former CIA analyst and Brookings Institution scholar whom he had called at home just days after the inauguration and asked to conduct a sixty-day review of American policy in Afghanistan and Pakistan. Eight days before he had pulled his intelligence chiefs into the Oval Office, Riedel had briefed him on his findings in a long meeting aboard Air Force One. He had told Obama that, in his estimation, al Qaeda was more dangerous today than it had been on September 11.

As Bob Woodward would report in his 2010 book, *Obama's Wars*, Riedel said, "Some al Qaeda watchers would argue that bin Laden, hiding in Pakistan, is irrelevant. He's stuck in a cave somewhere, and yes, he puts out these audiotapes once in a while, but he's more of a symbol than the commander of a global jihad. What I learned is that's just not true. He communicates with his underlings and is in touch with his foot soldiers. His troops believe they are getting his orders, and we know from good intelligence that they are . . . These guys are serious. They are clever, and they are relentless. Until we kill them, they're going to keep trying to kill us."

As Obama saw it, there was no way to defeat al Qaeda so long as its founder and spiritual leader remained at large. He was the soul of the organization. The president believed that bin Laden wasn't just evil, he was *charismatically* evil.

"He understood that with technology and modern media, the potential impact of a big event can magnify and leverage the power of even a small group," the president told me. "In that sense, although the notions of terrorism hadn't obviously developed or started with him, I think he had an understanding of the West and where our potential vulnerable points were that made him a singular figure, somebody who was uniquely capable of doing great damage to us."

Despite the simple life he preferred and his romantic notions of the past, bin Laden understood modern media and exploited it, Obama said. It gave him an influence far beyond the reach of his actual following. The September 11 attacks had shaken the world.

President Bush had felt the same way. Unable to squelch his Texas swagger early on, he had said he wanted bin Laden "dead or alive." But in the view of the Obama administration, the two wars Bush had launched gradually became usurping priorities. There is, as Donilon would put it, "limited bandwidth" in the White House. In the final years of the Bush administration, even though the man at the top still badly wanted bin Laden, the effort to find him was publicly downplayed in the way Riedel explained. It was said that bin Laden was out of touch. That he had been effectively sidelined and, so far as operations were concerned, rendered irrelevant. Unable to find him, the Bush administration had de-emphasized the importance of finding him.

The way Obama saw it, this was a mistake. America's war-making bureaucracy was vast, and without determined pressure from the White House, without an enumerated list of priorities that kept coming back and coming back until each item was crossed off, even urgent concerns got lost. Just keeping track of all the missions under way on any given day was more than a full-time job. There were U.S. troops on the ground in more than 150 countries around the world. When those missions turned hot, as they had in Afghanistan and Iraq, they devoured not just men and resources but the time and attention of the decision makers atop the chain of command. The essence of leading any very large enterprise was maintaining priorities, and while bin Laden had never slipped from the top during the Bush years, the list itself had become very crowded. The bottom line, as Obama put it to Panetta and Leiter, was that bin Laden's trail had gone cold. The president wanted it warm again.

Now, more than a year later, the agency finally had something to report. It had found an unusual compound just outside Abbottabad while looking for an al Qaeda figure who went by the name Abu Ahmed al-Kuwaiti, "Ahmed the Kuwaiti," a man known to have been a trusted aide and courier for bin Laden. Along with family, known associates, financial webs, and other networks, couriers had long been seen as potential cracks in the walls around the fugitive Sheik. Too wary to use cell phones or Internet links, bin Laden relied on couriers to distribute by hand his letters, poems, and occasional video and audio pronouncements. Reversing the paths to media outlets taken by these tapes or thumb drives always ended one or two steps short of their origin. The Kuwaiti might be one of those final links, perhaps even the courier who dealt with the Sheik directly. The search for him had lasted eight years. It had taken the CIA five just to learn his real name, which was Ibrahim Saeed Ahmed. And then the trail had led them to this very curious residence.

Panetta brought two of the agency's bin Laden team leaders with him to the Oval Office. The lead analyst, who would become known as "John" (his middle name), was a tall former college basketball player, now middle-aged, who had devoted himself to the hunt for most of the previous ten years. He had a broad chin and a big-featured face and looked more like an athlete than someone who spent most of his time before a computer monitor. At Langley, he reported to Michael Morell, who had risen to deputy director in the years since he had been briefing Bush.

The agency men handed around classified pictures and maps and analytical material, and walked the president and Donilon through their thinking in great detail—the reverse engineering that had helped them identify "Ahmed the Kuwaiti" and the suspicious nature of the compound itself. Panetta compared Abbottabad to a well-to-do northern Virginia suburb. The compound was eight times larger than any of the surrounding residences. Unlike most, it did not have any Internet or phone connections. The walls that surrounded it were built unusually high, topped by two feet of barbed wire. There were even walls around a patio at the back of the third floor. There was no way to see inside the house itself, from the ground or above. The windows were made of reflective glass or had been coated to achieve the same effect. The agency first learned that not only Ahmed and his family lived there, but also his brother Abrar and his family. They went by assumed names in the neighborhood, Ibrahim called himself Arshad Khan and his brother went by the name Tareq Khan. Both had been born in Kuwait, but ethnically they were tall, fair-skinned, bearded Pakistani Pashtuns. They had never been wealthy, but their compound appeared extremely pricey. And in addition to the high walls, it seemed the brothers observed extraordinarily strict security measures. They even burned all of their trash on-site. Other than to attend the local religious school or to visit a doctor, none of their children left the compound. In telephone calls to other far-flung family members, always made from locations distant from the compound itself, they lied about where they were living. The CIA had been known to misinterpret many things, but one thing it knew inside out was high operational security.

The agency had been investigating the compound quietly, snapping pictures from above and spying on it with agents on the ground—who couldn't see inside but who asked casual questions of those living nearby, always careful not to appear too curious. *Who lives in that big place? I wonder what the people who live there do?* That and telephone intercepts had produced two discoveries in recent weeks that the agency considered greatly significant, and persuaded Panetta that he ought to bring the discovery to the president.

The first was that living inside the compound on the upper two floors of the big house was a third family. No member of that family ever left the grounds. Its children did not even leave to attend school with the others. Neighbors in Abbottabad who knew of the Khan brothers and their families were not aware of this third one. And there were signs that the brothers, who ostensibly owned the place, *served* this hidden family. One or the other brother was always present, so the third family was never left alone. Ibrahim Ahmed and his family occupied the guesthouse on the grounds, and his brother Abrar and his family lived on the first floor of the main house.

The second discovery was that Ibrahim Ahmed was apparently still working for al Qaeda. Though he was known to have been close to bin Laden years earlier, the agency had no proof that he had retained the connection. Some of the detainees interviewed about him over the years had said that he had left the organization, in which case he might now be working for anyone with a need to lie low: An organized crime figure? A rich man with political enemies? A Saudi millionaire with a mistress or hidden second family? But in a telephone conversation with an old friend that summer, a call that the United States monitored, Ahmed was peppered with the standard questions—"What are you doing now? What are you up to?" At first he didn't answer. He dodged the questions. But his friend was insistent, and so he finally gave in, albeit cryptically. "I'm with the same ones as before," he said. His friend seemed to know immediately what that meant and, after uttering "May Allah be with you," dropped the subject. That suggested that whomever Ahmed and his brother were minding in Abbottabad belonged to al Qaeda.

These were the details presented to the president.

"This is the best lead we've had on bin Laden since Tora Bora," said "John."

Obama was familiar enough with bin Laden's background to have long ago stopped picturing him crouched in a cave or living in some sparse mountaintop camp. But to find him in a sprawling compound in an affluent neighborhood known for golf courses and cool summer breezes—they were all surprised by that. Still, the president wasn't especially hopeful. He knew he had been leaning hard on the CIA to come up with something, and demanding updates, so he had to expect they would bring him every scrap. This was a scrap. He found the information intriguing, but only in a general way. The connection to bin Laden was tenuous at best. He encouraged Panetta to press on. He wanted the identity of the hidden family nailed down. He also wanted a "close hold" on the lead, meaning it was not to leave his office. No one else in the military or intelligence chain was to be brought in yet. And they were not to seek help from Pakistan or tip their interest in the compound there . . . yet. The president left open the option of going to his purported Pakistani allies for help once they knew more. In the meantime, he wanted regular progress reports.

"Just emotionally," Obama told me, "I was not particularly optimistic about it. I mean, I think my general view was, okay, these guys are carrying out my orders to pursue every lead. Did I think at that stage that we had the goods? I think I was pretty guarded about not letting myself get overly excited about the prospects."

At that point, the president had been ordering drone hits and special operations raids to kill al Qaeda leaders for nearly twenty months. The skills of America's intelligence and military, honed over nine years of war, had given him tools no president had ever had. National Security Council meetings in this presidency were not just policy discussions. They regularly concerned matters of life and death for specific individuals. The capability developed over the previous decade armed the president with immediate choices about these prospective targets—people who had been found and identified and were now in the nation's crosshairs. They could be killed on his orders without placing a single American in jeopardy. There had been fifty-three drone strikes in Pakistan alone in the first year of his term. In 2010 there had been more than twice that number: 117. The numbers of strikes in Yemen, while fewer, had been steadily increasing every year, from two in 2009 to four in 2010. There would be ten the following year. Nearly every day the president faced immediate, deadly choices. Should this specific person be killed? Would killing him possibly involve killing others—others less culpable, perhaps others completely innocent?

Decisions like this had always come with the office, and sometimes had concerned questions of life and death for thousands, or even hundreds of thousands—one thinks of President Harry S. Truman making the decision to drop the atom bomb. But how many of these decisions concerned taking a single life? It gave the commander in chief a strangely direct role in the war. There were precedents. During World War II, American forces decrypted a Japanese message revealing that Admiral Isoroku Yamamoto, commander of the Japanese fleet, would be making an inspection tour of the Solomon Islands. His plane was intercepted and shot down, and he was killed. President Kennedy had notoriously plotted to assassinate Fidel Castro during the early 1960s. But these incidents were rare, and were undertaken at great risk. Toward the end of his second term, President Bush, and now Obama, had what was, in essence, a sniper rifle pointed at men regarded as significant terrorists. Obama was routinely presented with a brief on the target: who he was, how important he was, how dangerous he was, how much it might matter to be rid of him, and who else might die as a result. He had only to decide to pull the trigger. This was something new.

This war had demanded something new. After the 9/11 attacks, the two most obvious ways of fighting back had both been defensive: prevent the most dangerous kinds of attacks and prepare to cope better with smaller ones when they occurred. So the United States had spent billions on efforts to block known or obvious avenues of attack, and to improve emergency response. This is what the Department of Homeland Security and the Transportation Safety Administration had been all about. Another step was to secure materials worldwide, such as plutonium, surface-to-air missiles, and toxic biochemicals, that could be used to create especially powerful weapons. This approach is what had led, in part, to President Bush's invasion of Iraq—to secure Saddam's supposed arsenal of weapons of mass destruction.

As for offensive strategy—going after al Qaeda itself—this became immeasurably more difficult once the organization had scattered from its safe havens in Afghanistan. In solving this problem, the United States would bring to bear enormous resources of talent, wealth, and technology. The story of the previous ten years of war, viewed in this broad sense, had been the story of developing the right tools to destroy a terror *network*. It was still a work in progress in 2010, but it had come a long way. With the military's typical disdain for ordinary English, it had slapped an acronym on this capability. It was called "F3EAD" (Find, Fix, Finish, Exploit, Analyze, Disseminate). It stood for a remarkable fusion of instant global telecommunications, drones, computer-data storage, cutting-edge software, experienced analysts, stealth helicopters, precision munitions, and the operational skills of pilots and shooters who could execute strikes with great surprise and skill virtually anywhere in the world.

When Obama took office he inherited this unprecedented and still-evolving capability. The tool—particularly the use of drones—was proving to be lethal to al Qaeda. As much as it troubled those concerned about potential abuses—pinpointing and killing people by remote control was a scary futuristic concept—it was also, paradoxically, a fundamental advance in the humane pursuit of war. The three basic principles of lawful warfare had long been *necessity* (violence as a last resort), *distinction* (targeting the right people), and *proportionality* (not killing the wrong people). Very few would argue that the nation was not justified in using force to protect itself from Osama bin Laden and his movement, bent on suicidal acts of mass murder. Drones uniquely enhanced compliance with *distinction* and *proportionality*. The ability to soundlessly observe a target for days, weeks, or months before deciding to attack greatly improved the odds of hitting appropriate targets and avoiding inappropriate ones. There was no comparison with ground combat or even very precise bombs and missiles. If it was necessary to fight, then drones killed far fewer civilians than any previous war-fighting method, and they did so without placing American fighters at risk.

Obama had kept this capability on a tight leash. In most cases, he alone made the final decision to kill. In some cases, the decision was made by the CIA director. They would review the case against the targets and decide whether to shoot. Obama had directed the

Justice Department and the CIA's legal staff to draw up secret guide-lines that would mark the first step toward institutionalizing those controls, so that whoever succeeded him in office would inherit clear rules, clear precedent, and clear constraints. The administration had not made these guidelines public, which troubled many who were concerned about the growing use of drones. There was no doubt that within those strictures, whatever they were, Obama had proven himself willing to pull the trigger regularly.

This surprised many. Bush had brought to the White House a light dusting of military experience—he had served as a pilot in the Air National Guard during the Vietnam War period—but he was nevertheless seen by the military as one of them, a president who openly admired the armed forces and who was, to a fault, quick to authorize their deployment. He spoke their can-do vocabulary with a Texas drawl. His father had been a war hero and had served as the CIA director—the headquarters building at Langley was even named after George Herbert Walker Bush. Obama, on the other hand, was strictly civilian. His father was Kenyan. He was a liberal Democrat with an international upbringing—an academic and an intellectual. He had been an early, consistent, and outspoken critic of invading Iraq, which he had called a "dumb war." Indeed, he had initially geared his campaign for the Democratic nomination in 2008 as an antiwar candidate, attacking his foes in the primaries, Hillary Clinton in particular, for her early support of the conflict. Obama had also criticized the more controversial tools of the war—coercive interrogation methods, extraordinary rendition, military commissions, and indefinite detention—arguing that the nation's security should never trump its values. He talked a lot about the need for negotiating with enemies and the virtues of mutual understanding—not the kind of talk that rouses the troops.

Much of what most Americans heard from him during his scant twenty months in the Senate concerned hastening America's withdrawal from Iraq and spelling out his desire for a clearly defined exit strategy from Afghanistan. They had expected an all but pacifist president.

But the number of drone strikes in his first two years would be more than four times the total in Bush's two terms in the White House. And Obama's appreciation and enthusiasm for the Special Operations Command was clearly genuine. He seemed to fully embrace General Patraeus's line about going to bed each night with more friends and fewer enemies—with particular emphasis on the "fewer enemies."

Those who had been paying close attention to Obama were not surprised. He had been spelling out for years, in increasing detail, his willingness to wage war in general, and, in particular, his intent to wage war on al Qaeda. Just over a year after the September 11 attacks, as President Bush was gearing up to invade Iraq, Obama, still largely unknown outside of his Chicago district, was invited to speak at an antiwar rally in Chicago. He was one of the lesser speakers, and his talk wouldn't even get a line in the account in the next morning's *Chicago Tribune*. It was received with lukewarm applause. In his book *The Bridge*, David Remnick captures Obama's discomfort at the overall tenor of the rally, listening to the plaintive strains of John Lennon's "Give Peace a Chance" and leaning to one of the event organizers, Bettylu Saltzman, to ask, "Can't they play something else?" Giving a rousing speech that would excite the gaggle of tired lefties in Federal Plaza might make for a feel-good moment and some admiring local press, but it could also hurt his chances statewide. He had conferred with the consultants helping him prepare for his Senate run, trying to hone a message that, as Remnick wrote, "would express his opposition to an invasion of Iraq without making him seem disqualifyingly weak on terror." His advisers wanted him to speak—any African-American seeking statewide office in Illinois would need the Chicago vote. But he also had to transcend that audience.

So Obama's speech was very carefully thought out. It was an early effort at speechmaking and shows it. The speech was overly dramatic and derivative, echoing the famous "I Have a Dream" speech of Martin Luther King Jr. It showed careful political calculation but, given what we would see years later, it also expressed conviction. It also showed how far his thinking on the subject had evolved since his comments to the *Hyde Park Herald* the year before. His first words were: "Let me begin by saying that although this has been billed as an antiwar rally, I stand before you as someone who is not opposed to war in all circumstances."

Obama took note of the Civil War, "one of the bloodiest in history," which had driven "the scourge of slavery" from America. "I don't oppose all wars," he said. He noted his grandfather's service in World War II. "He fought in the name of a larger freedom, part of that arsenal of democracy that triumphed over evil, and he did not fight in vain," he said, and then repeated, "I don't oppose all wars."

He would continue to repeat that line as a refrain, imitating King's famous and stirring repetition of the line "I have a dream." It took cheek to borrow the most famous rhetorical device ever employed by King, the great practitioner of nonviolence, to proclaim his belief in the necessity of war.

"After September 11, after witnessing the carnage and destruction, the dust and the tears, I supported this administration's pledge to hunt down and root out those who would slaughter innocents in the name of intolerance, and I would willingly take up arms myself to prevent such a tragedy from happening again. I don't oppose all wars."

He went on to denounce the pending invasion of Iraq as a "dumb war," and a "rash war," but what those listening that day most remembered was his *affirmation* of war as just and necessary. His belief that some wars were worth fighting. The one against al Qaeda was one of them. It was a doubly bold speech for someone contemplating a run for the U.S. Senate, because it not only ran counter to the blanket antiwar sensibilities of his immediate audience but also bucked the decidedly pro–Iraq War sentiment of Illinois voters, most of whom were far to the right of the small group of protesters in downtown Chicago. Where the Iraq invasion was concerned, Obama was once more out of step with the nation, but where al Qaeda was concerned, he was no longer calling for some sort of global-welfare campaign. He was ready to "take up arms" himself in that war. In a more direct manner than he could have imagined, he would get his chance.

Three years later, after his victory in the 2004 Senate race and rapid ascent to national prominence, Obama was running for president. In August of 2007, he was still struggling. There had been excitement for him when he announced his candidacy in February, but things had quickly leveled off. He was running well behind Hillary Clinton, considered by many to be a shoo-in for the Democratic nomination, and also behind John Edwards, who was thought to be next in line in the unlikely event that Clinton stumbled.

At the time, the strongest thing Obama had going for him seemed to be that 2002 speech. Here was an attractive, smart, antiwar candidate at a time when America's patience for its adventure in Iraq was at an all-time low. Every Democrat in the race was opposed to continuing the war. They vied now only over who was more emphatically opposed to it. Obama had not been in the Senate when votes were cast to authorize the war so, unlike Clinton and Edwards, he could claim ideological purity on the issue. And the Chicago speech put him on record as having spoken out against it from the start. He was the premier antiwar candidate, and that's how he presented himself. The simple thrust of his attack on Clinton, in particular, was that she had gone along with Bush on the war, while he had taken the unpopular, principled stand and had been proved right. Over the course of the campaign Obama would be forced to spell out his thinking in more detail, and the picture would become more complex.

His rise was so meteoric that many felt it had come too fast. His opponents were both baffled and annoyed by the messianic luster that he and his campaign encouraged. The best way to push back was to convince voters that he was in too big a hurry. At age forty-five, with only half of his Senate term behind him . . . well, even if he was destined to be America's first black president, he wasn't ready for the job yet. He was one of the youngest men to ever seek the presidency.

So experience was the hammer, and Clinton lowered it whenever Obama gave her a chance. He gave her one after a CNN/YouTube debate on July 23, when he was asked if he would consider meeting with America's enemies without preconditions. The questioner, whose face was projected on a big screen, approvingly cited Egypt's President Anwar Sadat's courageous (and ultimately fatal) decision, in 1977, to initiate peace negotiations with Israel, and asked if any of the candidates would be willing, in the first year of their tenure, to meet *without preconditions* the leaders of Iran, Syria,

Venezuela, Cuba, and North Korea in an effort to "bridge the gap that divides our countries."

It was an easy question to dodge: *Negotiation is terribly important . . . I wouldn't rule it out . . . we have a history with these countries that didn't begin yesterday . . .* But Obama didn't dodge it. Up on the glitzy stage before glowing red, white, and blue screens, behind a spare, modernist podium of steel and plastic, he was the first of the eight candidates asked to respond.

"I would," he said.

A gasp rose from the studio audience, no doubt partly because of the directness of his answer. They were used to more maneuvering.

"My reason is this," he explained. "The notion that, somehow, not talking to countries is punishment to them, which has been the guiding diplomatic principle of this [George W. Bush] administration, is ridiculous . . . We may not trust them, they may pose an extraordinary danger to our country, but we have the obligation to find the areas where we may potentially move forward, and I think that it is a disgrace that we have not spoken to them."

Clinton, who answered next, promptly said that she would *not*. She explained that a lot of groundwork went into negotiations with unfriendly nations; that one did not rush into them. But, perhaps startled like everyone else, she didn't hit Obama too hard onstage. On reflection, however, and no doubt after her campaign strategists weighed in, she returned more harshly to the point the next day in interviews, labeling Obama's answer "irresponsible and frankly naive."

This was strictly politics. The United States had a long bipartisan tradition of negotiating with even its worst enemies, from John Kennedy—"Let us never negotiate out of fear. But let us never fear to negotiate"—to Richard Nixon's opening with China, to Ronald Reagan's famous "walk in the woods" with Mikhail Gorbachev. Obama's position was firmly in line with longstanding diplomatic practice. George W. Bush's post–9/11 policy—"You are either for us or against us"—was the exception, and a bad one. It removed subtlety from international affairs. It made no sense whatsoever for a savvy internationalist like Clinton to ignore the opportunity every newly elected president has to reset relations with hostile nations. Still, conventional wisdom held that you didn't admit such things. It made you sound soft. And *naive* was a word that worked against Obama.

It worked because many believed he lacked substance. He had yet to really define himself in detail on foreign policy or anything else. He had given a foreign policy address in April in line with his antiwar image, primarily calling for renewed internationalism, a greater willingness to seek consensus, and cooperation from other countries in pursuit of our national security goals. His remark about negotiating with enemies without preconditions made it easy for his critics to paint him as a complete pushover. It also suggested that Obama was a man who did not think things through carefully.

The "naive" label was troublesome. Soon enough the word had attached itself to him. TV pundits seemed unable to mention him without repeating it. Over the next few weeks his standing in the polls continued to fall as Clinton's rose.

Obama's staff fretted. Some wanted him to back off from his position, but he refused. "The thing is that I am right about this," he insisted in a meeting with his advisers Denis McDonough and Robert Gibbs. "Why would we *not* want to get into any negotiation that we could?" He asked them to schedule a national TV interview to reiterate his position, to underline it. It was, he felt, precisely the kind of message he wanted to send. He was offering to break with the past, to look at these foreign policy issues in a new way.

And he was just getting started. Obama was not about to let others substitute their analysis for his own. His approach to a problem was to look for a new solution, an original one. He believed much of the way America thought about defense issues was cast in archaic molds—the old divisions of left vs. right, conservatives vs. liberals, hawks vs. doves that had been set by the debate over Vietnam. He had been thirteen years old when that war ended. Much of the voting-age population of the country had not even been born. Nothing had shaken up that old dynamic as much as 9/11. Young people in particular were hard to classify in this regard. They tended to be far more liberal than their parents on most social issues—hence more likely to support Obama—but were also strongly supportive of robust military and intelligence efforts. As the candidate saw it, he was as hawkish as any American about defeating al Qaeda, but some of the tools traditionally associated with *doves*—tools such as negotiation and international cooperation—weren't just means of appeasing an enemy. They were essential to defeating this one.

A few weeks earlier, according to John Heilemann and Mark Halperin in *Game Change*, Obama had brought one of his close friends and old law professors, Chris Edley, to Chicago to lambaste his inner campaign circle for failing to let him do things *his* way. They were not giving Obama time and space in his frenetic campaign schedule to lay out his ideas in more detail.

"This is a guy who likes to think, he likes to write, he likes to talk with experts," said Edley, whose work on past Democratic campaigns and in White House service lent authority to his words. "You folks have got to recognize what he's in this for. He's in this because he wants to make contributions in terms of public policy ideas, and you've got to make time for him to do that . . . With all due respect to all you here, you should just get over yourselves and do what the candidate wants."

So in the days after the fallout from his *negotiate without pre-conditions* promise, it was decided that Obama would give another major national security speech. He did so at the Woodrow Wilson International Center, in Washington, D.C., on August 1, outlining his thinking on national security in some detail and in the process correcting the impression that he was "naive" or, worse, "soft" on national defense.

A National Intelligence Estimate that spring suggested al Qaeda had actually grown stronger in the previous six years. It noted that Pakistan had become the new safe haven for the terror group after the fall of the Taliban. All Democratic candidates had pledged change, but beyond promising to pull the plug on Iraq and end some of the more controversial intelligence-gathering methods (most of which had ended already), none had clearly articulated an approach to national security that differed significantly from Bush's.

Former Congressman Lee Hamilton introduced Obama at the Wilson Center gathering before an audience of a few hundred, many of them journalists. The speech had engaged all of Obama's foreign policy advisers, and every word in it had been weighed carefully. Tapped with the task of drafting it was Ben Rhodes, the former NYU graduate student who had watched from the Brooklyn water-front as the World Trade Center towers collapsed. He was now a top-level campaign worker with prematurely thinning black hair and a perpetual five o'clock shadow. Instead of setting to work on a first novel, he had joined Hamilton's staff just as the congressman was named cochair of the 9/11 Commission. Rhodes had helped draft policy proposals for the *Commission Report* and helped write the chapter entitled "What to Do?" One of the subheads in that chapter had been "Attack Terrorists and Their Organizations," and its first proscription was "No Sanctuaries." Of all the most likely places in the world to play host to terrorist groups, first on the list was Pakistan. Rhodes eventually helped Hamilton and his cochair, former New Jersey Governor Tom Kean, write a book about the commission's work. After serving Hamilton on the Iraq Study Group, which the congressman also cochaired, Rhodes joined Obama's Senate staff as a foreign policy adviser and speechwriter. He had helped draft some of Obama's talks about Iraq in the Senate, and had then signed on as a speechwriter in Obama's Chicago office. This was the first campaign speech he had been asked to draft, and it was a big one. It also returned him to a familiar theme.

In a telephone conference with Rhodes, McDonough, Samantha Power, and various other national security aides, Obama outlined seven points he wanted to make in the speech. These were distilled to five by Rhodes and Power. One of them concerned efforts to destroy al Qaeda. As for the issue of safe havens, Rhodes would remember Obama telling him, "Let's come up with the most forward-leaning formulation to make it clear that we are going to go after these guys, because that's the whole argument."

Before the crowd at the Wilson Center, Obama began by relating his own experiences on 9/11—hearing the first report on his drive into Chicago, standing on the sidewalk in the Loop eyeing the Sears Tower, watching the towers fall on TV. In the six years since then, the stirring sense of national unity and purpose engendered by the attacks had been squandered, he said. The Bush administration had started well, toppling the Taliban and chasing al Qaeda, the real enemy, from its bases in Afghanistan. But then it had dropped the ball. Instead of going after the architects of 9/11, who were on the ropes and on the run, the Bush administration had decided to invade Iraq and topple Saddam Hussein, a move that had quickly absorbed the nation's primary military and intelligence resources. The move had been "rubber-stamped" by Congress, he said, side-swiping his Democratic primary opponents. It was, he said, "A mis-guided invasion of a Muslim country that sparks new insurgencies, ties down our military, busts our budgets, increases the pool of ter-rorist recruits, alienates America, gives democracy a bad name, and prompts the American people to question our engagement in the world." Obama pointed to the new Intelligence Estimate as proof that al Qaeda had only changed its home address.

Once again, he pledged to end the Iraq War, not out of any pacifist conviction, but in order to refocus on the real enemy. His focus, he promised, would be on crushing al Qaeda. This was *the* mission 9/11 had compelled, a national priority that trumped peaceable relations with Pakistan or any other country. The enemy had been too broadly defined by the Bush administration, he said, a failing that not only had diminished the impact of our response but had fed into al Qaeda propaganda that America was at war with the entire Muslim world. The necessary war called for a much smaller focus: to find, target, and destroy the terror organization. To under-score his determination, Obama said he would respect no sanctuary and zeroed in specifically on Pakistan.

"Al Qaeda terrorists train, travel, and maintain global commu-nications in this safe haven," he said. "The Taliban pursues a hit-and-run strategy, striking in Afghanistan, then skulking across the border to safety. This is the wild frontier of our globalized world. There are wind-swept deserts and cave-dotted mountains. There are tribes that see borders as nothing more than lines on a map, and governments as forces that come and go. There are blood ties deeper than alliances of convenience, and pockets of extremism that follow religion to violence. It's a tough place. But that is no excuse. There must be no safe haven for terrorists who threaten America. We cannot fail to act because action is hard. As president, I would make the hundreds of millions of dollars in U.S. military aid to Pakistan conditional, and I would make our conditions clear: Pakistan must make substantial progress in closing down the training camps, evicting foreign fighters, and preventing the Taliban from using Pakistan as a staging area for attacks in Afghanistan. I understand that President Musharraf has his own challenges. But let me make this clear, there are terrorists holed up in those mountains who murdered three thousand Americans. They are plotting to strike again. It was a terrible mistake to fail to act when we had a chance to take out an al Qaeda leadership meeting in 2005. If we have actionable intelligence about high-value terrorist targets and President Musharraf won't act, we will."

That final line was the very last one inserted in the speech. Much deliberation preceded it. Rhodes had originally written, "If we have targets [in Pakistan] and President Musharraf won't act, we will." It was in keeping with the candidate's instruction to be as "forward leaning" as possible. But the issue of Pakistan was delicate. That unstable nation was critical to the war effort in Afghanistan. It was a nuclear power in one of the world's most volatile regions, and yet elements of its government, particularly its powerful intelligence agency, the Inter-Services Intelligence (ISI), were known to be in bed with all manner of Islamist radicals. Pakistan's President Pervez Musharraf had been walking a narrow line with the Bush administration, providing enough cooperation to avoid being branded an enemy but falling well short of routing extremists holed up in Pakistan's lawless northwest. Threatening to go after "targets" without Pakistan's cooperation made Obama's national security team nervous.

Nobody had been happy with the line in a pre-speech review at Obama's Washington headquarters. Present were Robert Gibbs, Susan Rice, Jeh Johnson, Rand Beers, and Richard Clarke, the campaign's premier consultant on security matters.

"Look, that is not how you talk about these things," said Clarke. He explained the importance of working with the tribes in Pakistan's northwest territories.

But the candidate was resolute. He wanted the line in. It said exactly what he thought, and what he planned to do as president. *I do not oppose all wars.* He was going to go after the real threat. So the discussion focused on the wording. Two caveats were added: "If we have actionable intelligence" and "high-value targets." This was to make it clear that Obama was talking about acting only in an exceptional circumstance, and only in a specific, limited way.

No matter. The careful phrasing was ignored. Obama had covered a lot of ground in the speech, reiterating his plan to get troops out of Iraq, pledging to reinvest in the effort against the Taliban in Afghanistan, and promising to give a major speech somewhere in the Middle East, within his first hundred days as president, to redefine the U.S. mission for that region. He also promised to close the prison at Guantánamo and to end Bush-era programs that "tracked" American citizens. But the line about going after targets in Pakistan got nearly all of the press. There was heat from every quarter.

Jeff Zeleny of the *New York Times* reported that Obama had "vowed to dispatch American soldiers to eradicate terrorist camps" in Pakistan.

The subhead on the story in the *Los Angeles Times* said, "He says he'd reserve the right to invade," and reporter Paul Richter wrote, "Senator Barack Obama said Wednesday that the United States should reserve the right to invade the territory of its Pakistani allies and withdraw U.S. financial aid if it believed Pakistani President Pervez Musharraf was failing to do enough to stop terrorists."

Liberals accused Obama of embracing the Bush administration's cowboy mentality. Conservatives faulted Obama for a supposed lack of sophistication: Didn't he understand the delicacy of our relationship with Pakistan? Even if that was his plan, didn't he understand that you don't talk about things like this?

Liberal blogger Jerome Armstrong was disappointed. "For progressive Democrats who want a more peaceful leadership in the world . . . [Obama's speech] fails the threshold of getting us out of picking fights in the Mideast, and discarding the Bush doctrine of preemptive attacks."

Conservative columnist William Kristol wrote that Obama was "frantically suggesting that he would invade Pakistan" in order to shore up his tough-guy credentials against Hillary Clinton.

On his radio show, Rush Limbaugh mocked Obama. He noted that Osama bin Laden had been exhorting his followers to overthrow Musharraf, and now Obama—"I get these guys confused," he said—had threatened to "invade Pakistan." Limbaugh added, "Poor Musharraf is going to get it on both ends if Obama is elected."

"It's a very irresponsible statement, that's all I can say," said Pakistan's foreign minister Khurshid Kasuri. "As the election campaign in America is heating up we would not like American candidates to fight their elections and contest elections at our expense." Kasuri said that President Bush had called to privately reassure Musharraf, terming Obama's comments "unsavory" and prompted by political considerations "in an environment of electioneering."

"I do not concur in the words of Barack Obama in a plan to attack an ally of ours," said former Massachusetts Governor Mitt Romney, who was then a front-runner for the Republican presidential nomination. "I don't think those kinds of comments help in this effort to draw more friends to our effort." He said, U.S. troops "shouldn't be sent all over the world," and called the comments "ill-timed" and "ill-considered."

Again, some in Obama's camp wanted the candidate to issue an explanation, but once again he refused. He had meant what he said. Obama told his staff that their public posture on the comment should be to shoot down any talk of an "invasion," but to stand behind his willingness to act unilaterally in Pakistan if the right occasion presented itself.

"I am not going to be lectured about foreign policy by the same people who were responsible for this catastrophic war in Iraq," he maintained, in response to some of the criticism. It illustrated, he said, his willingness to "think outside the box." The campaign released a memo by Power, reiterating the candidate's promise: "Conventional wisdom would have us defer to Musharraf in perpetuity. Barack Obama wants to turn the page. If Musharraf is willing to go after the terrorists and stop the Taliban from using Pakistan as a base of operations, Obama would give him all of the support he needs. But Obama made clear that as president, if he had actionable intelligence about the whereabouts of al Qaeda leaders in Pakistan—and the Pakistanis continued to refuse to act against terrorists known to be behind attacks on American civilians—then he will use highly targeted force to do so."

Despite this effort to explain, the supposed call to "invade" Pakistan quickly entered campaign lore . . . and evolved. Obama's eventual Republican opponent, Senator John McCain, would claim that Obama had threatened to "bomb" Pakistan.

"The best idea is to not broadcast what you're going to do," McCain said the following February. "That's naive. The first thing that you do is you make your plans and you carry out your operations as necessary for America's national security interest. You don't broadcast that you are going to bomb a country that is a sovereign nation and where you are dependent on the goodwill of the people of that country to help you in the war—in the struggle against the Taliban and the sanctuaries which they hold."

So in 2007 and early 2008, on the question of going after Osama bin Laden, Obama's call for direct, unilateral action was roundly condemned. It remained his plan, however, and as soon as he was elected he acted on it. As Obama settled into the job, his determination to pursue al Qaeda's leadership was plain. If bin Laden had empowered himself, or had felt chosen by God, Obama had been elected. He had sought and had been chosen by the people of the United States to make these life-and-death decisions.

The new president immediately began shifting resources from Iraq, where he was determined to systematically draw down U.S. involvement, to Afghanistan and Pakistan. Large numbers of drones began leaving Iraq and flying missions over the steep mountains of eastern Afghanistan and the lawless regions of northwest Pakistan. The Joint Special Operations Command, which had been operating out of Balad Air Base, in Iraq, relocated in the summer of 2009 to Jalalabad, Afghanistan, beefing up bandwidth at the new encampment to retain links between intelligence computers and analysts in Washington. And as we have seen, the number of drone attacks spiked. America's relationship with Pakistan grew more troubled.

When he was awarded the Nobel Peace Prize in October of 2009, just as he was deciding to send thirty thousand more American troops to Afghanistan, Obama had a chance to fully articulate once more his thinking about war.

Again Rhodes was pressed into service. This time Obama presented him with a handwritten first draft, which had three quotes from Reinhold Niebuhr, the American theologian who argued strongly for the necessity of war and who rejected pacifism as a sure prescription for tyranny. The emergence of fascism in Germany and Japan, and communism in Russia, had prompted Niebuhr to famously renounce his lifelong pacifism. That movement had enjoyed a resurgence after World War I, with its seemingly senseless slaughter of millions. Now, with the world teetering on the brink of an even larger catastrophe, pacifists, who included a good many Christian thinkers in Europe and America, argued that if enough people refused to serve in armies, states would be unable to wage war ever again. Niebuhr did not believe it. The passages Obama quoted were from Niebuhr's 1939 essay, "Why the Christian Church Is Not Pacifist," in which the theologian argues, "If we believe that if Britain had only been fortunate enough to have produced 30 percent instead of 2 percent of conscientious objectors to military service, Hitler's heart would have been softened and he would not have dared to attack Poland, we hold a faith, which no historical reality justifies." Niebuhr believed that just as men were imperfect, so, too, were states, and just as men must struggle to defeat evil in themselves, they must also struggle to defeat evil at large.

Obama had pronounced his willingness to "take up arms" years earlier. Now, armed with more military power than anyone in any other country, he was not just prepared to use it, he felt morally obligated to do so. Just as he had done before the antiwar audience in Chicago seven years earlier, he would use this pacifist platform to argue his belief in the moral use of violence. The Nobel Peace Prize itself had grown out of the same pacifist movement Niebuhr turned against in 1939. It was one of the award categories established by Alfred Nobel at the behest of his friend Bertha von Suttner, a well-known nineteenth-century Austrian novelist, pacifist, and eventual peace prize recipient. So it is not surprising that Obama looked back to Niebuhr's arguments as he prepared to accept the prize himself in Oslo.

His speech there was a brief lecture on the necessity of war, and a tribute to the use of force — American force above all — as the only practical means of achieving the peace prize committee's high ideals. He saluted two of the twentieth century's most famous practitioners of nonviolence, Dr. King and Mahatma Gandhi, but said, "I face the world as it is, and cannot stand idle in the face of threats to the American people. For make no mistake, evil does exist in the world. A nonviolent movement could not have stopped Hitler's armies. To say that force is sometimes necessary is not a call to cynicism — it is a recognition of history, the imperfections of man and the limits of reason."

Evil does exist in the world. As president, Barack Obama had been given an opportunity to take up arms against the enemies of the United States in a more direct way than had any previous holder of that office. He welcomed it. He did everything he could to push the matter. The CIA had long called whoever was in the White House the "First Customer," and on this issue there was no confusion about what the customer most wanted.

*　　*　　*

High in his seventh-floor office at Langley, overlooking the Potomac, Michael Morell had felt the same way for a long time. In his climb to the post of deputy director, he had run the agency's analysis division, and he knew that, despite their lack of success, they had never lost the sense of urgency. He still remembered flying around with President Bush on 9/11, the uncertainty and fear in the country, the way he had felt looking in on his daughters sleeping when he finally returned home. Even with two wars to fight, there had never been a want of manpower or of resources for finding bin Laden.

Still, he felt, Obama's push might have some effect. Morell's new boss, Panetta, for one, was now demanding those regular progress reports: at least one a month. In any large organization a demand for progress reports has an effect. No one wants to file a progress report showing no progress.

4

The Targeting Engine

There had been times, off and on, when the United States government knew where Osama bin Laden was. The CIA had been interested in him since 1991, after he moved from Afghanistan to the Sudan. Almost everywhere the agency looked in the expanding Sunni extremist world, his name came up. Not as a commander but as the go-to person for false documents, money, training, weapons, or chemicals that could be made into bombs. In December 1995, the agency created a small bin Laden unit, headed by Michael Scheuer.

A burly, confident man with a full beard and glasses who speaks with a flat Midwestern accent, Scheuer was less inclined than many in the CIA hierarchy to swallow his own opinions. He had not been a typical CIA recruit. A Buffalo native, he had worked as a rigger for Union Carbide while earning two master's degrees and then a PhD at the University of Manitoba, in Canada. He believed his bin Laden unit was the first ever established to hunt down an individual, and as the effort matured—as he learned more and more about bin Laden—he grew increasingly convinced of the danger al Qaeda posed for the United States. In time, his assessment of that danger outpaced his superiors'. His small group worked out of an office in a business center just a short drive from the main CIA campus at Langley. Scheuer named the office after his son Alec: "ALEC Station."

The best weapon they had for gathering intelligence at that point was rendition, the practice of arresting a suspect and turning him over to authorities in another country for interrogation. The practice enabled the agency to at least technically abide by rules against torture. The CIA obtained assurances that captives would not be abused, which some foreign governments likely honored more diligently than others. At that point the agency did not have the option of killing suspected senior terrorists: they had to be arrested and held somewhere. Rendition enabled the Clinton administration to avoid the legal difficulties of placing them in U.S. custody. As Scheuer would remember it, this was not so much a matter of explicit policy as it was policy by default. He would seek guidance from the White House about what to do with a target, and the answer would come back, "That's your problem." The problem was solved by willing governments in East Africa, the Balkans, and the Middle East.

Rendition did not, as it happens, produce the first big breakthrough for ALEC Station. That came in September 1996, when a Sudanese militant named Jamal al-Fadl, a former close associate of bin Laden's, turned up at the U.S. embassy in Eritrea offering to tell everything he knew about al Qaeda. He was flown to the United States and placed in the federal witness-protection program. He provided the first trove of fresh information about bin Laden and his organization—about its personalities, structure, and planned operations. His relevations ratcheted up interest in the group, which was clearly willing and able to launch major terror attacks.

By 1999, ALEC Station employed twenty-seven people, many of them women. They ran an unorthodox CIA office, very informal. People dressed casually. Because it maintained informants and contacts worldwide, the office was open twenty-four hours a day. Everyone worked long hours so few formalities of office life took hold. Scheuer would nap every afternoon in his office. As their sense of the threat posed by al Qaeda grew, so did their sense of mission. Some in the office, like Scheuer, passed up offers for promotions in order to stay with the work. Marriages broke up. The place had a cultish feel. Because Scheuer presided over so many dedicated women officers, some started calling his group "the Manson family."

They couldn't get bin Laden arrested in the Sudan, so they came up with a plan to harass him. He had a number of large projects under way there—road building, agricultural programs, and businesses. He was also actively underwriting terror attacks throughout the region. So ALEC Station proposed sabotaging his construction equipment. They wanted to spike engines with slurry that would force them to seize up. When the Senate Select Committee on Intelligence was briefed on the plan, one member objected: "If you do that, won't you be putting some Sudanese farmer out of work?" The project was scrapped.

Not long afterward, when the attempted assassination of the Egyptian President Hosni Mubarak was linked to al Qaeda, the Sudan was pressured by states in the region to expel bin Laden. He relocated to Afghanistan, where he declared his war on the United States. This move pleased ALEC Station, because the NSA could now listen in on phone conversations in Afghanistan; there was also an enormous archive of overhead imagery left over from the *mujahidin*–Soviet wars, and the CIA had many friendly contacts in that country. In 1997, Mullah Omar, the Taliban leader, invited bin Laden to live in Kandahar, at an experimental agricultural station called Tarnak Farms, south of the city. This was an area where the agency had an especially rich network of spies, a group it called "Tripoints."

For once they could watch bin Laden closely and listen to him and his people. Lacking the authority to kill him, Scheuer's group laid plans to kidnap him—that would have been in May or June of 1998, several months before the embassy bombings in East Africa. They intended to hold him in a remote mountainous area for inter- rogation and then fly him to an Arab state for imprisonment (unless the United States decided to prosecute him directly). They fleshed out a raid in detail, a snatch-and-grab mission inside Afghanistan employing a special ops team delivered by helicopter. But when the plan was run up the chain it was vetoed as too risky. American forces might get killed, and because bin Laden lived with his wives and children, some of the children might be harmed. Scheuer recalled being mystified by the decision. He asked, "How much more of a threat do you need before you finally do something?"

When Director George Tenet paid a visit to ALEC Station not long afterward, one of the women on Scheuer's staff confronted him angrily: "You and the White House are going to get thousands of Americans killed."

Tenet told them that he understood their anger, but that it would subside. By now the group's growing sense of urgency, cou- pled with its cultish image and high number of female staffers, had begun to work against it. They were seen as overly emotional and alarmist. Tenet's response reflected this subtle prejudice and ran- kled ALEC Station still further.

"You will all think clearer in a couple of days," he said.

In August, after the embassy bombings, Scheuer recalls being asked if the plan to kidnap bin Laden could still be pursued. The answer was no. Bin Laden knew that the chances of America taking action would grow after those attacks. He had gone into hiding. They had missed the chance.

By now, the United States was willing to use lethal force on bin Laden. President Clinton authorized two cruise missile strikes soon after the embassy bombings, one targeting Al-Shifa, a pharmaceutical plant in Khartoum thought to be developing chemical weapons, and the other targeting a bin Laden camp near Khowst. The missiles hit on August 20, fired from ships in the Arabian Sea. The CIA would estimate that twenty to thirty people were killed—but not bin Laden, who had reportedly left the Khowst camp a few hours earlier.

After that, the project for ALEC Station became pinpointing bin Laden long enough in advance to be targeted. They presented the White House with eight such opportunities, Scheuer recalled, and each time the strike was called off, primarily over concerns about collateral damage. The CIA man had always been prickly and eccentric. He was so much more willing to accept collateral casualties than his superiors—was so convinced that the threat posed by bin Laden warranted drastic, immediate action—that he had begun to be regarded with suspicion. He seemed obsessed.

In 1998, on the Sunday before Christmas, ALEC Station learned that bin Laden was staying in the Haji Habash house, part of the governor's palace in Kandahar. The CIA had a local spy who knew which wing of the building bin Laden was in, and even which room, because he had escorted him there. It was first-rate, firsthand intelligence, and a target that could easily be reached by Tomahawk missiles launched from ships in the Arabian Sea.

"Hit him tonight—we may not get another chance," advised Gary Schroen, ALEC Station's field officer.

Scheuer took it directly to the White House, along with Director Tenet and John Gordon, the deputy director. It was snowing. The three men drove from Langley into D.C. together, but inside the White House only Tenet was allowed into the meeting, which the Clinton administration's principals joined by teleconference. Scheuer and Gordon waited outside for hours. The missile strike was not authorized. According to *The 9/11 Commission Report*, there was concern that as many as three hundred people might be killed or injured, and that there was thought to be too great a chance of bin Laden moving at the last minute, as he had before. There was also a mosque nearby that might have been damaged. The CIA men drove back up the George Washington Parkway, disappointed yet again. Scheuer was particularly upset by the administration's worry about damaging a mosque.

The next day, with the opportunity gone, Scheuer wrote to his field officer, Schroen, that he had not been able to sleep. "I'm sure we'll regret not acting last night."

"We should have done it last night," Schroen wrote back. "We may well come to regret the decision not to go ahead."

Scheuer's frustration got the better of him. In 1999 he drafted a memo to the heads of the CIA, complaining about the risks being run to collect timely information, the hours of hard work that went into each targeting opportunity, and the unwillingness of the government to take action.

"[It seemed wrong to] me, to some extent, the idea of continually sending your officers into harm's way to gather information that is credible and usable and to find the government not willing to use it to defend American people for reasons that [exist only in] their own minds," he explained years later in an interview for this book. "You know, how racist is it to think that 1.4 billion Muslims are going to rise up and attack the United States because some shrapnel hits a stone mosque in Kandahar? You have to have zero respect for the humanity or the common sense of the Muslim world to expect something like that to happen. And yet, that's the excuse these brilliant Harvard-trained people come up with."

He was relieved of responsibility for ALEC Station. As he recalled later, he was told, "We want you to tell your people that you are burned out and don't worry, we're going to give you a medal and a monetary award."

Scheuer said he told them, "Stick it in your ass."

Everything changed after 9/11, of course. Then the questions all became, Why hadn't the United States acted against bin Laden more aggressively when it could? "Obsessives" like Scheuer and his "cult" at ALEC Station looked prophetic, not overly emotional. The United States had missed its chance to get bin Laden before his biggest plan bore fruit.

After the invasion of Afghanistan there were battlefield leads that pointed American forces toward a rugged redoubt in Tora Bora, which translates to "Black Cave." It was in the far easternmost part of the country, near the border with Pakistan, and was reputed to have a byzantine maze of caves, natural and man-made. It was also reputed to be bin Laden's hideout. When American forces and Afghan militiamen took it in 2001, over a five-day siege, they found lots of small caves and some bunkers, but nothing like the fortress they had imagined. It turned out to be another place the Sheik had recently left.

The best reports said he had fled over the White Mountains into Pakistan, probably before the assault even began. After that . . . nothing.

No, not nothing.

Start with thousands of small bits of information. Names, lots and lots of names. Sightings. Rumors. Interrogation transcripts. Phone numbers. Phone calls. Dates. Addresses. Geographic coordinates. Aerial photographs. Ground surveillance photos. Videos. Faces. Iris images. Gaits. Maps. Fingerprints. Old diaries. E-mails. Web sites. Social media. Text messages. Tweets. Old-fashioned letters. Blogs. News reports. Broadcasts. Bills. Payment schedules. Traffic tickets. Rent payments. Credit card numbers. Charges. Bank account numbers. Deposits. Withdrawals. Transfers. License numbers. Passport numbers. Police reports. Arrests. Travel itineraries. Everything and anything that can be transformed into data. When you're looking for one person in a world of seven billion, and when that one person does not wish to be found, you cast a wide net.

After 9/11, and after bin Laden escaped Tora Bora, it is safe to say that the United States government was fully engaged in hunting him down. Engaged to a degree that makes the uphill battles of little ALEC Station seem like a basement hobby. The Obama administration might invoke "limited bandwidth" and competing priorities to explain why these efforts fell short, but the truth is that every agency and branch of the vast U.S. military-industrial complex was now fully invested. What did that mean? It meant that finding and eliminating bin Laden was not just a preoccupation of a small group working in a storefront near Langley. It was a central goal. No one would be left waiting in the hall at the White House ever again for permission to strike. But finding bin Laden had also become exponentially more difficult. Tools and networks and units had to be developed to find, fix, and finish al Qaeda and other terror networks like it. What would evolve—this thing they called F3EAD—is worth examining in more detail.

You begin with scraps. Anything that can be transformed into data, those names and numbers and other types of information partially enumerated above. All of that and more, intel from every pipeline: detainee interrogations, HUMINT (human intelligence), SIGINT (signals intelligence), GEOINT (geospatial intelligence), and even something called MASINT (measurement and signature intelligence, which converted into searchable data highly technical things like radar or chemical or sound). Each bit is a potentially useful dot in a vast matrix. Collection flowed from a blizzard of agencies, large and small—CIA, FBI, NSA, NGA, and many more. The SEAL and Delta Force warriors ransacked the hideouts they raided for everything that might contain a lead—they called it "pocket litter." Who knew which stray fact might lead to bin Laden? Or if any of them ever would? At times the CIA had dozens of analysts working on bin Laden full time, but the sheer number and variety of leads was daunting. There was always a good chance, perhaps a better than even chance, that the Sheik would live out his days in hiding and die peacefully in bed, surrounded by his wives and his many children and the devoted members of his intimate circle, perhaps after leveling one last broadside at the "Head of International Unbelief"—thumbing his nose as he entered paradise. For those who believed in such things, evading the grasp of American justice would lend credence to his claim of divine guidance.

In the end, finding bin Laden would illustrate the most banal of truths about intelligence work. More than genius or courage, it is about effort and patience and will. It is also, of course, about money and time—but when we are talking about a goal assigned top priority by not one but two presidents of the United States, and where time and resources are, in effect, bottomless, it boils down, ultimately, to a steady application of will. President Bush famously kept a chart of wanted terrorists in a desk drawer and would personally X out those who were captured or killed. Bin Laden was always "Number One." At his regular daily briefings, Bush would routinely ask, "How're we doing?" and everyone knew what he was talking about. It was the same with Obama. After that impromptu meeting in his office with his new intelligence chiefs in 2009, he would bring it up at nearly every security briefing.

"Are we any closer?"

"What have we learned?"

An intelligence network like America's is not one but multiple bureaucracies, each with its own specialty—listening, observing, photographing, sensing, probing, analyzing. The strength of such an overlapping structure is that things get looked at more than once, and from every conceivable angle. And the strength of bureaucracy—everyone knows about the weaknesses of bureaucracy but rarely do we consider its strength—is in its limitless capacity for work. Steady, unceasing work, like the trickle of the river that ever so slowly carves a gorge. Hour after hour, day after day, year after year, here was an effort that would consume large chunks of the careers of analysts—analysts replaced at intervals with fresher eyes and ears and minds who would eagerly set off down stale trails with new vigor.

Now add supercomputers. Convert those millions of bits of intel gathered from all over the world over years of effort into bytes, and suddenly the impossible, finding the needle in a million haystacks, becomes at least a little more probable.

So when we trace the trail to Abbottabad, this is what we are talking about—a sophisticated targeting engine. Viewed backward, from bin Laden's hideout to the scraps of intel that led to it, the trail seems obvious. Tracing it from end to beginning obscures the level of difficulty: the years of frustration and patient effort, the technological innovation, the lives lost, the mistakes made, the money spent. Just the special ops piece of the story unfolded over a quarter of a century of trial and error, beginning with the improvised mission to rescue American hostages in Iran in 1980.

After Iranian students seized the U.S. embassy in Tehran in November 1979, President Jimmy Carter undertook months of fruitless diplomatic efforts to free the more than fifty Americans held hostage there. During that time, the army's newly formed counterterrorism unit, Delta Force, cobbled together a daring effort to rescue them. They borrowed helicopters from the navy used for minesweeping, and marine pilots unused to the kind of flying required. The mission called for the choppers to fly to a rendezvous point in the desert outside Tehran, called Desert One, refuel the choppers from large fixed-wing aircraft flown in by air force pilots, and then proceed to a hiding place near the city. The following evening Delta Force would emerge from hiding, raid the embassy compound and free the hostages, then assemble in a soccer stadium across the street from the embassy in central Tehran, where they would be picked up by the helicopters and flown to an airport that was to have been seized by U.S. Army Rangers. From there, the rescuers and hostages would be flown out of the country.

This extraordinary bold and complicated mission never made it past the rendezvous point in the desert. Sandstorms damaged choppers and forced several pilots to turn back. With too few helicopters to proceed, the mission was aborted.

As the aircraft maneuvered to fly quietly out of Iran, one of the choppers collided with a plane on the ground, and both exploded, killing eight American servicemen. The disaster ruined hopes of keeping the aborted rescue effort secret. The subsequent embarrassment condemned the hostages to many more months of captivity, handed Iran a large propaganda coup, (they claimed an American "invasion" had been thwarted by God), and likely destroyed Carter's hopes of being elected to a second term.

That episode would bear a striking similarity to the one that killed bin Laden, and it would illustrate how far the talents and tools of the special ops community had come. That 1980 disaster, in effect, created the Joint Special Operations Command, by demonstrating cruelly what this nation could not do. Progress can be further traced back to the heroic and bloody firefight in Mogadishu in 1993, the battle documented in *Black Hawk Down*, which resulted when another special ops raid spun off track. Thousands of missions, successful and unsuccessful, large and small, honed the men and machines and tactics that would target the Sheik.

That raid could not be launched until bin Laden was found. Finding him meant reconstituting human spy networks dismantled in the complacent years after the Cold War, when spying was considered unseemly and unlawful and a threat to personal liberties and human rights. After 9/11, the public rediscovered the value of spies on the ground and of eyes and ears overhead. It would speed the development of unblinking aerial platforms and telecommunications networks that would allow constant, real-time surveillance unheard of in the past.

Four months after the attacks, former Admiral John Poindexter was appointed to head a new initiative he had helped devise called Total Information Awareness, which sought to use supercomputers to amass unimaginably huge databases in order to, in essence, collect, as its name suggested, *everything*. With the right software, you could mine that data in order to identify and locate potential terrorists. The admiral's history of lying to Congress during the Iran-Contra episode did not engender confidence, nor did the inherently scary, Orwellian notion of the government compiling vast pools of data about American citizens. In that sense, the name, Total Information Awareness, was a fatal public relations blunder. The bald, white-mustachioed Poindexter was called the "Pentagon's Big Brother," and worse. Congress scotched the program as originally conceived. Poindexter found employment back in the private sector, and the remnants of the project, which was barred from collecting information on American citizens, was tactfully renamed *Terrorism* Information Awareness.

As wrong a choice as Poindexter was to lead this project, and as tone deaf as he may have been in its presentation, he had the right idea. He had been thinking about it for decades. One of the computer's great contributions—this ability to store and manipulate vast amounts of data—seemed mundane but was in practice so revolutionary that it was transforming modern life, whether performing a Google search, stocking the shelves at a Walmart from an international supply chain, shipping packages anywhere in the world overnight, or mapping the human genome. So why not put that capacity to work tracing a terrorist network—recognizing clues in what would appear, even to teams of skilled analysts, to be random events?

Poindexter's concept did more than survive. It would come to undergird the entire war effort: storing every scrap of intel about al Qaeda and related groups gathered by the nation's very active military and spy agencies, transforming them into data, and then plumbing that data for leads. The hunt for bin Laden and others eventually drew on an unfathomably rich database, accessible to anyone in the world with the proper security clearance, whether a marine officer at an outpost in Afghanistan or a team of analysts working in Langley. Sifting through it required software capable of ranging deep and fast and with keen discernment—a problem the government itself proved less effective at solving than were teams of young software engineers in Silicon Valley. A start-up called Palantir, for instance, came up with a program that elegantly accomplished what TIA had set out to do. Founded in 2004 by Alex Karp and Peter Thiel—the latter is the billionaire cocreator of Paypal and an early Facebook investor— Palantir developed a product that actually deserves the popular designation Killer App. Newly minted software engineers from the best computer schools in the country were put up in a seven-thousand-square-foot workspace in Palo Alto. It was stocked with junk food and video games and nicknamed "the Shire," the home of the Hobbits in Tolkien's *Lord of the Rings*. (The company itself is named after a magical stone in the Tolkien saga that confers special powers of sight and communication.) The software produced from this very unlikely source would help turn America's special forces into deadly effective hunters. Palantir is now worth billions, and has contracts with, among others, the CIA, the NSA, the Defense Department, the Defense Intelligence Agency, the FBI, the National Counterterrorism Center, and the Department of Homeland Security.

The pace and urgency of war have always accelerated the development of technology and encouraged novel uses of devices that already exist. After rapid initial success toppling the regime of Saddam Hussein in Iraq, American forces found themselves under increasing attack by Sunni extremist groups, the most violent of which was a new branch of al Qaeda, under the direction of an innovative killer named Abu Musab al-Zarqawi. His group mounted a campaign of roadside bombs and brutal suicide attacks, many of them designed to kill Iraqi civilians indiscriminately—the sort of attacks that bin Laden, in hiding, considered mistakes. Indeed, the mass killings eventually helped turn the Sunni majority in Iraq against the insurgency, marking the turning point in the war. But at the same time, under the direction of General Stanley McChrystal, JSOC was hammering away on insurgent cells of the local al Qaeda killers with increasing effectiveness, mounting mission after mission in rapid succession, capturing and killing at a pace that such operations had never before been able to sustain. They found Saddam Hussein hiding in a hole in the ground in late 2003. Zarqawi himself was killed by an American bomb in 2006. McChrystal's success, considered to be one of the major military accomplishments of modern times, was something he called "collaborative operations," by which he meant the fusion of "special operators"—teams of elite shooters from every branch of the service—with this new computational ability, which amassed data from all of the other inputs. The task force built a massive database at Camp Victory in Iraq, and then another at Bagram in Afghanistan, blending the big picture with the small. It meant bringing a different kind of warrior to the front, one more accustomed to clicking a mouse than pulling the trigger.

Guy Filippelli was one of them. A young army captain, a West Point graduate with a master's degree from Oxford, in 2005 he was asked by his commander in Afghanistan to visit the walled-off facilities of the task force—the special ops unit—and show them what he could do with his computer. Filippelli calls himself a geek. He had started writing computer programs as a high school student before heading to West Point's growing computer science department. He was helping the command staff at Bagram design systems to better control "information flow," plugging intel collected from the sites of raids in the field and from the interrogations of detainees into a growing national terror database. He arrived inside the cloistered walls of the task force full of enthusiasm for his work, certain his lecture would excite these frontline troops. The shooters and their staff could not have been less impressed. Filippelli's subject matter was highly technical and abstract, cutting edge, and very cool to him, but he was talking to a roomful of soldiers whose adrenaline rush came from . . . free falling from high altitudes or getting shot at. Their world was the extreme opposite of virtual. So the next time the young captain got a chance, this time with a smaller group of soldiers, he tried a different tack.

"Listen, I know you guys are a thousand times better at this stuff than I am and are probably already doing all this, but let me show you what I'm doing and I'll be out of your hair in ten minutes."

At first it was something easy. The task force was used to simply locking up suspects in the detainment facility as they awaited questioning. Filippelli had built a database for detainees, and had also mapped the facility's population by tribal affiliation, background, kinship, and other factors. Putting a detainee in the wrong place, for instance, with a group from his own village, meant that his comrades would rapidly coach him. Filippelli could show how those poorly placed were significantly less useful afterward in interrogation. So where you put them in the facility was important.

"Look," he said. "You've picked up this guy. Why did you put him with *these* guys? You could have done this . . ."

And with that, he closed his laptop and started for the door.

"Thanks for your time," he said. "Let me know if there's anything else I can do for you."

"Wait," the men protested. "Tell us a little more about this."

Gradually, he found himself working more and more with the task force, showing them how crunching data could vastly improve their efficiency. The applications went way beyond storing detainees. The name of the game in warfare is to learn faster and act faster than the enemy. So, as Filippelli and others doing the same kind of work came to see it, the contest had to do with time cycles. If it's a detainee who could be held for, say, only twenty-four hours, how do I use that time most efficiently? What questions should he be asked? What do I need to learn in order to ask him the best questions in the time allotted? And that was just one piece of the puzzle. Looking at the larger mission, the special ops teams needed to get inside the information cycle of their enemy. In the past, after a successful night raid where a member of an insurgent cell was killed or arrested, by morning, or even within a few hours, every critical member of that group would know about it and would have taken evasive action. Information spread quickly. Cell phones would be ditched, computer discs destroyed, bomb-making facilities moved—the bad guys would scatter. But if you could get *inside* that response time—if you could beat their information cycle and learn enough from the first raid through either interrogation or, say, scrutinizing a seized cell phone or hard drive—you might be able to launch a new raid or even multiple raids before word of the first one had gotten out.

The databases enabled local scraps to be instantly cross-checked with the larger data pool. Warrior geeks like Filippelli would examine the pocket litter, and plug that into the national collection; it was like jumping from the middle of the woods to a panoramic view of the forest. The warrior geeks helped connect the dots for the shooters, lifting order from disorder. Soon enough, the teams were doing it for themselves. Armed with such rapid intel, the teams got very fast indeed, going out on multiple missions every night, easily lapping the enemy's information cycle. They had, in strategic terms, "seized the initiative." This capability turned terrorist hunting from a passive endeavor, characterized by long periods of intel collection and analysis and preparation, punctuated by occasional raids, into an aggressive endeavor. To stay alive, the bad guys had to stay in constant communication with each other and keep moving—two activities that actually made them easier to find. In Iraq, under McChrystal in 2007 and 2008, JSOC teams began dismantling networks at an ever increasing pace, taking them down before they knew what hit them.

McChrystal would be handed the entire Afghan command soon after Obama's election, turning over JSOC to Vice Admiral William McRaven, who signed a secret agreement in early 2009 with the new CIA director, Leon Panetta, spelling out guidelines for expanded cooperation. So at the same time Obama was pushing the CIA to find bin Laden, JSOC was deepening its relationship with the spy agency worldwide.

The right weapon had evolved. Just nine years earlier, President Bill Clinton had complained to General Hugh Shelton, then chairman of the Joint Chiefs, about his lack of options in going after Osama bin Laden. "You know, it would scare the shit out of al Qaeda if suddenly a bunch of black ninjas rappelled out of a helicopter into the middle of their camp," he said. It was the wish of a man who had more experience with the military in movies than real life. In order to rappel into an enemy's camp, you first had to know where it was and who exactly was there. From time to time, as we have seen, the United States had obtained reasonably current intel about bin Laden's location, but the ability to act swiftly and effectively on that knowledge, at acceptable levels of risk, did not yet exist.

Now it did. No matter how one felt about the wisdom of invading Iraq, or the seemingly unending conflict in Afghanistan, a near decade of combat had matured a generation of warriors and tools, battle tested and custom-made for finding and killing terrorists. This is what author Bob Woodward had hinted at when he caused a stir in a 2008 interview with *60 Minutes* by referring to a "secret operational capability." It briefly inspired wild speculation about a crash military research program like the Manhattan Project in World War II that produced the atom bomb. Some imagined a "terrifying radar cannon" or a "thermal signature" device that could effectively fingerprint a target from twenty thousand feet. But there was no one secret weapon. The new tool was *everything*: reconstituted human spy networks, supercomputers, state-of-the-art software, global surveillance, and elite commando units.

There was, however, one more critical piece, one of the most dramatic developments in the history of modern warfare. One that began not at some secret lab with cutting-edge scientists, but on an airstrip in Hungary, with an air force colonel they called Snake.

James Clark had planned on a career in politics when he graduated from Catholic University in 1973. He had it all mapped out: law school, legal practice, then a run for Congress . . . But he had accepted an ROTC scholarship to help pay for school, and when he graduated the air force invited him to fly fighter jets. It was a thrill he found hard to leave behind, so his four-year commitment turned into ten, and then ten turned into a career. His call sign was "Snake." He was based in Taszár, Hungary, in 1995 when he got the chance to play with something then called the Gnat. It illustrated how a good idea doesn't always require a blinding stab into the unknown, because the Gnat was basically a glider with an Austrian skimobile engine. It would improve, of course: its surveillance tools would become state-of-the art and its engine virtually silent. Its hover time would greatly lengthen and its optics would become astonishing. It would eventually carry its own missiles. Called the Predator, it rapidly became the most sought-after weapon in the air force's multibillion-dollar arsenal.

The drone, or, as the air force prefers, the UAV (unmanned aerial vehicle), was not new. Radio-controlled aircraft were used during World War II. President John F. Kennedy's older brother, Joe, was killed on a secret mission when his specially engineered B-24, designed to fly itself to a German target after Kennedy had bailed out, exploded prematurely. Drones had been used in Vietnam, and the Israelis had used them to good effect over Lebanon's Bekaa Valley in 1982. Several of the Israeli models were purchased by the CIA, which turned them over to the San Diego defense contractor General Atomics for further development. Clark got four of them in Hungary during this experimental phase. He housed them in small tents out on the runway at Taszár. They were an immediate hit. Soldiers had long sought the ability to see over the next hill and the Gnat gave them a sixty-mile panorama from a platform that could stay airborne more or less permanently, flown in twelve-hour shifts. Manned aircraft could stay aloft for only as long as a pilot could stand it, or until his fuel ran out. Satellites provided a nice view when they happened to be passing overhead, and were in great demand, but they were expensive and few, and not always overhead. Once Clark's Gnats started flying missions over Kosovo they never stopped. Demand for them grew and grew. They have been in continual action ever since.

As the air force saw it, the problem during the Cold War had not been finding the enemy; they were, for the most part, in plain sight—tanks, missile silos, armies, and so on. The problem was how to attack them. The war that began in earnest after 9/11 posed the opposite problem. Al Qaeda terrorists made easy targets, if you could find them. At most they were holed up in compounds with a few armed guards. So a capability that allowed you to silently watch a target from fairly close range over days, months, and even years, in real time, was suddenly as valuable, if not more valuable, than a multimillion-dollar piece of hardware in orbit around the Earth.

General James Poss, working with Clark, commanded the first Predator mission over Iraq early in 2001, when the UN was policing a no-fly zone. The Iraqis would occasionally shoot at American planes patrolling the no-fly zones, aided by a large, clumsy Russian Cold War–era portable radar device called "Spoon Rest." It was mounted on a large van with twelve giant antennae shaped like coat hangers on top. In other words, they were hard to miss. Except that after nine months of trying, the air force could not find any of them. How could something so big and distinctive remain invisible? Whenever an American plane detected it was being tracked by radar, the force would direct an AWACS—Airborne Warning and Control System— to fly over and scan for a Spoon Rest van. None was ever seen. Could the Iraqis be dismantling them after each use? The old Soviet manuals said a unit could not be taken apart in less than twenty minutes, and the AWACS would get overhead a lot faster than that. The air force tried spotting them with a U-2, which also turned up nothing. Poss tried everything he could imagine. He had every large building in the vicinity surveyed. He tried pattern recognition analyses to try to predict where they were likely to show up. Nothing.

The Predator found the answer on the first try. Able to silently watch an Iraqi town where a Spoon Rest van was known to operate, it saw the Iraqis drive the distinctive van through the central market and park it under a bridge. All of the Spoon Rest vans were quickly located and destroyed.

There were other uses for drones. Before the U.S. bombing campaign began over Baghdad in 2003, Poss and Clark flew an old

Predator they had planned to retire low and slow over the capital, prompting the Iraqis to fire up the radar at all their antiaircraft installations. This enabled the air force to map the city's defense system. When the Predator ran out of fuel they plunked it in the Tigris River, prompting the Iraqis to claim they had shot down an American fighter. They never recovered the aircraft. The next day, Poss and Clark did the same thing, but they miscalculated the fuel levels. Instead of splashing it into a lake on the outskirts of the city, the drone made it only to the water's edge. Alerted again by claims that an American jet had been shot down, film crews the next day recorded the recovery of an old drone painted with graffiti, without a bullet hole in it.

These first experimental models could only transmit TV signals along a line of sight, but before long Predators were bouncing their feed off communications satellites, which meant the view from above could be monitored and analyzed from anywhere, in real time. This was the real breakthrough. Drones provided not just a view from above—balloons had been floated over Civil War battlefields to accomplish that. The revolutionary change came when drone surveillance was tied into the existing global telecommunications system. This allowed the U.S. military to mount "caps," or permanent stable observation platforms, over whole cities. Tie that capability into supercomputers, with software capable of recognizing the "signature" of a specific target—say, a red pickup truck with a dent on its right rear fender—and you had the ability to track a target night and day.

By 2010, fleets of UAVs—which today include Predators, Reapers, Global Hawks, and a growing variety of others—were part of a worldwide integrated network that enabled remote operators at bases in the United States to fly missions almost anywhere in the world, funneling imagery and sensory data for analysis back to computers at Beale Air Force Base in California and CIA headquarters in Langley. The number of drones was well into the thousands, enough to sustain as many as sixty-five caps at once. For a selected target, the unblinking eye could establish things as simple as: How many people live in a compound? When do they wake up in the morning? When do they go to bed at night? What kind of weapons do they have? The air force was now using drones in teams, producing a system it called Gorgon Stare, that could cover an area four kilometers square—an area the size of Fairfax, Virginia. The image would not have to be monitored continually by human beings; it could be monitored by computers, which never get bored or distracted and are serenely undaunted by complexity. If, say, a vehicle belonging to a suspected terrorist was recognized by the computer—because it had some distinguishing feature that enabled the computer to track it—then the movements of that vehicle could be followed over a small city for months, or even years, permitting a detailed map of the suspect's travels. Combine that map with cell phone tracking, with human intelligence, and you can begin to assemble a detailed and accurate chart of your target's connections, or his network. Improvements in optics had enabled such observations from a great distance, so that the UAVs themselves would not have to be directly over a target. They could "stand off," well outside the restricted airspace over a country such as, say . . . Pakistan.

The trail to Abbottabad that seemed so clear in retrospect represented a triumph of dot connecting. In this case, it began with a name. It was not even a real name, and the reference was to someone reported, falsely, to be dead.

The name Abu Ahmed al-Kuwaiti was first mentioned to authorities in Mauritania by an al Qaeda operative, Mohamedou

Ould Slahi, who went by the nom de guerre "Abu Musab." Slahi was a veteran *mujahid*, having fought twice in Afghanistan: first against the Russians and then against the regime left in place when the Russians departed. He had sworn allegiance to bin Laden and was living in Germany in late 1999, pursuing a degree in electrical engineering, when he befriended two of the young Arabs who would become 9/11 hijackers: Ramzi bin al-Shibh and Marwan al-Shehhi. The two were looking to join the jihad in Chechnya, but Slahi advised them first to travel to Afghanistan for training. Joined by Mohammed Atta, who would become the leader of the 9/11 group, the young Mauritanian helped them make travel arrangements to Karachi, launching them on the road that would take them to the United States and flight training. Performing this service placed Slahi at the origins of the 9/11 plot, and he was thus a highly wanted man after the attacks. In just ten days he was located living in his home country and was brought in for questioning by Mauritanian authorities. He was arrested in November 2001 and underwent extensive questioning in Mauritania and then in Jordan, where he claims he was tortured, and probably was. He has been imprisoned at Guantánamo Bay since 2002.

In telling the story of his travels and battles with the *mujahidin*, one of the names Slahi mentioned—one among many—was this Abu Ahmed al-Kuwaiti, whom he said had been killed. It was obviously a pseudonym. The name meant "the Father of Ahmed from Kuwait." It was just one name among thousands that were daily being entered into what would become the Terrorism Information Awareness database.

The same pseudonym, and person, would be fleshed out in more detail more than a year later by a true believer named Mohammed al-Qahtani, a baby-faced young Saudi who had pledged himself to al

Qaeda and had planned to join the 9/11 hijackers as "muscle"—one of the enforcers trained to seize the plane and keep the passengers under control on the way to impact. He had arrived in Orlando about a month before the attacks—Mohammed Atta was waiting there to pick him up—but was turned away by an immigration officer, whose suspicions, even in that relatively unwary time, were aroused by the fact that Qahtani had a one-way ticket and could not speak English. When Qahtani grew indignant, he earned himself a return flight to Afghanistan. Denied martyrdom, he rejoined bin Laden and fought in the battle of Tora Bora. Fleeing that encounter, he was arrested crossing the border into Pakistan with other *mujahidin* in December of 2001. Qahtani claimed he had been in Afghanistan to learn the art of falconry. He was turned over to American authorities, who eventually matched his fingerprints with the young Saudi who had been denied entry to the United States in Orlando the previous August. This made him a subject of great interest.

Qahtani was interrogated relentlessly at Guantánamo from early November of 2002 until January of 2003. A daily log of his ordeal reveals a grinding effort to break down the young man's resistance. He displayed heroic defiance. There were repeated hunger strikes and attacks on his guards and interrogators—he frequently spat at them, head-butted one, and threw himself bodily at others. When doctors tried to administer IV fluids he tore out the needle, and when his hands were strapped to his chair he got the IV line in his mouth and bit it in two.

The Obama administration has claimed that torture played no role in tracking down bin Laden, but here, in the first two important steps down the trail, that claim crumbles. At best it demands a very narrow definition of the word. Slahi's prosecutor refused to pursue charges against him before a military commission because he found they were based on statements made under torture. And in Qahtani's case the coercive methods employed are clearly documented and public, and would be described as torture by any disinterested person. Indeed, it was his case that prompted the Department of Defense to draw up guidelines to curb interrogation excesses.

In time Qahtani succumbed to this pressure, however it is defined, and dropped his falconry story and began describing his work with al Qaeda in detail. One of the many names he mentioned as part of bin Laden's inner circle was this same Abu Ahmed al-Kuwaiti. He did not know the man's real name, but said he was not only alive and well but had worked closely with Khalid Sheik Mohammed, al Qaeda's Number Three, and had given Qahtani some preliminary computer instruction at an Internet café in Karachi, showing him how to communicate with the group's leaders once he was in America. As Peter Bergen reported in his excellent account, *Manhunt*, Qahtani was taught to compose a letter on an e-mail account, and then store it as a draft instead of sending it. His colleagues, armed with a password to the same account, could then log in and retrieve the draft e-mail without it ever having been sent, presumably avoiding America's watchful eye. Qahtani would also describe Ahmed the Kuwaiti as a "courier."

So now the name had come up twice, from two different men in two different countries, separated by more than a year. No one was yet paying attention to it. Many of the early detainee interrogations were not widely distributed, even within the agency—the importance of the single, enormous database would rise only when the software to exploit it appeared in a few years. In the early years of the hunt, even with dozens of analysts working full time, even with President Bush's list in the drawer of his desk in the Oval Office and his constant prods of "How are we doing?," and even with the help of the computers, it was nearly impossible to keep up with the flood of tips and "Elvis sightings." There was a $25 million reward offered by the State Department for information leading to bin Laden, and an additional $2 million put up by an airline trade association and the pilots union, so passing along a tip was like buying a lottery ticket: you can't win if you don't play. Tall, slender, olive-skinned Arab men were seen on every continent. The analysts did not have high expectations for any of these leads, but given the national priority assigned to the task, every single one had to be taken seriously. It was a powerful time suck.

In that context, a detail offered up under duress by Qahtani, one that would later prove key, was years away from being recognized as significant. Qahtani himself was not that big a deal. He was a foot soldier, one of thousands rounded up in Afghanistan as they fled across the border. All of them were questioned, and their answers were all swept into the growing database. Qahtani merited more attention than most, though. He was an Arab fighter, after all, and, unlike most detainees, he had been a member of al Qaeda. He had fought at Tora Bora and had tried to enter the United States shortly before the attacks, and if he had not been turned away he might have played a role in them himself. But he was still just muscle, a foot soldier. There was no reason to believe he could point out the location of Osama bin Laden. His mention of this Ahmed the Kuwaiti was noted. The supposed "courier" had helped prepare Qahtani for the 9/11 mission and apparently had worked closely with Khalid Sheik Mohammed, so he was potentially significant. But it was still just a fake name. Whoever the Kuwaiti was, by 2003 his pseudonym remained just another drop of intel in what was fast becoming an ocean of data.

Then Khalid Sheik Mohammed himself was arrested in Pakistan just a few months after Qahtani started talking. This dark, burly,

hairy man was easily the most important al Qaeda figure ever appre-
hended—the terror group's Number Three, its operations director
and the primary architect of 9/11. His arrest stirred a great deal of
excitement. Here was someone who could provide a map of the entire organization, possibly cough up the hideouts of bin Laden and
al-Zawahiri, or at least lead them closer, and perhaps reveal ongoing
plots before they matured into new incidents of mass murder. Khalid Sheik Mohammed got the full treatment. He was interrogated
aggressively by both Pakistani and American forces. In between 183
waterboardings at a secret CIA interrogation center in Poland, he
was asked about many, many names. One among the many was
Ahmed the Kuwaiti. And in addition to the volumes of information Khalid Sheik Mohammed provided—some of it true, some of
it false—he acknowledged that such a character existed, but said the
man was unimportant and had retired from al Qaeda years earlier.

So it was not as if the teams of analysts at the CIA were now,
in 2003, looking at this fellow called "the Kuwaiti" as an important
lead. But having been thrice acknowledged, albeit thrice acknowledged under torture, the prospect of his being fiction—someone
made up by a detainee spinning stories—became less likely. He
existed, or had existed. He may have been dead but was probably
still alive. He may even have been, or might be, a member of bin
Laden's inner circle—perhaps even a courier. Even so, the name
wasn't a real name, and it was one of a multitude. It was not yet a
lead, because to know so little doesn't lead or point anywhere.

The teams looking into the matter were smart, dedicated, and
possessed the agency's studied, nondescript style. They were members of a kind of university of analysis, working under the direction
of Michael Morell. When the effort settled into a routine, there
were more than twenty analysts, men and women. There were more

women than usual for this kind of job, partly because the CIA had undertaken to achieve a better balance of gender, but also partly because women were considered especially good at this kind of patient detail work and had a reputation for being sensitive to subtleties that eluded many men—the same insight that had guided Scheuer's staffing of ALEC Station. The teams tended to be on the youthful side of middle age, and the analysts had the look of people who commute to a job in a cubicle and spend long working hours before a computer screen or in meetings. They got a chuckle out of the depiction of CIA agents in books and movies—jumping from airplanes, leaping from rooftops, speeding through European capitals in sports cars under fire. They were mostly bookish sorts, but seemed less like academics than like accountants or junior business executives. Indeed, that's probably what they would tell you they did for a living if you asked. Ego and eccentricity were suppressed, sublimated by the clandestine nature of the job.

The Elvis sightings had slowed and then pretty much stopped by 2004. Bin Laden seemed lost. The teams turned more attention to sorting through the accumulated data—sorting it, devising ways to improve how they attacked it. There was his family, his huge family, with a dizzying number of kin and in-laws, any one of whom might become a conduit for a message to his mother (bin Laden had always been very close to her, a point of potential weakness). As the head of al Qaeda, he was known to be sending and receiving messages constantly. People were supplying him with food, medicine, and information . . . what methods did he use? And those video and audio statements? Who in his inner circle was known to make such recordings? The recordings were scrutinized with great care. What kind of wallpaper is that behind him? What sort of plants are in the room? What is he wearing? Analysts were far more interested in the trappings of bin Laden's statements than in anything he had to say. Why, if he was living in a cave in the wilds, were his robes so clean? There was a "media" team that focused on clues like that. And who delivered these offerings to Al Jazeera and other outlets? That was the job of the courier team. The agency got to where it could track the chain of couriers back to Number Three—it was Khalid Sheik Mohammed and then his replacement, a Libyan, Mustafa al-'Uzayti, who went by the nickname Abu Faraj al-Libi—but there the trail always went cold.

In January 2004, Kurdish police arrested Hassan Ghul, a known al Qaeda figure, trying to enter Iraq with money and bomb-making schematics. He was carrying a letter from bin Laden to Abu Musab al-Zarqawi, the murderous leader of al Qaeda in Iraq, the local franchise that was just beginning its bloody campaign against Americans and the Iraqi citizenry. During Ghul's interrogation the name Abu Ahmed al-Kuwaiti surfaced once more; Ghul described him as an important courier, one of the Sheik's most trusted aides. There were now four mentions of this mystery man, who was looking more and more real. But who was he? What sort of person would he be? The most valuable sort in such a role, if bin Laden were hiding in Pakistan, would be someone fluent in both Pashto and Arabic. Did the Kuwaiti fit that profile? If so, how do you track a nickname?

The public line offered during the remainder of the Bush years was that bin Laden was probably living in a cave somewhere in Waziristan. The CIA teams had stopped believing that in 2002. There were no sightings or even rumors of his presence in the northwest Pakistani territories—not a single report. There were also many stories suggesting that he had a serious kidney disease, and these, too, were discounted early on—these were the stories bin Laden himself had attempted to disprove by feasting before the Pakistani journalist

Mir. The CIA rejected them because the logistics of dialysis would have been too difficult to sustain, and the Sheik appeared hardy enough in his videos.

When the analysts weren't slugging away on their computers, they were in meetings, proposing theories and arguing about theories. Detailed profiles were worked up. How would bin Laden be living? Who was likely with him? How big was his household? Where would it be? What might it look like?

The four most promising avenues seemed to be family, organization, finances, and couriers. The agency had committees focusing on each. And each of these avenues was generating its own collection of data—names, numbers, photos, interviews, etc. . . . all of it swelling the database, the great pool of potential leads. The work ground on, day after day, week after week, year after year. And nothing seemed especially promising.

The arrest of Abu Faraj al-Libi in May 2005, in Pakistan, raised hopes once again for a breakthrough. The second al Qaeda Number Three to be captured, it was known that he had been in direct communication with bin Laden in the years since the 9/11 attacks. But while he provided a lot of information after his capture, he offered nothing that directly helped the bin Laden teams. He did, *indirectly*, provide some help, however. Among the many people al-Libi was asked about was the Kuwaiti. Al-Libi said he had never heard of him.

That was interesting. Five different detainees had been asked about him now. Four said they knew of him. Three placed him close to bin Laden (although one of those three said he was dead), and one, Khalid Sheik Mohammed, said he had left al Qaeda. Now al-Libi, who had been with al Qaeda for more than twenty years, said he had never even heard of the man. How could he know nothing about someone Khalid Sheik Mohammed had readily acknowledged? The organization was not that big. Here's what the analysts gathered: their two most important captives either minimized the importance of the Kuwaiti or denied his existence altogether. This might mean that Ahmed the Kuwaiti was very important indeed. Bin Laden was the crown jewel. If the most important captives would protect anything, it would be information that might lead to him. That was one possible explanation. Add the fact that the Kuwaiti had dropped off the map . . . just like bin Laden. For the first time the CIA teams began to consider that the Kuwaiti was with the Sheik even now—his primary conduit with the rest of the world.

So among the various avenues still being explored intensely, the Kuwaiti became more important. Again, the name was just one of many and was just an alias. It would be five years before they managed to connect it with a real person. In 2007, the agency learned that the Kuwaiti's real name was Ibrahim Saeed Ahmed. It will not say how the connection was made. It might have been as simple as an informant, perhaps someone detained and being interrogated in another country, or it might have emerged from the wizardry of its supercomputers—from the Terrorism Information Awareness database—after some conversation on a cell phone somewhere in the world triggered the right connection. One senior official said that the information came from a "third country." Morell would tell me later, "You could write a book about how we figured it out." It is a book he is not ready to see written.

However the connection was made, by 2007, in light of the increasing usefulness of human intel networks and the enormous TIA database, a real name was a huge step forward. A real man had a history. Ahmed came from a large Pakistani family that had moved to Kuwait. He and his brothers had grown up speaking Pashto and

Arabic. One of his brothers had been killed fighting against the Soviets in Afghanistan. A man with a large family had relatives who had telephones and mail delivery and computers with Internet connections. A man like Ahmed had a network that could be mapped and monitored. With the ability to pore rapidly over every scrap of data and find links in terabytes of intel, one might, say, notice a suspicious cell phone number that made calls home to Kuwait from Pakistan, and then locate the cell towers where the signal originated and comb through the reams of numbers that pinged that tower, looking for telltale patterns of usage. You could also begin routinely recording the conversations on that cell phone, although there is no evidence that anyone was interested enough to listen in just yet.

There still wasn't that much excitement over Ahmed the Kuwaiti. Again, he was just one of a great number of potential leads, many, many of which looked a lot more promising. Most of the analytical effort focused on finding the new al Qaeda Number Three or other key operational players, which had the added benefit of possibly thwarting ongoing plots. The Kuwaiti was peripheral. Much of what they had heard about him over the years suggested that he had dropped out of the organization altogether. His past associations would have been enough to explain why he kept out of sight. Perhaps it was the renewed pressure generated by President Obama in 2009, or perhaps just a decision by the teams to crank up the courier angle. It might have been that there was no change at all, that the patient collection of information and the growing sophistication of the software used to explore the TIA database finally delivered a key. But in June of 2010, because of either some change in his cell phone or its service package or some improvement in their own capability, the United States was able to pinpoint the phone's location when it was in use. This meant they could find the Kuwaiti, and watch him.

What they found, and what immediately provoked even more curiosity at Langley, was that Ibrahim and his brother Abrar were extremely careful. They would use their phones only in the car. Ahmed drove a white Suzuki Jimny with a spare tire mounted on the back, which could be watched from above. It turned out that before even turning on his phone he would drive for at least an hour from what turned out to be that very curious compound in Abbottabad. Ibrahim and his brother were using assumed names, Arshad and Tareq Khan. That was interesting, but there could be many explanations for it. Ibrahim's past associations alone might account for it. It was possible they were involved in some sort of illegal enterprise. Drug smuggling was big business in the Afghan-Pakistan border areas. Or maybe they were still working for al Qaeda.

These insights were sufficient to ramp up interest. If Ahmed the Kuwaiti was still a courier, perhaps he could lead them to where bin Laden was hiding.

The brothers' recorded phone calls now got close attention. Neither gave away anything in conversation about what they were doing but, significantly, there was that business about telling lies even to close family members about where they were living. And in one of Ibrahim Ahmed's calls came the brief exchange that appeared to confirm that he was still working with al Qaeda.

"I'm with the same ones as before."

Now his compound in Abbottabad had the agency's full attention.

5

"Please Make Sure to Keep the Children and All of the Families Away from the Areas That Are Being Photographed and Bombed"

Fall, 2010

Nine years after his most spectacular success, things were not going as Osama bin Laden had foreseen. He was cut off from his followers, frustrated, and his organization was fraying. The 9/11 attacks had been both his greatest achievement and his undoing. Toppling the World Trade Center towers and crashing a commercial jet into the Pentagon had not, as he supposed, sent the United States into a spiral of fear, retreat, and ruin. It had instead set al Qaeda and himself on the run from a patient, determined, and deadly pursuer. The movement had been fragmented physically and conceptually. It had become less his organization than a franchise, a banner waved by men who did not share his precise, divine insight, and who sullied its name with acts that killed, maimed, and alienated those he sought to defend and convert. The holy cause had gone off the rails. In isolation, he could no longer steer it himself. But the Sheik had not given up. The divinely inspired don't.

So he wrote letters, windy letters that filled many pages, a steady stream of them that were passed along a chain of couriers to the men he recognized as his deputies. Despite the oppressive reality, his letters offered consistently hopeful assessments of al Qaeda's opportunities. They contained detailed instructions promoting men to positions made vacant by virtue of an arrest or drone attack, bestowed or withheld his official blessing on start-up organizations in other countries, requested more detailed updates and information, mourned the dead, and critiqued, guided, and motivated his increasingly far-flung troops. He himself had little else to do. He would either tap away on the keyboard with his long, delicate fingers or dictate to one of his wives. He paced.

"In the name of God most merciful," he began one letter in October, 2010 to "Sheik Mahmoud" Atiyah Abd al-Rahman, one of his most faithful, long-serving soldiers, "may God protect him. I hope that this letter finds you and your family are in good health. I offer my condolences to you for the death of our beloved brothers. May God have mercy on their souls and consider them among the martyrs."

A Libyan, al-Rahman had sought out the Sheik in Afghanistan more than twenty years earlier, when he was a teenager determined to fight the great Soviet military machine. Even today he had a youthful, permanently unkempt look, with pale skin and a beard so sparse that it grew only in wisps on his jaws before thickening under his chin. Until recently, al-Rahman had been living in relative safety in Iran, serving as bin Laden's emissary to that country's mullahs, with whom bin Laden had an uneasy relationship. One of the Sheik's three wives and some of his twenty-two living children had been in Iran for years, either imprisoned or living under "protective custody." It was a matter of interpretation. Al-Rahman had helped broker their release, and was now back in the tribal regions of western Pakistan, somewhere in North or South Waziristan, ready to assume an operational role.

As it happened, there was an opening. The Sheik must have been grateful to have al-Rahman back. Drone attacks on al Qaeda forces in Waziristan had so thinned its ranks that the group was finding it hard to retain anyone in the critical Number Three position —operations commander, beneath only the Sheik himself and al-Zawahiri. Anyone pledged to al Qaeda was now a marked man, but this was especially true for its Number Three. The job required suicidal commitment. Unlike the organization's most infamous leaders, the operations commander had to be in constant touch with the group's rank and file, plotting actions, moving money, and training recruits, and the more active you were the more likely it was that the American satellites, drones, or raiders would find you. Number Threes did not last long. There had been 9/11 planner Khalid Sheik Mohammed, who was found and arrested in Pakistan in 2003. His successor, Abu Faraj al-Libi, was arrested in 2005, and al-Libi's successor, Hamza Rabia, was killed later that year by a drone strike.

Next up, Sheik Saeed al-Masri, had been killed in May of 2010. The Americans were getting better. The rain of death was accelerating. Al-Rahman, stepping in for the late al-Masri, would die within the year, less than a month before his successor, Abu Hafs al Shahri, would likewise be killed in a Predator strike. And his successor, Abu Yahya al-Libi, would be killed in June 2012.

By now, every letter the Sheik composed from his cramped third-floor office in Abbottabad began with prayers for the martyrs and lists of condolences.

"This is the path of jihad," he intoned stoically in another letter to Atiyah Abd al-Rahman, his new Number Three. "God said, 'You will sacrifice your money and yourself for His sake.' They strike us and we will strike them back."

The limitations of this movement were more apparent. And while bin Laden politely asked his followers to launch more attacks on the United States, there was no longer any way for al Qaeda to make such ambitious arrangements. The 9/11 attacks had taken years to prepare, and had involved substantial international travel, long months of training, money, and close coordination. When the plan had been set in motion, the group was a peripheral concern for the United States and the Western world. Michael Sheehan, the U.S. ambassador for counterterrorism in the waning years of the Clinton administration, had felt like he was butting his head against a wall trying to get people to take bin Laden and his group seriously in the late 1990s. Michael Scheuer and "the Manson Family" of analysts at ALEC Station were regarded as alarmist, and wore themselves out with frustration.

This was no longer the case. America had spread an invisible web of surveillance that registered seemingly everything that stirred. Death rained continually. It was dangerous for the organization's leaders to move from one house to another, much less put another international plot in motion. And yet here was the Sheik still dreaming his big dream. His own men, even those who shared his vision, were discovering that their revered leader lived in a fantasy. He was still urging them to "hunch forth and stain the blade of lances red." Bin Laden had become the crazy officer waving his sword and rallying depleted troops to run headlong into withering fire—before him, mind you, not behind him. He sent them broad strategic analyses and called for specific missions that were wildly unrealistic, even screwy.

"I asked Sheik Sa'id, Allah have mercy on his soul, to task brother Ilyas to prepare two groups—one in Pakistan and the other in the Bagram area of Afghanistan—with the mission of anticipating and spotting the visits of Obama or Petraeus to Afghanistan or Pakistan to target the aircraft of either one of them," he wrote. "They are not to target visits by U.S. Vice President Biden, Secretary of Defense [Robert] Gates, Joint Chiefs of Staff (Chairman) [Michael] Mullen, or the Special Envoy to Pakistan and Afghanistan [Richard] Holbrooke. The groups will remain on the lookout for Obama or Petraeus. The reason for concentrating on them is that Obama is the head of infidelity and killing him will automatically make Biden take over the presidency for the remainder of the term, as it is the norm over there. Biden is totally unprepared for that post, which will lead the United States into a crisis. As for Petraeus, he is the man of the hour in this last year of the war, and killing him would alter the war's path. So please ask brother Ilyas to send to me the steps he has taken into that work."

Bin Laden diagnosed their primary problem not as the deadly American pursuit, which it was primarily, but their own lack of focus. And he had become a scold.

"After the war expanded and the *mujahidin* spread out into many regions, some of the brothers became totally absorbed in fighting our local enemies, and more mistakes have been made due to miscalculations by the brothers planning the operations."

Too many operations against Americans had inadvertently killed Muslims. He criticized two specific efforts, both by local jihadists affiliated with al Qaeda: the first being the unsuccessful attempt on the life of Afghanistan regional commander General Abdul Rashid Dostum in January 2005. The suicide bomber in that case had blown himself up outside the Ghocha Park mosque in Dostum's hometown of Sheberghan, where the general and his retinue had been praying during the annual Eid al-Adha festival. About twenty people had been injured. The other was an attempt to kill Pakistani General Muhammad Yusef Khan, in June 2004, again setting off a bomb at a mosque. Both had killed many Muslims, and both, bin Laden wrote, "bear extreme negative impact on the partisans of the jihad . . . It is extremely sad for an individual to fall into the same mistake more than once."

The campaign of terror led by al Qaeda's franchise in Iraq had killed eight times more Muslims than non-Muslims, according to a 2009 study. Bin Laden saw this kind of information reported on satellite TV. The bloodshed was thought to have caused many Sunni groups opposed to the U.S. invasion to turn on al Qaeda. This had been a clear tactical error, and a moral one. The rule was that one did not kill Muslims unless there was no other way to get at legitimate targets.

"[This] has resulted in the killing of Muslims (we ask God to have mercy on them and forgive them, and compensate their families)."

Bin Laden was now not so sure that the rule allowing even this exception to killing brother Muslims was valid. He wanted such rationales "revisited based on the modern-day context, and clear boundaries established for all the brothers, so that no Muslims fall victim except when it is absolutely essential . . . Here is an important issue that we should pay attention to: carrying out several attacks without exercising caution, which impacted the sympathy of the Nation's crowds toward the *mujahidin*. It would lead us to winning several battles while losing the war at the end. It requires an accurate criterion for the ramifications of any attack prior to carrying it out; also weighing the advantages and disadvantages, to then determine what would be the best attack to carry out."

Even successes troubled him. During a siege in Khobar, Saudi Arabia, in May 2004, a large group of terrorists took hostages from two oil company installations and killed nineteen foreigners. The attackers were part of the "al Qaeda in the Arabian Peninsula" branch, based in Yemen. They had asked each of the hostages if they were Muslims, and slit the throats of those who were not. Most of the attackers were killed in a rescue operation, and the incident helped provoke a brutal Saudi crackdown on extremists.

The Sheik now cautioned against mounting attacks like these and others inside Arab countries.

"The regime shall have a huge reaction toward the *mujahidin*; this would lead to defending themselves and avenging the regime," he wrote. "The brothers and the regime would then engage in a war that we did not begin against it, because the power of the brothers is not ready for it." The right strategy was to defer conflict with local Arab states, such as Yemen and Iraq and Saudi Arabia, "to avoid wasting our energy with these regimes at this stage [and] . . . losing the sympathy of the Muslims toward us . . . We are the ones defending the Muslims and fighting their biggest enemy, the Crusader-Zionist alliance."

It was now enough that the "general public" considered the victims Muslims, even if bin Laden, with his purer standards, did not. Killing those who fell into this category, while morally defensible, was a strategic error. Better that future attacks should come in places far removed from the Middle or Near East, he said. He mentioned South Korea in particular.

"Among the opportunities to be exploited in targeting the Americans is the state of security laxity found in countries where we have not carried out any attacks."

The Sheik often lectured in these letters, trying to steer his organization back to its central goals. He worried not only that local al Qaeda franchises had drifted away from his guidance, but that its mission was being diluted on targets and concerns he regarded as peripheral.

"By God's grace, jihad is under way on several fronts [Iraq and Afghanistan and, to some extent, Pakistan], and these are sufficient, by His will and His glory, as well as by the steadfastness of the *mujahidin* there, to perform the functions of bleeding the head of the infidels, America, such that it is defeated, God willing. Then the Islamic Nation will be able to expel that which has stricken it with weakness, servility, and degradation. The plague that exists in the nations of Muslims has two causes: the first is the presence of American hegemony and the second is the presence of rulers who have abandoned Islamic law and who identify with the hegemony, serving its interests in exchange for securing their own interests. The only way for us to establish the religion and alleviate the plague . . . is to remove the hegemony. . . . After this phase comes the phase in which the second cause—rulers who have abandoned

Islamic law—are toppled, and this will be the phase in which God's religion is established and Islamic law rules."

Proceeding too hastily in local regions like Yemen undermined the movement's long-term goals, he argued. He saw the Taliban as a cautionary tale in this regard.

"A man might measure the results of establishing a Muslim state before toppling its enemies against the . . . fall of the Islamic emirate in Afghanistan, which we pray to God does not happen again."

In this October letter to al-Rahman, and in several others composed around the same time, the Sheik offered a sweeping assessment of the cause, his organization, and the world. He remained stubbornly optimistic, despite his circumstances. If America was the greater enemy, he considered Pakistan the one closer at hand, and he saw the natural disasters and political strife that year as a hopeful sign.

"As for the local enemy, as you know, they are in big trouble and the government is in danger of falling, especially after the floods [of the previous July] and the increase of the numbers of those who are suffering from the financial crisis." The floods, he wrote, were "God's punishment" on Pakistan for "its sins," but he urged al-Rahman that no one from al Qaeda should say this publicly, "because of the case of the Jewish man with the sick child, whom the Prophet invited to Islam, but did not tell him that his son was sick because he was not a believer." Best not to insult Pakistan.

He relished the conflicts between his two enemies: Pakistan and the American-led NATO coalition in Afghanistan. In recent months Pakistan had closed the border to Afghanistan, shutting down main supply lines for American forces there.

"Through the generosity of God, the situation is moving in the direction of the *mujahidin*. You should be patient and strong and God will reward us."

Given the persistent American pounding, it was time for all but the most disciplined "brothers" to leave Waziristan. He recommended that the others begin moving back into Afghanistan, urging al-Rahman to instruct them to leave their cars behind, because the Americans might otherwise start targeting houses, and that would "increase casualties among women and children." Bin Laden was very particular about protecting the lives of innocent Muslims. He urged his followers to move on "cloudy days, so that their flight would not be readily detected from above." He sent instructions concerning his grown children, the ones who were not in hiding with him, detailing precautions they should take when traveling, and where he wanted them to go. He had lost two of his elder sons, Saad and Mohammed, to the cause already. The Sheik considered himself an expert on security, especially on avoiding overhead surveillance, advising that travelers be moved from car to car inside tunnels, and that the brothers plant large trees around their bases of operation to provide cover from overhead cameras. He warned that tracking and eavesdropping devices might be "so small that they can be put inside a medical syringe."

Gone from these letters, full of condolences and the need for vigilant security, is the bravado of his younger years. Now and then the Sheik would digress for a moment to fondly recall that glory. He reminisced to al-Rahman, his current Number Three, about that moment in their shared story.

"[The attacks] filled Muslims with sympathy toward their fellow *mujahidin*, as it became perfectly clear that they are in the vanguard and are the standard-bearers of the Islamic community in fighting the Crusader-Zionist alliance that has caused the people to endure various forms of pain and degradation. One indication of that is the wide-scale spread of jihadist ideology, especially on the Internet, and the tremendous number of young people who frequent the jihadist Web sites—a major achievement for jihad, through the grace of God, despite our enemies and their efforts."

But those enemies and those efforts had kept him on the run or in hiding. He had been disowned by his large extended family. Most of his closest associates were either dead or in prison. He had been certain that America would not dare to directly confront him and the Taliban in Afghanistan. He had boasted to a Pakistani journalist, "I want the Americans to proceed toward Afghanistan, where all of their misconceptions and illusions will be removed. I am sure, however, that the Americans will not come, because they are cowards. They attack only the unarmed and weaker people."

The United States did come to Afghanistan, and they had defeated the Taliban. Despite the costs they were still coming. In addition, the United States had done something the Sheik could never have imagined. They had elected a black man president, a man with the name Barack Hussein Obama. It sounded like a Muslim name. And for almost two years now, Obama's words and policies had helped weaken the anti-Americanism that fueled al Qaeda's cause, while his drones killed off its membership.

Worse still, the indiscriminate brutal tactics of al Qaeda and its self-anointed affiliates had alienated millions of Muslims, those bin Laden meant when he referred to "the people" or "the Nation." This was the hardest thing for him to swallow. All this had happened, he believed, because he had lost control. His isolation had made it impossible for him to shape the group's image and message, and because al Qaeda had failed to make further dramatic strikes inside America, its significance waned. The attacks he had rejoiced over, that had seemed the start of something glorious, had instead set him back further than he had been when he had started. His world now consisted of two upstairs floors of a house in Pakistan that he and his family never dared to leave.

The house stood inside a large triangular-shaped compound at the end of a dirt road about a half hour drive north of Islamabad, the capital of Pakistan, in a neighborhood called Bilal Town. Abbottabad was in a basin surrounded on all sides by the rugged Sarban Hills. The drive from the capital was uphill, and Abbottabad's relatively cool air made it an escape for well-to-do residents of the big city during the brutally hot summer months. There were several golf courses nearby. One mile away was Pakistan's large military academy at Kakul.

The compound was new, and even though Bilal Town was an affluent neighborhood, at thirty-eight thousand square feet it was many times larger than any of the surrounding ones. Its walls were built of cinder block that had been plastered in the front. They were as high as eighteen feet in some spots, topped with barbed wire. The main house was a large white three-layer box, with a third floor that appeared to have been an afterthought, which was only two-thirds as tall as the first and second. This truncated floor was odd. It had windows on only the north wall: a large one at the center filled with glass coated with an opaque reflective material, and four small rectangular ones just under the overhanging roof, similarly coated. Most of the house was painted white, and the windows on the second story were shaded with simple white awnings. The Sheik and his large family lived on the upper floors. Bin Laden himself was rarely seen even by the other two families who shared the compound and who ostensibly owned it—the brothers who called themselves Arshad and Tareq Khan.

Locked away and losing control, bin Laden had not given up, nor had he retreated from life. Two of his first four wives were still with him, and he had taken one more. His most recent, Amal, a Yemeni a quarter century younger than him, shared a mattress with him on the cramped third floor. The two older ones—Khairiah and Siham—waited their turns with him downstairs. There was not, as later events would show, perfect harmony in these domestic arrangements. There was a container of Avena syrup on his kitchen shelf, an oat-based folk remedy that promised arousal to the sexually depleted male. It might even have done him some good, because the cramped hallways of his upstairs cloister were crowded with twelve children, the youngest, Hussein, just two years old. The Sheik's own father had taken twenty-two wives, so by comparison the son was a restrained polygamist who, by most accounts, labored to meet his responsibilities to each wife, even to those who had left him. He had acquiesced in the desires of Najwa and Khadijah to divorce him. He knew the difficulties of his chosen path and did not push it on them or his children. But he personally never wavered in his commitment to the cause. He was soft-spoken, but hardly an easy person to live with. Marriage was no equal partnership for the Sheik. His faith stressed strict patriarchy, and bin Laden was its obedient servant. He ruled his family. He not only made all the decisions, he liked to instruct, and like most men who possess the ultimate truth he liked to hold forth. He gave frequent in-house lectures to his wives about the correct way to raise and discipline children. And there was a daily religious homily.

There was no stoop yet to his tall, lean frame, and daily pacing sessions behind the high walls of his compound gave him at least a modicum of exercise. He walked beneath a tarp suspended over the compound's vegetable garden that deflected direct sunlight and shielded him from prying eyes. The Sheik had been athletic in his youth, playing soccer and volleyball. He was vain about his appearance. The whitening of his hair and beard bothered him. The most wanted man in the world worried less about being recognized than *not* being recognized. On TV, that is. He had been in such deep hiding that few outside his immediate family had seen him in person for years. But his self-made videos and the periodic pronouncements smuggled out by couriers were seen everywhere. It would not do for him to appear old. Given fundamentalist Islam's ban on depicting the human form, there were only a few images of the Prophet Muhammad, but no one better appreciated the power of pictures than the Sheik, and those of the Prophet that did exist generally showed him young and virile, with flowing robes and a dark beard. He had mimicked those images all his life. So now he dyed his hair and beard black for his taping sessions, with results that were predictably amateurish. The color was too uniform and dark. He looked like a caricature of himself: Osama bin Laden with a cheap dye job.

He had plenty of time to think. He could picture what must be done but could no longer make it happen. Al Qaeda's name had been so usurped and muddied by younger, less careful warriors in Iraq, Yemen, and elsewhere—men less constrained, as he was, by the strict dictates of faith—that bin Laden apparently thought of changing his group's name. Among his papers were long lists of possible alternatives, most of them amusingly clumsy in their English translation, but all attempted to identify the group closer to his religious ambitions. Increasingly, affiliates were fighting local wars over local problems, and ignoring the Sheik's overarching vision. This was no small matter. The path he saw was immutable, and perfect, and straying from it meant nothing less than failure. He weighed al Qaeda's every act and public comment with mounting dismay.

Take the case of Faisal Shahzad, the young man coached by bin Laden's followers in Waziristan to explode a car bomb in Times Square. No doubt Shahzad's attempt was an example of bin Laden's men trying to follow his instructions—he repeatedly urged renewed attacks in the United States at iconic, well-populated locations. Times Square fit the prescription perfectly, as did Shahzad. He was the son of a wealthy and prominent Pakistani air force officer. He had been raised in luxury and given the best of international educations. After marrying an American woman of Pakistani descent, settling in Connecticut, and fathering two children, he applied for and completed a program to become an American citizen. Then he'd traveled to Pakistan and received training on how to set off the bomb. A young volunteer with an American passport must have seemed a godsend to the besieged plotters in Waziristan. But alert Times Square sidewalk vendors had thwarted Shahzad's mission and the would-be bomber was arrested. Just before he was sentenced to life in prison, a judge had asked Shahzad about the oath of allegiance he had sworn to the United States when he was made a citizen.

"I sweared," he said, "but I didn't mean it."

This bin Laden found offensive, despite the fact that years earlier he had taken the opposite viewpoint about breaking an oath in an argument with his mentor Abdullah Azzam, who had opposed bin Laden's plan to bomb a bus full of tourists in Pakistan.

"[Shahzad] was asked about the oath that he took when he obtained American citizenship," he wrote to al-Rahman. "And he responded by saying that he lied. You should know that it is not permissible in Islam to betray trust and break a covenant. Perhaps the brother was not aware of this. Please ask the brothers in Taliban Pakistan to explain this point to their members. In one of the pictures, brother Faisal Shahzad was with commander Mehsud [Hakimullah Mehsud, who would be killed by a drone strike in 2012]; please find out if Mehsud knows that getting the American citizenship requires taking an oath to not harm America. This is a very important matter because we do not want *mujahidin* to be accused of breaking a covenant."

The Sheik seemed to have little appreciation for the murderous pressure on his followers in the field. He wanted more attacks on America, but he had no new ideas. Instead, with quaint courtesy and diligent thrift, he pushed for a duplication of the 2001 attacks. He wrote: "It would be nice if you would pick a number of the brothers, not to exceed ten, and send them to their countries individually, without any of them knowing the others, to study aviation. It would be better if they are from the Gulf states, as study there is at the government's expense. They have to be picked with the utmost care and with very accurate specifications, one of which is that they are willing to conduct suicide actions and are prepared to do daring, important, and precise missions that we may ask of them in the future. So please pay top attention to this matter due to its utmost importance. Establish a mechanism to monitor and follow up on the brothers going to study aviation so that we reduce the chances of them slackening from conducting jihad. . . . It would be nice if you would ask the brothers in all regions if they have a brother distinguished by good manners, integrity, courage, and secretiveness, who can operate in the United States. He should be able to live there, or it should be easy for him to travel there. They should tell us this without taking any action and also tell us whether or not he is willing to conduct a suicide operation."

He concluded his letter of October 21 to Rahman by inquiring after the growing lists of "widows and orphans."

"Please make sure to keep the children and all of the families away from the areas that are being photographed and bombed. I pray to God Almighty to protect you and all the brothers around you. May He grant you success. May God's peace, mercy, and blessings be upon you."

He signed with an old nickname, "Your brother Zamray."

At the time he was writing this, after all those years in hiding, after his rigorous routines of self-protection had become rote, after not a whisper of suspicion that anyone outside his inner circle knew of his whereabouts, the Sheik had every reason to feel secure.

Except he wasn't.

6

Disguised Uncertainty

Winter 2010-2011

At the White House in the fall of 2010, Ben Rhodes noticed a growing number of meetings to which he was not invited. As with the Nobel Prize acceptance speech, Rhodes had become Obama's go-to writer for speeches and statements explaining his decisions as commander in chief. Rhodes's official title was "Deputy National Security Adviser for Strategic Communications and Speechwriting." His hair had thinned on top, he rarely did anything but work, and he dressed every day in a suit and tie, but at thirty-two he had a job that anyone with his interests would envy. There were not many high-level national security discussions from which he was barred.

His desk was deep in the warren of small offices in the West Wing, just downstairs from the Oval Office and the primary corridors of power. Windowless and closet-like, his and the other offices of the national security staff were as humble as the jobs were important. Rhodes's space was just big enough for his desk and chair, a waist-high bookshelf, and one more chair opposite the desk. It was as spare as an intern's quarters at most law firms. Rhodes helped the president craft speeches, shape security policy, and decide how to frame critical issues for the public. He knew that John Brennan, the president's chief counterterrorism adviser, had been holding frequent meetings now for months, and that Donilon, the president's national security adviser, often sat in. The mystery sessions were simply called "John Brennan's group." Ordinarily there were cameras that monitored the conference rooms so that staffers and secretaries could keep track of where people were, but for John Brennan's group the monitors went black. Rhodes wondered about that. Was the country about to be attacked again? Was it something serious related to nuclear weapons? There was a very short list of things that would engender that level of secrecy *within* the basement offices of the White House. One of the thoughts that occurred to him was that maybe they had found bin Laden.

After getting briefed in late summer on the compound in Abbottabad, Obama had left his intelligence chiefs with instructions to nail down who was living in it and report back. These regular reports documented heroic efforts to scrutinize the residence from afar. Using a variety of tools, including agents on the ground and surveillance platforms that were far enough away to avoid any possibility of notice, the agency was now able to flesh out life in the compound in far more detail. Other than occasional visits to the mosque, or taking their own children to the madrassa, the religious school attached to it, the "Khan" brothers kept to themselves. No one except a local handyman was ever invited inside the compound walls. Among the most religious people in Bilal Town—and the Khan brothers were clearly that—it was not uncommon to hide women away behind high walls and locked doors. Longer observation confirmed that the children of the hidden family, the ones who did not attend the madrassa, were seen to leave the compound only when one of the brothers took them to the doctor for a routine visit or treatment for some minor ailment or scrape. This would give the CIA an idea.

There was no way to catch a glimpse of the hidden family upstairs. The walls were high, the windows opaque. Only one member of the family could be seen regularly, a tall man in traditional Pashtun dress and prayer cap who took daily walks inside the compound walls. He walked in brisk small circles around the vegetable garden, part of which had a tarp stretched overhead to shield the patch of ground from direct sunlight—or, perhaps, one could imagine, to shield the walker from eyes in the sky. Overhead cameras were able to get images of him anyway, but they were not very good. The agency did not want to risk putting a drone or observation aircraft directly overhead for fear of tipping off the residents—or the Pakistani government, which it feared would amount to the same thing. The angle or altitude of the standoff cameras made it impossible to get a clear look at the walker's face. He appeared to be tall and thin. Efforts were made to more accurately gauge the man's height by measuring his stride and the shadow he cast, but the calculations were only precise enough to confirm what they could see for themselves: he was tall.

Brennan, for some reason he cannot fully explain, and that may have been no more than wishful thinking, felt in his bones that this was bin Laden. They called the man "the Pacer." Perhaps Brennan was inclined to believe it already, given the extraordinary lengths taken to hide this man, but as soon as he saw an image of the Pacer . . . he knew. We recognize people by many things other than their facial features and hair color, or their size and shape. We sometimes recognize someone we have seen before at just a glance, a glimpse out of the corner of the eye, something in the way they carry themselves or stoop or tilt their head or swing their arms. Brennan is a big wide man, imposing and stern, a former CIA officer who had been involved in efforts to go after the al Qaeda leader all the way back to when ALEC Station was up and running. He had been based in Saudi Arabia at the time, butting heads with Scheuer over how much or how little the Saudis' help could be trusted. He had worked closely with the Saudis after the 1998 East Africa embassy bombings. And he had seen Predator images of the Sheik taken from overhead in Afghanistan during that period, a tall man in robes surrounded by security, striding confidently. This was a different setting, Abbottabad, and the clothes were different, but here was the same man, the same walk. There wasn't hard evidence he could show to convince anyone else, but Brennan felt he *recognized* the Pacer.

Panetta briefed the president periodically through that fall, and in December his deputy Morell, "John," the head of the CIA's bin Laden team, and several others met with Donilon and Brennan at the White House. There was no breakthrough to report. The images of the Pacer were not clear enough to remove all doubt. None of their efforts had managed to pierce the compound's walls. An agency team was now living in a house in Bilal Town. They noted everything they could see, but they couldn't see much. They watched the comings and goings of the Ahmed brothers. They counted the laundry that was hung out to dry. They had determined that the hidden family was large: three wives, a young man, and ten or more children, several of them teenagers or young adults. The number of wives and children corresponded with their theorizing about who might surround bin Laden on the run. He had always kept most of his family with him. The analysts still could not prove that the mystery man was bin Laden but, then again, there wasn't a single scrap of information that ran counter to that theory, either. Sometimes when you are looking hard enough at something, when you are ready for anything that might shoot down your hypothesis, and nothing comes . . . lack of disproof begins to feel like proof.

"We think we have the best intelligence case for the location of bin Laden since Tora Bora," Morell told Donilon.

So, on December 14, just before Obama left for his annual holiday trip with his family to Hawaii, Panetta visited him in the Oval Office.

Obama listened and weighed the evidence. He was impressed. Now that there were actually "eyes on" the compound the whole prospect seemed more real, and all the new intel fit the puzzle neatly. Obama was struck, just as the others had been, by actually being able to see the mystery man. You couldn't tell exactly who it was, but something about actually seeing the target moving inside the high walls, hiding from the world, registered with him.

"At this point, you're saying to yourself, this is all circumstantial, but it's hard to figure out what the explanation would be for that particular pattern," said Obama. "And so at that point I think there's a part of me that's thinking this might be for real."

Still, the president was cautious. He told Panetta, "For all we know this could be some sheik hiding from one of his wives."

He wanted more. He instructed Panetta to get creative, to figure out a way to nail it down. He said to continue keeping a tight lid on it. And he also instructed Panetta to start preparing options for action.

*   *   *

As closely as the secret was held, Bill McRaven had gotten wind of it back in November. Those monitors might have been blacked out for meetings inside the NSC's offices, and McRaven was now spending most of his time in Afghanistan, but it was hard to keep the JSOC commander completely out of the loop.

He had worked in the White House himself. It was when he was just beginning to work his way back from his severe jump injuries, his body adjusting to the plates and pins that now held his pelvis together. He'd gotten a surprise phone call in October 2001, from Wayne Downing, a former four-star general who had led the Special Operations Command. The two men had gotten to know each other during the years before Downing's retirement. The general had just been asked by President Bush to unretire and take up a position in the White House as a kind of counterterrorism czar—an ill-defined special assistant role designed to bring some measure of coordination to the multiple agencies and services involved in the new war. Before he even officially accepted the job, Downing called to ask McRaven if he would come to Washington to help.

"You bet," said the SEAL captain.

A few weeks later, Downing caught up to the still hobbled SEAL as he was driving across the country from San Diego to his new desk job in Norfolk, Virginia.

"Hey, I've taken the job," Downing said. "Can you be here on Monday?" That was just four days away.

"Yeah, I think so," said McRaven.

When he showed up at the White House in his wheelchair, Downing told him simply, "Figure out what you're going to be."

It was a terrific opportunity for any military officer, especially one who had years earlier abandoned the idea of advancement in order to stay in the field, jumping out of planes and working deep underwater. The chance was not lost on McRaven. It seemed clear from the beginning that, in the long term, finding and taking down a furtive terror organization would require the kind of creative, cross-disciplinary skills long practiced by special ops. If every new war demanded that the military rethink how it fights, McRaven was already a few steps ahead. He had written a book on the subject while attending the Naval Postgraduate School in Monterey, California, entitled *Spec Ops: Case Studies in Special Operations Warfare: Theory and Practice*. It was a rare military graduate thesis to be picked up by a commercial publisher—the Presidio Press, which published it in 1995. In the book, McRaven had studied eight special operations missions, from the German attack on the fortress of Eban Emael in 1940, prior to the blitzkrieg of Belgium, to the Israeli raid at Entebbe, Uganda, in 1976, the raid that prompted President Carter to request creation of a similar counterterrorism unit for the U.S. military. McRaven had visited the sites of these raids, interviewed many key participants, and pieced together his own understanding of why they had succeeded or failed. As he did so, he crafted a way of thinking about such specialized missions. Now he would have a seat at the table, a chance to apply those ideas to America's newest military challenge.

The very idea of "special ops" had long been regarded critically by the conventional military. The elite, secret units that conducted these operations sucked up enormous resources and key personnel for occasional acts of amazing derring-do. When such missions worked they seemed almost magical, as in the Entebbe raid, where Israeli commandos flew 2,500 miles to Uganda, surprised a much larger force, and rescued 102 hostages, killing all of the Palestinian hijackers who had seized a commercial French airliner. When they failed, as in the rescue mission to Iran in 1980, they nearly always seemed harebrained in retrospect. They were daring by definition. The idea was to attempt something bolder than the enemy could reasonably anticipate. The men involved accepted great personal risk, and those in command gambled their reputations and careers on the outcome. And it was in the nature of the work that failures made a huge splash while successes, except in rare instance like Entebbe, were often, by design, unadvertised and unnoticed.

The debacle in the Iranian desert had prompted the creation of JSOC, which is based at Fort Bragg, North Carolina. Much blame for the failure fell on the clumsiness of efforts to borrow from various service branches unused to working together. So the mission had navy helicopters flown by marine pilots carrying army special operators deep into Iran to link up with air force piloted planes and crews. This motley force had left behind a desert staging area littered with destroyed aircraft and incinerated American bodies. Though one of the most spectacular failures in American military annals, the effect was not to kill special ops but to expand it. JSOC was created to integrate elite units from every branch into a smooth fighting force, and to equip them with the kind of vehicles and weapons needed for small, unorthodox missions. It brought together the army's Delta Force and 75th Ranger Regiment, the air force's Special Tactics Squadron, and Navy SEAL teams. Since the Iran mission had broken down trying to deliver the force to the target, the Night Stalkers, the 160th Special Operations Aviation Regiment, was stood up at Fort Campbell, Kentucky, where special choppers were designed and tested, and where the military's best helicopter pilots trained specifically for special ops missions.

McRaven's thesis, which would become part of the curriculum at the Naval Postgraduate School, set out the core concept of special ops: that a small, well-trained force can deliver a decisive blow against a much larger, well-defended one. He defined such a mission as one "conducted by forces specially trained, equipped, and supported for a specific target whose destruction, elimination, or rescue (in the case of hostages), is a political or military imperative." Refining the key elements to success for such missions, he prescribed, in a nutshell, "A simple plan, carefully concealed, repeatedly and realistically rehearsed, and executed with surprise, speed, and purpose."

President Bush's two large wars, each requiring hundreds of thousands of conventional soldiers, gradually proved the point that special ops was the most useful tool against al Qaeda. The tremendous effort and innovation that went into finding and fixing a target relied on men capable of executing the third F in the acronym F3EAD, the *finish*. The model McRaven had developed in his thesis primarily dealt with assaults on larger, well-entrenched enemy positions, but the principles of the lightning raid—simple, secret, and well rehearsed, executed with surprise, speed, and purpose— would prove devastatingly effective against an enemy that hid itself in a civilian population, in large part because pinpoint raids, as opposed to aerial attacks or direct assaults by conventional forces, avoided killing and injuring innocent bystanders. It also allowed for onsite collection of intelligence, which was essentially for feeding the target engine. Over the next decade, McRaven would get a chance to refine his strategies and put his theories into practice at a pace he had never imagined.

His two years in Washington before returning to a field command enabled him to combine necessary physical rehab with some high-level career rehab, developing the kind of relationships that are necessary to achieve flag rank. Rank was not something McRaven actively sought—indeed, years earlier, even before his accident, he regarded himself as the last person in the navy likely to become an admiral. But in just a few years he was back on his feet, serving in Iraq as deputy to JSOC commander General McChrystal, admiring the fusion of rapid intel and shooters his commander had implemented, and occasionally accompanying his men on night raids—the kind where you could drive or walk to the target. No more jumping out of planes, roping out of helicopters, or long marches in full pack for McRaven. During those years, first under McChrystal and then commanding JSOC himself, the admiral would help forge this new capability into the nation's premier war-fighting instrument. The JSOC force itself doubled in size, to nearly four thousand men and women. It became, in effect, a fifth branch of the U.S. military, an army within an army. It was global, operating in secret in more than a dozen countries, and had been freed from strict mission-by-mission oversight from Washington. The need for speed trumped the desire for close control, so commanders like McChrystal and McRaven were given the authority to launch at least routine strikes without seeking approval all the way up the chain.

Through the first decade of the century, McRaven and his men had carried out more special ops missions than any such unit in history. He estimated that by the time he was summoned to Langley in January 2011 to be officially briefed on the Abbottabad discovery, he had been personally involved, commanding either remotely or on the ground, in *thousands* of them.

By early 2011, the CIA had its own small armies in the field. After 9/11, the nation had recovered quickly from its misgivings about spying and covert action. Agency operators, most of them former military, had worked ever more closely with JSOC throughout the wars in Iraq and Afghanistan. When Panetta and Morell returned from the White House meeting with Obama in December, the one where he directed them to start thinking about taking action, the first units they considered were their own.

The two broad options were to bomb the compound or to send a raiding party in. The latter would be far more complicated. It would require planning and rehearsal, and involve a variety of special talents, so the instinct was to develop that option in-house. This had the advantage of keeping the now four-month-old secret contained. Outside the agency, those who knew about the compound, or who were supposed to know, could still be counted on two hands. There was the president, of course, and a few top members of his foreign policy staff, including Brennan and Donilon. The director of National Intelligence, James Clapper, had been told. At the Department of Defense there were only four people, Secretary Robert Gates, Chairman of the Joint Chiefs Michael Mullen, Vice Chairman General James "Hoss" Cartwright, and Undersecretary of Defense for Intelligence Michael Vickers.

The CIA teams were excited about the mission and were ready to do it themselves . . . soon. But Panetta and Morell had time. The president had also told them to work harder on identifying the mystery man. Before committing themselves to using their own operators, they wanted to at least consult with McRaven.

All the JSOC commander knew before getting the call was that the CIA had a new lead on bin Laden. He had heard that before over the years, and in each case the lead had failed to pan out. Early in the war in Afghanistan his men had spent a lot of time chasing bin Laden's ghost. This time he was told that the lead seemed better than most, but McRaven didn't think much of it until he was summoned to Langley. That had not happened with any of the previous leads. At the conference table in the deputy director's office, McRaven and one of his top aides met with Panetta, Morell, and the heads of the CIA's own strike force. He was shown pictures of the compound. No one had glimpsed the inside of the buildings. Everything was heavily couched in maybes. Morell made it clear that they were not certain that bin Laden was really there, and they weren't sure yet what course the president would decide to take, if any. But on that qualified basis, they launched into a tactical discussion. If you were going to hit that target, how would you do it?

The CIA men had had a head start. They sketched five different options. That fact alone was telling. McRaven could see at a glance that there was really only one way to do it. He had ruled out a bombing option immediately. Whatever the advantages in simplicity and reduced American risk, his educated guess was that it would take upwards of fifty thousand pounds of ordnance to destroy a compound of that size and make sure bin Laden, if he was there, wouldn't survive. You had to consider the possibility of tunnels or an underground bunker—like the one where Saddam had been hiding. That explosive power would kill everyone inside the compound and quite a few people nearby.

A ground raid, on the other hand, posed relatively few problems. His men had been hitting compounds like this every night for years, often a dozen or more a night. This one was unremarkable. It had a three-story residence, a smaller outbuilding, and high stone walls all around it. The layout and location of the compound clearly indicated to him the right way to assault—a small helicopter-borne force.

He kept this thinking to himself as the CIA unit commanders described the options they had worked up. When it was his turn to comment, McRaven congratulated Panetta and Morell on developing such a strong lead and proceeded to walk them through how JSOC would do it. You would need a team big enough to secure the compound once you were inside. The primary challenge was its location. Abbottabad was in a "denied" space 150 miles from friendly territory, which meant that delivering the force to the target and safely extracting it without triggering a shooting war with Pakistan would be the biggest problem. It was, as the admiral was fond of saying, "sporty," but doable. It would increase the complexity of the mission, and complexity multiplied the number of things that could go wrong. But those problems aside, how to actually raid the compound and the buildings were old hat. The tactics McRaven's teams had developed were built on years of trial and error, missions that had worked and those that didn't. A lot of good men had died perfecting these skills. He ran through for the CIA men how his team would proceed, and why. He even suggested the right man for the mission, his SEAL Team Six commander, who had earned a legendary reputation—he had led the mission that had killed three Somali pirates in 2009, rescuing an American freighter captain. McRaven explained that the most valuable thing his team would bring to the mission was experience. No matter how well the operation in Abbottabad was planned, long experience taught that something would go wrong. Something *always* went wrong. What you needed were men who could think on their feet and make good decisions under pressure, men who had seen all manner of snafus and survived. No one in the world could rival JSOC's seasoning. The SEAL team he had in mind had just rotated back to the United States and could get to work on the mission right away.

Morell and Panetta were impressed. Their guys were good, but McRaven's men were the pros.

"If the president decides to do this on the ground," Panetta told Morell, "then JSOC are the guys to do it."

Panetta pushed the agency to come up with creative ways to get a better look inside the compound, without much luck. The agency team spent hours kicking around possibilities. No idea, no matter how outlandish, was rejected without serious discussion. Was there some way to flush the residents out of the compound? A fire? A stink bomb? A summons to emergency prayer? Panetta kept a chart, and every suggestion was logged on to it. A suggestion was not crossed off until it was either tried or seriously discussed.

Was there a way to position a camera closer, say on a tree that could peer down over the walls? What about one farther away on high ground but with better optics? How about sewage lines: could a listening device or a camera be threaded in that way? There was a tree inside the compound. Could they put a small camera or listening device up in it somehow? Some of these ideas were tried but yielded nothing of value. The tree inside the compound was chopped down before anyone could figure out a way to get at it— spooky, because it was as if someone inside the compound had seen the director's chart. One by one, the schemes either fizzled or were discarded. They were extremely careful not to tip their hand. The compound had clearly been designed to hide the family inside, and designed well. It would not take much to spook them. Any hint that they were under surveillance would blow everything. Morell lived in fear of waking up one morning to discover that, overnight, the compound had emptied.

One creative idea may have grown out of the observation that the only time any member of the hidden family emerged from the compound was when a child was taken to the doctor. The agency got the idea of opening a free hepatitis B vaccination clinic for children nearby. Maybe they could draw some of the hidden children out that way. They found a Pakistani doctor, Shakil Afridi, whose passion was setting up such clinics all over the country. He would go door-to-door notifying residents and persuading them to bring their children in for shots. Agents approached Afridi and offered him a substantial sum—something in six figures worth of American dollars—enough to sustain his program for some time. All he would have to do in return was give them the needles he used. They never told him why they wanted the needles, but the plan was to recover DNA from them and analyze it. The CIA had DNA samples from close relatives of bin Laden. If genetic material from one of the hidden children closely resembled it, it would come very close to proof positive that the Sheik was the father. The clinic would be real, the inoculations completely legit. The children of Abbottabad would emerge healthier and the agency might get the confirmation it needed. The agents did not hide their affiliation from Afridi; he was told that the CIA was funding the program.

Over the next few months, as planning proceeded at Langley and in the White House, Afridi set up the clinic. He went door-to-door, inviting everyone to bring in children. He inoculated many. But when he knocked on the door to the big compound in Bilal Town, no one answered.

No one would ever answer.

Planning for either an air or a ground assault on the compound proceeded through February. Despite Panetta's push for an answer, the CIA was no closer to the identity of the Pacer. McRaven's man was drawing up detailed plans in an unmarked office on the first floor of the agency's printing plant, and the air force was plotting out a B-2 mission to obliterate the compound in one blinding strike. All of this required enlarging the circle of knowledge. Michèle Flournoy, the undersecretary of defense for policy, was read in by her boss Mike Vickers, and she began working closely with General Cartwright. The various deputies were now meeting every week, usually at the White House but sometimes at the CIA, getting updates on the intelligence-collection efforts and discussing every possible permutation of a raid. These "deputies" meetings were usually attended by Cartwright, Morell, Vickers, Robert Cadillo, the deputy director of National Intelligence, and sometimes John Brennan and deputy National Security Adviser Denis McDonough. Toward the end of the month, McRaven sat in on a few of these sessions, prepping for a March 14 principals meeting with Obama, where they would formally present the president with recommendations.

As usual, the national security agenda was full. An earthquake and tsunami three days earlier had caused widespread death, destruction, and dislocation in Japan, and the U.S. military was mobilizing to deliver humanitarian assistance. There were sweeping popular protests in Egypt, as the "Arab Spring" spread across the Middle East—an inspiring but potentially treacherous period of change in a region whose stability had long been vital to U.S. interests. In mid-February, Obama had called for Egypt's longtime president Hosni Mubarak to step down, and was now weighing options for some kind of limited intervention in Libya, where dictator Muammar Gaddafi's long-standing regime was being pressured by increasingly violent protests. And in Pakistan itself, a CIA contractor working out of the Lahore consulate, Raymond Allen Davis, had shot and killed two armed men on the street when he said they had tried to rob him. He was under arrest and facing murder charges, and the United States was having the devil of a time trying to extract him. Local frustration over American policies in Pakistan had warped the incident into a standoff, with demonstrators and some prosecutors demanding that the CIA contractor be prosecuted and punished. So at the same time options were being prepared for various ways of violating Pakistani sovereignty with a raid on Abbottabad, the White House and State Department were engaged in delicate discussions over Davis.

It was in this context that Obama met with the National Security Council to formally consider the CIA's case. It was time to start making the important decisions. Obama was acutely aware that the longer he delayed, the more people were read in on the secret—and greater became the likelihood that it would leak, or that something critical would change. The group met in the White House Situation Room, where much of the drama over the next two months would unfold.

The Situation Room is a few steps down from the ground floor of the West Wing, the largest in a complex of small meeting rooms, and is hardly what a set designer would imagine as the decision center for the world's only superpower. Long ago nicknamed "the Woodshed," it was installed by President Kennedy after the Cuban Missile Crisis to create a secure command center fully wired for global telecommunications. It is windowless and cramped, much smaller than the dining room in most grand residences. Much of the mahogany paneling that gave the room its nickname was removed in a 2007 renovation to make it easier for electronic technicians to get at the cables and wiring. Now its beige walls are hung with flat video screens. The ceiling is low and lined with harsh recessed fluorescent lights. The room is all but filled by a long mahogany table at its center, polished to a high gloss. Around it are thirteen high-backed black leather chairs. The blue carpet beneath has a yellow border around the edges, on which are lined smaller black leather chairs for deputies and staff members. The president sits at the north end of the table beneath the circular presidential seal. There is no chair at the opposite end, which is open to afford a clear view of a video screen that reaches from tabletop to ceiling. There are leather desk pads at each place around the table for the secretaries of defense and state, the national security adviser, the vice president, the director of National Intelligence, the chairman of the Joint Chiefs, the president, and, for nearly all of these sessions, the CIA director and his deputy and various others. Until his work in the field took him away, Admiral McRaven was present.

Above all, one is struck by how intimate the space is. When full, as it was for many of these meetings, the top leadership of the nation can be said, without exaggeration, to be huddled.

By early March the agency had determined that the Abbottabad compound held a "high value target," and that it was most likely Osama bin Laden. "John," the team leader at the CIA and the most veteran analyst on the trail, was close to convinced. He put his confidence level at 95 percent.

The president surveyed confidence levels around the room. Brennan felt about the same as "John," but others were less certain — some far less certain. The opinion had already been "red-teamed" three times — worked over by agency analysts assigned to poke holes in it: at the Counterterrorism Center, by Brennan's staff, and by a group within the CIA. Four senior leaders at the Directorate of National Intelligence had reviewed the case and written out their own opinions. Most seemed to place their confidence level at about 80 percent. Some were as low as 40 or even 30 percent. Obama then asked Morell, who was seated in a chair against the wall behind him, under the presidential seal.

Morell had come to admire Obama's decision-making skills. He had worked with President Bush up close almost every day, and he had admired him, too, but the two men were very different. Morell and others who worked closely with Bush believed he was widely underestimated. He was plenty smart. He was not as eager as Obama to ingest written reports, but he did read them, and he was a good listener. He grasped the nut of an issue quickly, asked sharp questions, encouraged lively debate, and then, unhesitatingly, often on the spot, made a decision. Obama, on the other hand, had a level of study and contemplation that he kept private. He liked to pore over written reports and, after initiating a discussion of opposing views, would generally retire before coming back with a decision.

One thing in particular impressed Morell about Obama. Morell had given and sat through thousands of presidential briefings by now, enough to know the in-house tactics of policy makers. Advisers had a way of narrowing the choice to option A or option B, and then steering the president to the one they preferred. It was all in how the issue was framed. This method didn't have a chance with Obama. He would listen to A and B, ask a lot of good questions, and more often than not propose an entirely different course, option C, which seemed to emerge wholly formed from his head. He had done this just a few days earlier in a widely reported instance concerning Libya. It came during a prolonged policy discussion over what the United States should do about Gaddafi's apparent intent to slaughter rebels and civilians who were contesting his regime. In that case, option A was just to stand back and not get involved.

The consequences would be awful but U.S. military intervention in a third country (Iraq and Afghanistan still being very much live wars) would be hugely unpopular domestically and might, in Libya, where there was no clear idea what would emerge after Gaddafi, end up making things worse. Option B was to intervene militarily on the side of the rebels, essentially do whatever had to be done to prevent them from being systematically slaughtered by the regime. There were strong views on both sides, but the first option was clearly the one favored by most of the staff. Obama then proposed an option C, the course he would eventually pursue. This called for the United States to spearhead air attacks on Gaddafi's forces for a few days, and then let a coalition of European and Arab countries take over. U.S. forces would step back from most combat missions after the initial thrusts but, through NATO, continue providing critical air support and patrol a no-fly zone. Morell thought it was brilliant.

He now placed his own certainty that the Pacer was bin Laden at 60 percent.

"Okay, this is a probability thing," said Obama. "Leon, talk to me about this."

The director explained that ever since the agency's erroneous call, a decade earlier, that Saddam Hussein was hiding weapons of mass destruction, a finding that had kicked off a long and very costly war, the CIA had instituted an almost comically elaborate process for weighing certainty. It was like trying to contrive a mathematical formula for good judgment. Analysts up and down the chain were now asked not only for their opinion, but to assign it a confidence level—high, medium, or low. Then they had to explain why they had assigned that level. What you ended up with, as the president was finding, and as he would later explain it to me, was not more certainty but more confusion.

Obama said as much, and then turned in his chair and looked at the deputy director.

"Michael, what do you think?"

Morell had thought a lot about it. He had been personally involved in the finding about Saddam's supposed weapons of mass destruction, and had felt more certain about *that* than he felt about *this*.

"People don't have differences because they have different intel," he said. "We are all looking at the same things. I think it depends more on your past experience." He explained that counterterrorism analysts at work on al Qaeda over the past five years had enjoyed a remarkable string of successes. They had been crushing the terror group inside Pakistan, and they had directly or indirectly prevented further terrorist attacks inside the United States So they were very confident. Those who had been at work longer, like him, had known failure. They knew the fragility of even the soundest-seeming analysis. The WMD story had been a bracing lesson. He bore responsibility for it.

"Mr. President, if we had a human source who had told us directly that bin Laden was living in that compound, I still wouldn't be above 60 percent." He said he had spent a lot of time on both questions—WMDs and Abbottabad. He had seen no fewer than thirteen analytical drafts on the former question, and at least as many on the latter.

"And I'm telling you, the case for WMDs wasn't just stronger, it was *much* stronger," he said.

This kicked off more discussion about percentage levels of confidence. The president listened, but he had already pretty much made up his mind.

"One of the things you learn as president is you're always dealing with probabilities," he told me. "No issue comes to my desk ` ` is perfectly solvable. No issue comes to my desk where there's one hundred percent confidence that this is the right thing to do. Because if people were absolutely certain then it would have been decided by somebody else. And that's true in dealing with the economic crisis. That's true in an order to take a shot at a pirate. That's true about most of the decisions I make during the course of the day. So I'm accustomed to people offering me probabilities. In this situation, what you started getting was probabilities that disguised uncertainty as opposed to actually providing you with more useful information."

Obama had no trouble admitting it to himself. If he acted on this, he was going to be taking a gamble, pure and simple. A big gamble.

If they were successful, and if the Pacer was bin Laden, then killing or capturing him would mark a clear and central victory in the war al Qaeda had started almost ten years ago. It would deliver on the promise Obama had made campaigning four years earlier, the one where he said he would take a shot unilaterally in Pakistan if he got a good chance, the promise that nearly everyone had criticized, including some, such as Hillary Clinton and Joe Biden, who were now in the room helping him to decide. That promise in some ways had *defined* his national security strategy. So success would be a demonstration of justice achieved at great cost and sacrifice, and with tremendous skill. It would be a satisfying achievement for America and the world, an emotional turning point, but more, it would vindicate the determination and skill of everyone who had given of themselves—in some cases *all* of themselves—to the struggle. On a practical level, it would be the single greatest blow yet to an organization still scheming to take American lives.

If he tried and failed, however—and they had not yet begun to calculate all the spectacular ways it might fail—then some brave

American warriors might lose their lives attempting something that might turn out to be a major national embarrassment. Failure would likely be as prestige-enhancing for al Qaeda as Desert One had been for Iran's mullahs in 1980. Bin Laden's stature, which had waned considerably since 2001, would get a new boost, the kind that translated into more money, more recruits, and more attacks. Success might bump up Obama's political standing at home for a few weeks, but failure could brand him as an ineffectual commander in chief, and doom his chances for a second term as surely as Desert One had doomed Carter's.

Either way, success or failure, there would be an outraged Pakistan to deal with. American relations with that difficult, nuclear-armed nation were already strained nearly to breaking. Whatever he decided, Obama later told me, was going to be a judgment call based on circumstantial evidence, piecing together patterns. There was still a possibility that this was some warlord from Afghanistan who had set up shop, or that this was a drug dealer from the Gulf who valued his privacy or had a mistress or a second family. There were other stories that might have explained the pattern. The calculation the president had to make was whether it was probable enough that bin Laden was there to justify the risks, given the importance to America's national security.

So as the conversation around him about levels of certainty wore on, the president, who usually did more listening than speaking in these meetings, interrupted.

"This is fifty-fifty," he said. That silenced everyone. "Look guys, this is a flip of the coin. I can't base this decision on the notion that we have any greater certainty than that."

So, if he decided to act, what were his options? Obama was presented with two. The simplest, and the one that posed the least risk to American forces, was to reduce the compound to dust, along with everyone and everything in and around it. To do the job right, the air force had calculated that would mean raining as many as thirty or more precision bombs from a high-flying B-2, or launching a comparable number of missiles. This would be enough to guarantee that anything breathing on, in, or near that plot of earth would be killed. It would vaporize everything above ground and pulverize anything below. There would be minimal worry about encountering Pakistani air defenses—a lone high-flying B-2 Stealth bomber would be long gone before the country knew it had been hit. With no ground forces there was no chance of mixing it up with that nation's army or police. It would be a mighty, sudden stroke from a dark sky that would leave nothing but a big smoking hole in the middle of Abbottabad—which, wasn't going to sell very well. Collateral damage would make the Pakistani fury all the more righteous. But it would get the job done.

Obama asked how many people were living at the compound and was informed that there were four adult males, five women, and nearly twenty children. He asked about the houses that were close to the compound in the neighborhood. Those, too, would be completely destroyed, along with every resident man, woman, and child. This really gave the president pause. America was not going to obliterate them on a fifty-fifty chance of also killing Osama bin Laden.

So the president scrapped that plan immediately. He said the only way he would even consider attacking the compound from the air was if the volume and precision of munitions was such that the blast area would be drastically reduced.

Then McRaven explained the ground option for the first time. His team had not yet fleshed out the mission completely. The one thing he could tell the president for sure was that if his team could be delivered to the compound, they could clear it and kill or capture bin Laden with minimal loss of life. The admiral delivered this opinion with the kind of confidence that can come only with long experience. He wasn't trying to sell it. He had been in these meetings back in the early years after 9/11, and he had seen how various factions or branches or agencies had worked to sell their approach to the president. This was not like that. He was surprised, given the importance of this mission and the risks it entailed, that the discussions were not more rancorous. Panetta and Brennan had set the tone from the beginning. In every meeting he had attended, options were laid on the table and discussed, pro and con. McRaven had told his aide on the project: "We may end up doing this thing, we may not. In the end we're going to do what's best for the country. If it's dropping one bomb on the compound, then that's what we're going to do." So he presented the still-sketchy ground operation as a simple statement of fact. Without bringing any more people into the planning loop, he said, "I can tell you that we can succeed on the raid. What I can't tell you yet is how I get in and how I get out. To do that requires detailed planning by air planners who do this for a living and assess the air defense capabilities of that country and who can plot and route how we would get in and how we would get out and what obstacles we would face getting in and getting out.

"So I am not recommending a raid," he told the president. "I am telling you that if I could get in, we could execute a raid. Getting out might be a little sporty. I can't recommend a raid until I do the homework."

Even if he had done the homework, the admiral felt no need to push for the raid. He believed everyone in the room would come to that conclusion on his or her own. The facts would steer them to it. He also believed the president would not let this opportunity slip. The bombing option was too loud and messy, too many innocents would be killed, and in the end you would not have any way to prove you had killed bin Laden. After a strike like that, with the big smoking hole in Abbottabad, Pakistan would be understandably furious. There would be no chance that an American team would get the chance to sift patiently through the rubble looking for DNA. Actually getting bin Laden was the only thing that would make the blowback from Pakistan worth it. But you would have to be able to show that's what you had done. Nothing would accomplish that short of having his corpse or living person in custody. Only that would eliminate any mystery about why you had done it. The risks were greater whenever you sent men in on the ground, but his men were more than capable, and he knew Obama knew it. He had also learned that this president was not unduly risk averse. He had been favorably impressed over the previous two years. Obama had made the final call on almost every major mission JSOC had undertaken in that time, and he was not timid. He would always listen without tipping his thoughts to discussions of the military and political risks, then he would retreat for a time, a few hours or until the next morning, and would generally come back to say, "I gotta go do it." The only time he said no was when the risks were prohibitively high. Understanding that the president had a broader range of responsibilities than he had as a military commander, McRaven had come to trust Obama's judgment. The president counted the real risks for the men on the ground more heavily than the political risks, which is what any military officer wants from the commander in chief. In a few cases where even McRaven's superiors had advised waiting—had said, "It's a little too risky"—it was the president who had come back to say, "No, okay, let's go do it." So the admiral did not voice his own thoughts about which way to go. There was no need.

Panetta had another thought about the raid option. If bin Laden was not in the compound, the SEALs might be able to depart without creating a major disturbance. The people living there and the neighbors would have a story to tell, for sure, but because the mission was conceived as CIA covert action, the United States could simply deny it. Such a denial would hardly fool the Pakistani government, but it would make the thing less of a poke in the eye. Deniability pushed the mission into the gray area that had sustained secret American operations in Waziristan for years.

When the meeting ended, Obama asked the air force to work on developing a more surgical strike, and also some "targeted stand-off options," which meant missiles or, more likely, drones. But the president also wanted a fuller picture of what a ground raid would look like. Could they deliver the force without setting off alarms? Could they get in and out without the need for going to war with Pakistan's air defenses?

"Sir, it's just me and one other guy right now and this concept that we've got to come up with," said McRaven. "I can't tell you whether or not this will work. I can't tell you until I pull the team together and we do the rehearsals, and then I can get back to you."

So McRaven was sent off to do his homework.

This meant running what he called "all the trap lines." There were a lot of variables. The Abbottabad compound was relatively large at thirty-eight thousand square feet. Bigger meant more people.

On a normal-sized compound in Afghanistan, McRaven was used to sending in seventy men. You had to be able to strongpoint the perimeter and every door and window. There was a three-story house and an outbuilding. So you had to get the right force there. You had to get them there without being detected. It was a long way in and a long way out, so you had to be able to refuel before flying back, which meant a staging area somewhere outside the city where you could set down larger choppers carrying fuel and a quick reaction force. The helicopters all had their specifications, depending on altitude and temperature and other factors, so you had to figure out how many men they could carry. At the end of the day it was all about load. Pounds cut into airtime. The more choppers you used, the larger your presence and the greater the likelihood of being discovered, or of mechanical or pilot malfunction—ghosts of Desert One. He wouldn't have the final calculations until they started rehearsing, but he could tell right away that they were going to have to go in heavier and with fewer men than he would like.

Two weeks later, at the end of March, he was back in the Situation Room with a full plan. McRaven now told the president that he was completely confident that his men could execute the raid. His air planners had worked out entering Pakistan's airspace without being seen by means of two stealth Black Hawks, secret aircraft specially designed to fly silently and avoid radar detection, followed by two big MH-47E Chinooks carrying fuel and a backup force, which would set down in Kala Dhaka, fifty miles northwest of Abbottabad. The Black Hawks would deliver the "operators" to the compound and, when they had finished taking it down, fly them out to the Chinooks and refuel before flying back to Afghanistan. He said it was likely they could do this without tripping any alarms. McRaven said that if his men could get on and off the compound within thirty minutes, there was a good chance that they would encounter no organized Pakistani defense. There was always a possibility that a small armed police unit—a couple of guys armed with AK-47s—might stumble on them. It was even possible that the compound had its own nearby defenders. But forces that small would not pose a serious threat to his men.

If it happened this way, then the obstacles were minimal. But what if the Pakistanis were more alert than they imagined? What if something significantly delayed them at the compound? The admiral was grilled hard at this second meeting. Many in the room were skeptical of the response time he projected for the Pakistanis. Didn't he realize how close the compound was to the military academy? Less than a mile. That there was an army facility and an Inter-Services Intelligence compound nearby? McRaven was aware. He explained that proximity in this case did not guarantee a speedy reaction. Even if some low-level soldier or cop or agent was awakened or alerted to something fishy going on at the compound, it would still take time for any kind of coordinated response. The Pakistani forces adhered to a rigid command structure, with lower-ranking men rarely acting without permission. It was a command philosophy the U.S. military discouraged but was typical of many militaries around the world. Most young officers would prefer to get in trouble for doing nothing than for doing something wrong. That calculation was built into the thirty-minute estimate. That was about as fast as they could do it, the admiral said. But what if he was wrong? What if the Pakistani forces responded faster than he imagined they could? What if something happened on the compound that slowed *his* men down?

McRaven explained that if a significant Pakistani force showed up before his men could get out, then there was going to be a gunfight. He didn't want to get into that gunfight. His men would win it, but in the process lose the war. That scenario would give the Pakistanis the high moral ground. There were big political ramifications whenever American forces killed a single Pakistani soldier or policeman. They didn't know for sure that bin Laden was there, after all. As soon as the admiral had brought more of his planning team in, he had told them that rule one was they were going to do everything conceivable to avoid killing Pakistanis. It had been a priority at every point in the planning. If they got in and out fast, there would be no problem, but he could readily imagine a scenario that might delay them. If they got on target and were not able to find bin Laden, but they thought he was there hiding from them, behind a false door or false wall—something they had encountered often—then what would they do? Did they just hop on the helicopters and leave? Suppose they had his wives and other key people who confirmed that bin Laden was there somewhere? The answer was no, they would not leave. They had come too far and were too close at that point to give up. At that point, they had to be prepared to strongpoint the compound and start tearing things apart until they found him. Which would mean overstaying their limit. There was a strong potential for that, perhaps even a likelihood, and every extra minute upped the chances of a confrontation with Pakistani troops.

"So at what point in time do you stop trying to find him?" McRaven asked hypothetically. "And now you are surrounded by Pakistanis, what do you do?"

The admiral's answer was surprising. He recommended that if it came to that, his men would just hunker in and wait for Washington to work things out with Pakistan's leaders.

"You go to them and say, 'Okay, guys, this was the one we've been telling you about for umpteen years, that if he was there we were coming. Well he's here. We haven't killed anybody. We're holed up. Let's talk about this.'"

That, McRaven thought, might buy them thirty more minutes. After that, he wouldn't be dealing with a local response, but with the entire Pakistani chain of command.

Here's where the thinking of an admiral differed from the thinking of a president. As far as McRaven was concerned, his men could fight their way out of anything. There was a Quick Reaction Force nearby in case things got unexpectedly hairy. So they could fight their way off the compound. But then you had the rendezvous in Kala Dhaka, and then four American choppers flying out of Pakistani airspace, which was patrolled by F-16 fighters. Protecting the helicopters would now involve facing down the Pakistani air force. Again, this was something the U.S. Air Force could handle, with its superior fighters and air-to-ground capability, but . . . well, the fight would now be very sporty, indeed. The admiral thought this was a scenario to be avoided at all cost. After two years in Afghanistan, where the bulk of his force had moved from Iraq, he was acutely sensitive to the delicacy of the Pakistani relationship. It would not likely withstand a trail of dead Pakistanis and downed fighters and burning ground-to-air stations. So at the point where the raiding force inside the compound found itself surrounded, he suggested they should decline the fight. They would strongpoint the compound, hole up, and wait for Washington to work things out with Islamabad. They were, after all, American soldiers on a mission that Pakistan, ostensibly, supported . . . apprehending the world's most wanted terrorist. Someone in the White House or at the State Department would then get on the phone with General

Ashfaq Kayani, the Pakistani army chief of staff, or President Asif Zardari, and explain the situation. Ask, *How do we extract ourselves from this without killing a lot of people? We don't want dead guys; you don't want dead guys.* This is how McRaven imagined the conversation might proceed. The very fact that they preferred standing down to getting into a gunfight demonstrated that they intended no harm to Pakistanis and posed no threat to that nation.

The president saw it differently than the admiral. He was not going to have any such conversation with Pakistani authorities. Counterterrorism adviser Nick Rasmussen would later describe the president's response to McRaven's suggestion as "visceral."

"I thought the possibilities of them being held, being subject to politics inside of Pakistan, were going to be very, very difficult," the president explained to me. "I did not want to put them in a position of that kind of vulnerability."

If he were going to deal with an outraged Pakistan, which he would have to do in almost any event, he would do it without a force of brave Americans in the middle.

Just days earlier, Obama had finally brought to a close the difficult wrangling over CIA contractor Davis, who had been released only after the United States negotiated a $2.4 million deal for the families of the men he had killed. The incident had stirred up a small furor in Pakistan, where much of the public and the leadership was already fed up with American intrusions on their sovereignty—publicly, at least. Unofficially, the country's top leadership was a lot more flexible, but there was only so far you could push them.

Where this mission was concerned, Obama wasn't going to count on Pakistani goodwill, because there appeared to be little to spare. Like many countries in that part of the world, Pakistan's leadership was less a coherent hierarchy than a collage of overlapping interests. Part of the art of managing that relationship was in balancing those interests. It was an important relationship. Most of the supplies and fuel for the American war effort in Afghanistan flowed across Pakistan's border. Even though al Qaeda terrorists had taken refuge in the country's northwestern territories and had the tacit sympathy of powerful factions in its leadership, the United States depended upon the government's silent support to continue its drone campaign. And Pakistan was a nuclear power, a thing never to be forgotten. Its stability was vital to the security of not just the region but the world. With tempers in Islamabad already hot, imagine handing the Pakistanis a small force of elite American soldiers. Imagine trying to negotiate their exit with them trapped inside a compound with hostages or dead bodies, one of them quite possibly Osama bin Laden. The SEALs could all end up dead or held hostage. It wasn't hard to imagine.

"And I also had confidence, based on my subsequent conversations with McRaven, that they could get out of there without engaging the Pakistani military," the president explained. "There was a good enough chance of them being able to get in and get out, even if something went wrong, even if it wasn't bin Laden, that they could hold off the Pakistani military, which we anticipated couldn't respond faster than a certain period of time, so that the likelihood of a firefight erupting between the United States and Pakistani military was very slim. And in that situation, I just wanted to get them out of there, and then we would deal with the fallout knowing that those guys were back here safe."

So Obama told McRaven that if his SEALs went in, they were coming out. Bin Laden was an imperative that outweighed the relationship. If the Pakistanis sounded an alarm and responded faster than they anticipated, so be it. There would have to be a confrontation. He told the admiral to be fully prepared to fight his way out.

But the president had not decided on the raid yet. The air force came back with a plan for smaller bombs and smaller blast circles. They could hit the compound without harming people living in homes outside its walls, but the lesser assault meant that they could not guarantee taking out anything underground. There would still be a lot of bodies, women and children included, and no way to tell if one of the dead was bin Laden.

But there was another air option, one that appealed especially to Cartwright, one of Obama's favorite generals. It had been Cartwright who had come up with a middle path the year before when Obama was caught between launching a large counterinsurgency campaign in Afghanistan and essentially pulling the plug on the American mission. Cartwright had proposed sending a much smaller force than the Pentagon was requesting, one capable of conducting counterterror operations, but not large enough for the nation-building exercise contemplated.

Cartwright's new proposal for Abbottabad was to target the Pacer alone. Wait for the tall man dressed in *shalwar kameez* and prayer cap to emerge for his daily exercise around the vegetable garden and shoot him down with a small missile fired from a drone. It would require great precision, but the air force could do it with the equivalent of a sniper drone. There would be no smoking hole in the center of Abbottabad, no dead wives and children, little collateral damage, if any, and there would be no potential dead or wounded SEALs, no chance of a sticky standoff against Pakistan's armed forces at the compound.

It felt too good to be true. The guys who operated these things felt pretty good, but there was a strong whiff of testing stage about it. And what if it worked and you dropped the Pacer in his tracks? What then? How would you know that you had killed Osama bin Laden? And what if you hadn't? What if you had dropped some cheating sheik from Dubai? How would you know? It meant that the uncertainty that surrounded this mission would live on, and that in some sense bin Laden would live on, even if it *had* been him. And it was strictly a one-shot deal. If you missed, the Pacer and his entourage would vanish.

There was one strong clue that Obama had already made up his mind. McRaven had said that his team would be ready to conduct the raid by the first week of May, when the moon would vanish for a few days over Abbottabad and the nights would be black— the way JSOC liked them. No one said anything, but that window seemed to impose a hard deadline. The drone option had no urgency. It was a daylight opportunity, and the Pacer walked every day. You could take the shot whenever you wished. So why did everyone feel that the moon's cycle was so important?

Obama told McRaven to start full-dress rehearsals and to be ready to go when the nights turned black. He also told Cartwright to get ready to attempt the drone strike. He wanted both options kept alive until he made a decision.

But to those who knew him, there was little doubt which way he was leaning.

7

"Adhering to These Precautions"

April 2011

In what would prove to be the final weeks of his life, events had overtaken the Sheik. There were popular uprisings throughout the Middle East. The tectonic shifts of what would be called the Arab Spring were remaking his world, country by country, but the revolutions bore little resemblance to his visions or his methods. The insignificance of al Qaeda in these events was widely noted. This worried him.

He had much to worry him that April, and he spelled it all out in another of his long letters, dated April 26 but likely begun well before then, again to "Mahmoud," Atiyah Abd al-Rahman. The letter would never be sent. This was his sixth spring confined in Abbottabad. His caliphate had shrunk to the confines of his high compound walls, to the cramped and crowded space of the house's upper two floors. On the upper floor, when he stood with his prayer cap on, his head was just inches from the ceiling. His days and nights followed very familiar routines, rarely broken: meals, his seven daily prayer sessions, his readings, his brisk daily walk around the vegetable garden, teaching poetry to his children and grandchildren, and the regular sermons and lectures to his three wives.

Much of the rest of the day, he was in front of his TV, absorbing the startling news by satellite from all over the world. Tyrants had been overthrown or were besieged in Egypt, Tunisia, Libya, Yemen, and Syria. There were rumblings elsewhere. It was a groundswell of Arab pride, Islamic fervor, and passion for democracy that no one had foreseen, and that certainly *he* had not foreseen. Bin Laden felt sidelined, felt it like some kind of punishment, and was troubled. The great awakening he had longed for and predicted was happening without him.

"I protest to God so much about my isolation and being alone," he had written in a different letter, "that I worry people will tire of me and [my ideas] will become old and worn out to them! But I protest only to God."

He worried. His vision for the Middle East was a return to a model many centuries old, the ancient caliphate, where all true believers would be united in a single holy nation, a strict Islamist state run according to principles of the Koran as interpreted by Qutb, by himself, and by other like-minded religious scholars. His methods, the suicide attacks on infidels designed to spread fear and confusion, had been superseded by popular, mostly nonviolent, mass movements, crowds of joyous, angry, brave protesters singing and chanting defiantly, demanding freedom and change. He had a lot to say about all of this, tapping at his computer keyboard with his long, thin fingers in his tiny third-floor office alongside a crude wooden bookshelf, or pacing and dictating. He had recently dyed his beard and donned more elegant robes to record a new video statement that would go out with this packet of letters. In one to al-Rahman he raced to catch up with the Arab Spring, to interpret the events in light of his own immutable beliefs, and to instruct his followers on how to think about the changes and what posture to take toward them. He saw the revolutions as a partial fulfillment of his prophesies—he dubbed them "half solutions"—but potentially hazardous to the ultimate goal, insofar as much of the popular support came from young Arabs "tainted" with softer notions of Islam, or, even worse, Western secular views of tolerance, human rights, and democracy. He still spoke of "the Nation" as his vision of a unified Muslim empire.

"To start, I want to talk about this most important point in our modern history, the launching of the Nation's revolution against the tyrants, which I ask Allah to make the impetus for a revival of the dignity of the religion and its glory. What we are witnessing in these days of consecutive revolutions is a great and glorious event, and it is most probable, according to reality and history, that it will encompass the majority of the Islamic world . . ."

The influence and control of the United States was being cast out.

"And the Americans worry about that, which is great; the secretary of state indicated in her visit to Yemen that, 'We worry that the region will fall into the hands of the armed Islamists.' . . . the fall of the remaining tyrants in the region became certain, with the will of Allah, and it was the beginning of a new era for the whole nation. These events are the most important events that the Nation has witnessed for centuries . . . and it is known that comprehensive popular movements inevitably change conditions, so if we redouble the efforts to direct and educate the Muslim people and caution them from half solutions, while taking care in providing good advice to them, the oncoming stage will be for Islam, Allah willing."

The rise of the Muslim Brotherhood in Egypt, for instance, troubled him, because the organization was not, as he saw it, purely devoted to his brand of strict and violent jihad. He was hopeful that the group was coming around, noting news reports of growing militancy within it, especially among the young. "So the return of the Brotherhood and those like them to the true Islam is a matter of time, with the will of Allah. The more attention paid to explaining Islamic understanding, the sooner their return is, so preserving the Muslim movements today and adjusting their direction requires effort and attention, keeping in mind the necessity of being kindly to the sons of the Nation who fell under misguidance for long decades."

The role of al Qaeda now, he explained, would be "the duty of guidance and advice, which is connected to the fate of the Nation."

The Sheik complained that his recommendation years earlier to establish "a number of scholars and wise men" to guide the emergence of the caliphate had been ignored, and that this now helped explain why the Arab Spring was progressing along improper paths. Now, at this "pivotal moment," he wrote, "it is incumbent on us, the *mujahidin*, to fulfill that duty and to plug that gap as much as we can, which became one of the utmost duties after faith, so that the Nation is liberated with the will of Allah and the religion regains its glory. There is no doubt that the duties of the *mujahidin* are numerous, except that this great duty should take the main share of our efforts so that we do not shortchange it, and expose the Nation's shake-up today to what the revolutions against Western occupation got exposed to in the past."

In the past, such revolutions had been co-opted by corrupt, Westernized, secularized dictators like Saddam Hussein and

Muammar Gaddafi, or had, as in Afghanistan, been toppled by Western intervention. Bin Laden argued that he and his followers were the ones with the right vision, with the God-inspired vision to lead the changes. Contrary to interpretations of the Arab Spring that claimed al Qaeda was irrelevant, the Sheik argued that it had been his efforts that prepared the way. It was al Qaeda that had "bled down the head of international apostasy"—that is, America—"and emboldened their Muslim brothers to rise up against the regimes it had propped up for much of the last century. The most important thing for now was to end conflict between Islamist factions, at least temporarily, and for every Muslim to join this great rising tide.

"So we have to get into expanding the programmed and directed media, and our efforts in directing the Nation's research and deciding on a specific plan that we all discuss, as the oncoming stage is important and very dangerous and does not tolerate the apparent differences in our directions," he wrote. "Initially, I would see that one of the most important steps of the oncoming stage is inciting the people who have not revolted yet, and encouraging them against the rulers and their methods, indicating that it is a religious duty and a logical necessity, so the arrows are concentrated on toppling the rulers without discussing the differences in issues, while paying maximum attention to spreading awareness and correcting the understanding. We should tell the brothers in all the regions to pay attention to spreading the book *Misunderstandings About Islam* by Sheik Muhammad Qutb. Please inform Sheik Yahya [Abu Yahya al-Libi, who would be killed in a drone strike in little more than a year] and the other brothers who have expressive abilities . . . and inform me of their opinions without missing any of them, as every voice that can contribute in this stage should not be excluded."

Bin Laden now set down a list of "general points," asking that a video statement he had recorded on a thumb drive about the Arab Spring, and which he would enclose, be given to Al Jazeera for broadcast, and seeking advice about an essay he had written on the same subject. As for the al Qaeda brothers in various countries undergoing dramatic change, he wrote, "It would be nice to remind [them] to be patient and deliberate, and warn them of entering into confrontations" with other Islamist factions. He foresaw, correctly, that the newly elected governments in most states would "belong to the Islamic parties and groups, like the Brotherhood and the like, and our duty at this stage is to pay attention to the call among Muslims and win over supporters and spread the correct understanding, as the current conditions have brought on unprecedented opportunities . . . The more time that passes and as the call increases, the more the supporters will be of the people [who agree with al Qaeda's goals], and the more widespread will be the correct understanding among the coming generations of Islamic groups."

The Sheik had a lot to say in this letter. He moved from sweeping political commentary and advice to a host of detailed instructions for the far-flung branches of his organization. He had read or heard that some members of al Qaeda in Yemen were experimenting with the use of poison gases, which worried him. He advised that they proceed only with great care, alluding to his concern about tactics that killed Muslims as well as infidels. He expressed worry over "the political and media reaction against the *mujahidin* and their image in the eyes of the public." He wondered why he had not heard anything from "the brothers in Iraq" and instructed those touting an al Qaeda affiliation in Somalia (whom he had opposed granting official status) to release a female hostage and some of the others they held, and then wait to kill the remainder until after the revolution in Libya had resolved itself, and until after national elections were held in France. He wanted the "brothers in Somalia" to concentrate more on economic development in that ravaged country, and to temper strict enforcement of the harsher measures prescribed by shariah law. Citing the Prophet, he said, "Use doubts to fend off the punishments."

The letter went on and on, offering guidance for safely moving specific members of the organization from country to country, about the travel of his twenty-year-old son, Hamza, and other things.

And in this same letter the Sheik found time to hammer home some advice about staying hidden. After more than nine successful years on the run, he considered himself to be an expert on the subject.

"It is proven that the American technology and its modern systems cannot arrest a *mujahid* if he does not commit a security error that leads them to him," he wrote. "So adherence to security precautions makes their advanced technology a loss and a disappointment to them."

As troubled as he was by world developments, he personally felt safe, very confident in his security methods. But he knew that not everyone was capable of his discipline. There were those who could stay hidden and those who could not.

"There is a percentage of people who cannot do that, and those need to be handled in a different manner than the others, and it may be better to provide them with an opportunity in the field," he wrote. In other words, these people were disposable. "As for those whom you have observed as being disciplined and capable, you arrange homes for them on the outskirts of the city . . . and they will be with trusted companions, and the companions will have some work as cover, as if they lived from it, especially for those who live close by and have observing neighbors."

He was describing his own situation, his compound just outside Abbottabad, and his trusted followers the Ahmed brothers, who, under their assumed names, Arshad and Tareq Khan, said they worked in the transportation business. To evade the Americans, it was best to live exactly as he lived. There was, however, one constant problem. Children.

"One of the most important security issues in the cities is controlling children, by not getting out of the house except for extreme necessity like medical care, and teaching them the local language; and that they do not get to the yard of the house without an adult who will control the volume of their voices, and we with the grace of Allah have been adhering to these precautions for nine years . . ."

Nine years since 9/11.

He had five more days to live.

As the Sheik was writing this letter, his last, as he was boasting of his security prowess, adhering to his precautions—albeit with the problem posed by children and grandchildren—he was in the crosshairs of the United States. In the terms used by the American military, he had been *"found* and *fixed."*

For the *finish,* President Obama had ordered the two remaining options to be more fully developed and wanted both to be ready by the first week of May. The ground option was time sensitive. In addition to there being no moon in the first few days of May, it was also mid-spring, which meant nighttime temperatures at four thousand feet were still cool enough to avoid overheating the choppers.

The Black Hawks would have to maneuver and hover over the target after having flown low and fast for an hour and a half en route from Jalalabad. They would arrive hot and heavy.

Four choppers would make the trip into Pakistan: the two Black Hawks to deliver the twenty-four-man raiding party directly to Abbottabad and two much bigger MH-47E Chinooks to haul fuel bladders and a twenty-four-man Quick Reaction Force to a remote spot outside of the city. A fifth chopper carried a larger reserve force, Plan C, in case the forward troops needed more help—this force was even larger now that the president had ordered McRaven to be prepared to fight his way out. It would remain just inside the Afghan border ready to launch if needed. All of the choppers were outfitted with stealth and sound-damping technology. The loads had been finely calibrated to get the most performance at Abbottabad's altitude and expected air temperature. Waiting a month would push the mission into early summer and warmer weather, which would up the stress on the aircraft and probably require changes—more choppers or fewer men. McRaven had moved this force into position in Jalalabad, and they would be ready to go on Obama's command.

The other alternative was called the "air option," and it had been reduced to Cartwright's advocacy of a one-shot try—a single shot from a drone. That could be done whenever the Pacer showed himself and the order was given.

It would be hard to overestimate the importance of this mission, not just to America—getting Osama bin Laden would be like closing an open wound—but to Obama's presidency. He would formally announce his run for a second term in early April, and it was by no means a sure thing. A stubbornly sluggish economy had steadily eroded his popularity. His relationship with Congress, never good, had been at an impasse ever since the November elections had erased the Democratic majority in the House and substantially reduced it in the Senate. He had been labeled a big-spending, old-fashioned liberal, even a socialist, at a time when the United States had accumulated massive debts and Republicans were signing oaths to oppose any tax increases, promising to finally end the era of "big government." Obama the bridge builder—what he'd said he hoped to be on taking office—had become a deeply polarizing figure.

Much of the negative assessment was still grounded in the notion that he was somehow *inauthentic*. He was not really an American. For some, the suspicion was quite literal. They argued that his Hawaiian birth certificate had been faked. Or that he was not a Christian, as he professed and that his twenty years of churchgoing affirmed. No, he was secretly a Muslim. Most people didn't buy these stories; there was overwhelming evidence they were false. But such beliefs colored or swayed the perceptions of even sensible voters, who suspected subtler shades of inauthenticity—who suspected that Obama, with his lefty, Harvard elitist, internationalist, interracial background, was not fully committed to bedrock national principles. He was less a believer in personal liberty than government power. That he was not a true believer in the American experiment, in the Constitution, but was more in the mold of European social democrats, who preferred a society and economy managed by government, by smart people like him. The president's famously "cool" personal style still hurt him, too. His attempts to halt the 2008 financial collapse had unloosed a flood of federal spending, and although that approach had simply continued the policies of his Republican predecessor, and were believed by most experts to have at least partly worked, the economic recovery was slow, people were discouraged, and budget deficits were scarily large, with the president seemingly bent on making them larger still. His biggest legislative triumph, national health care, had seemed to hurt him politically more than it helped him. It had cemented the perception of Obama as a closet socialist, or at least a traditional big government, big spending, big taxing liberal. National health care added a whole new social program to the roster of those already bankrupting the country, his critics claimed. It was denounced as unconstitutional, proof of Obama's secret, un-American agenda. His shrillest political opponents had created so much doubt over his unusual ancestry and upbringing that the president had found it necessary to release the complete 1961 file from the Kapi'olani Maternity and Gynecological Hospital in Honolulu in order to prove that he possessed the most basic qualification for the White House, citizenship by birth. It satisfied all but fringe critics that he was truly American, but it didn't persuade many that he wasn't engaged in a plot to turn America into a European-style state.

Perhaps the most effective counter to this suspicion of inauthenticity was his performance as commander in chief. Obama had effectively and aggressively defended America. During the campaign he had skillfully associated his rise with that of another young, charismatic, tough-minded Democrat a half century earlier. He had cultivated the family of John F. Kennedy, winning the endorsement of Senator Ted Kennedy in the months before Kennedy's death, even orchestrating a powerful endorsement from Caroline Kennedy, who compared him with her father. But now Obama was in danger of being too much in the model of JFK, a spellbinding orator and stylish young leader with only a callow grasp of national leadership. It had been President Lyndon Johnson, after all, who had come along after the assassination to shore up Camelot's legacy; it had taken his hardheaded mastery of power, of Congress, to enact the signature legislation Kennedy himself had been unable to achieve. Killing bin Laden would be one accomplishment that even Obama's worst critics would acknowledge. Here was the one arena where a president could decide and act without outside political interference, especially given the covert nature of the enterprise. Within that arena differences of opinion were strictly subject to his judgment and decision. The most significant criticism of his performance as commander in chief had come from his own former supporters. After promising to close the military detention center at Guantánamo Bay, a symbol of the Bush administration's presumed abuses of power, Obama had failed to overcome congressional opposition to transferring detainees to prisons in the United States. On the big issues he had kept his campaign promises. He had ramped down and would soon end America's involvement in Iraq, and in this he had broad public support. While initially boosting American forces in Afghanistan by 30,000 troops, he had concluded that efforts to build a functioning central government there were unlikely ever to succeed and had quietly reversed direction. He was determined to end America's large-scale military commitment there, too. He had been criticized for not decisively jumping into the Libyan revolution, and then for not doing so more directly, but the NATO–led intervention on behalf of the rebels—what Obama's critics had termed "leading from behind"—was already starting to look like a smart strategy. In a country weary of two long wars, there was little or no opposition to Obama's minimalist, pragmatic approach to using America's military power. Even the Republican candidates already battling for the chance to unseat him in 2012, who missed no chance to fault Obama, rarely spoke of national security concerns.

Getting bin Laden would be the capstone. It would be a milestone emotionally and strategically.

"I thought it would be cathartic for the American people to know that we stay with something," the president told me. "We don't let it slip. I thought that was important. Once I got into office, we were making significant progress against high-value targets in al Qaeda below bin Laden—the lieutenants, the captains, the field generals, we were taking them out pretty systematically—so there was a sense that we understood that the organization was getting hollowed out, and that if we could get the guy at the top, then we might be in a position to strategically defeat the organization. As long as bin Laden was still out there, though, even if we were making a whole bunch of progress at the lower levels, their capacity to reconstitute itself, I thought, would still be pretty significant."

It would inevitably have political benefits, too. No one involved with Obama's handling of the bin Laden effort saw the slightest hint that politics shaped his thinking, but there's no question that success would help, and that a public failure would hurt. It was *the* thing that President Bush, for all his bluster, had been unable to do. Obama was a skilled politician. There was not a move he made that did not include a measure of calculation, even if only in understanding the stakes. No one understood the stakes better. Killing or capturing the author of 9/11 would register with every American, of every political stripe. It would be a thing that transcended politics in an age where very little else could. There were very few things he might accomplish as president that would compare. Getting bin Laden would not completely destroy al Qaeda or end the threat of terror attacks, but it would be a huge step in that direction. It would slam shut the door on a painful national trauma. It would feel . . . perfect. He had argued from the beginning that it was the correct military response. It was the thing he had promised to do if he got the chance. So while Obama had not yet officially made up his mind about the compound in Abbottabad, and had tipped his hand to no one, those close to him believed he would go for it. He was leaning that way, and because of his confidence in McRaven he was leaning toward doing it on the ground.

Raiding the compound was the riskiest option. It posed a slew of hard questions that the air option did not. One of the most interesting was what to do if bin Laden was not killed but *captured*. The success of Obama's drone war had meant that very few high-value targets ever found themselves in American custody any more. It had prompted speculation that this president was less interested in capturing al Qaeda figures than in killing them, or even that JSOC was under orders to avoid taking prisoners.

"Our basic attitude was that, given his dedication to his cause, the likelihood of surrender was very low," the president explained. "We also knew that there would always be the possibility of him strapping on explosives and trying to take out a team with him. So I think people's general attitude was, if he's going to surrender, he better be naked and on the ground. Had that occurred, then we would have arrested him and held him. I won't go into all the details of what those various steps would have been, but ultimately, we would have brought him to justice. We would have brought him back here."

This, too, had to be thought through. Did they *want* a captured bin Laden? If they had him, what would they do with him?

What to do with high-profile terrorists had been a hot political issue for years. Congress had done nothing to resolve the problem. Bush had locked most of them away—like Khalid Sheik Mohammed and Abu Zubaydah—at Guantánamo, and talked about military tribunals somewhere down the line. But some, like the shoe bomber Richard Reid and the would-be Times Square bomber Faisal Shahzad—the latter of whom had betrayed his citizenship oath, an idea that troubled the Sheik—had been arrested and tried in federal courts and were now serving life sentences. Attorney General Eric Holder's announced intention to put Khalid Sheik Mohammed on trial at the federal courthouse in lower Manhattan had generated so much political protest that the administration had been forced that very month to back down and announce that he would instead face a military tribunal at Guantánamo.

In the unlikely event that bin Laden surrendered, Obama saw an opportunity to resurrect the idea of a criminal trial.

"We worked through the sort of legal and political issues that would have been involved, and Congress and the desire to send him to Guantánamo, and to not try him, and Article Three," the president told me. "I mean, we had worked through a whole bunch of those scenarios. But, frankly, my belief was if we had captured him, that I would be in a pretty strong position, politically, here, to argue that displaying due process and rule of law would be our best weapon against al Qaeda, in preventing him from appearing as a martyr."

Bin Laden in custody might give him the political capital he had lacked with Khalid Sheik Mohammed. It might be the very thing to end all the confusion over what to do with top-level terrorist detainees, and to end it in the right way. Obama believed that placing these terrorists before a judge and jury in a criminal court, affording them the full rights of criminal defendants, would showcase America's commitment to justice for even the worst of the worst. It would present bin Laden to the world not as a heroic holy warrior but as the ill-informed fanatic and mass murderer he was. The president had to do more than just imagine these scenarios. It was one more outcome that needed to be thought through completely and planned for.

Obama added, "I think it's important to emphasize, having made those plans, our expectation was that if, in fact, he was there, that he would go down fighting."

McRaven's men did their first rehearsal on April 7. They worked on an isolated acre deep inside the sprawling wooded grounds of Fort Bragg, where a faithful mock-up of the three-story Abbottabad house had been built. Chairman Mullen and Michael Vickers were among those who came down from the Pentagon and CIA to watch.

For the first practice session, the SEALs rehearsed the critical piece of the mission: hitting the compound and target house at night. They approached aboard two Stealth Black Hawks. One unit roped down to the roof of the building and assaulted it from the top down. The other roped into the compound and assaulted from the ground floor up. This part of the operation took only about ninety seconds to complete. The delivery choppers moved off while the men did their work, and then swooped back in to pick them up. The speed and coordination were impressive. They did this twice.

In part, McRaven was putting his men through this demonstration in order to impress. They had done this sort of thing so many times they could almost do it blindfolded. McRaven had hand-picked shooters from SEAL Team Six. It was a Dream Team: men who, in the thousands of raids he had overseen, had shown they did not rattle, had shown they could handle themselves coolly and intelligently not just when things went according to plan, but when things went wrong. Those situations required quickly assessing the significance of the error or malfunction or whatever unexpected event had occurred, and then making the necessary adjustments to complete the mission. The core talent required was the ability to adapt, to think for yourself and make smart decisions. These were men who had proved it over and over in combat. They did not really need to rehearse, but rehearsals have other uses. McRaven wanted the assembled brass to see how good they were, how fast, how certain. He wanted them to witness the speed and coordination firsthand, to hear the sounds of the rotor blades and of the flash-bang explosions and of the weapons being fired, and to be able to imagine themselves on the receiving end of it. He wanted them to meet the men, touch their equipment and weapons, talk to them, get a sense of how professional, how experienced, and how confident they were, and then to carry that experience back to the White House—"*Mr. President, they just did a rehearsal that will knock your socks off!*"

SEAL Team Six had rotated home not long before. The men on these elite special operations teams went to war in shifts. For most of the last ten years they had been regularly deploying to Iraq or Afghanistan for three to four months, where they maintained a very high tempo, going out on missions every night, sometimes two or three times a night. Each unit had its own embedded combat support, administrative staff, and logistical teams that traveled together, every one of them handpicked. When deployed they lived for the most part sequestered from conventional troops, either at their own forward operating bases or on a portion of a larger base that was sealed off. The work was deadly serious. The men would spend the day getting their rest, cleaning their weapons, working out, and getting ready to go back out. They had their own TV and Internet access, but under rules that were far more restrictive than for most soldiers. Their pace and discipline were severe. They would blow off steam for a few months at home and then go back. When they were deployed, it was all business.

It was a demanding but extremely satisfying way of life. The men who achieved membership in these units tended to stay. Many found it hard to adjust to doing anything else. The skills required were not readily applicable to other kinds of work. And when you have been part of life-and-death operations for years—adrenaline-pumping missions where you risked your life, shot to kill, and where some of your good friends gave their lives—and when you believe that your work is vital to the security of your country, it is hard to find anything else that compares. When you work every day with people who are the very best at what they do, and when you enjoy the silent admiration of everyone you meet, even if they had only a vague idea of what you do—well, there is nothing quite like it.

On average, the operators were a decade or more older than most soldiers. Most were in their early thirties, veterans of several tours in regular units or "vanilla" special forces teams, as opposed to "black ops." Some were in their forties, which skewed the average age to thirty-four. Some of the men in these units would joke that their biggest worry wasn't so much getting shot by the enemy as it was throwing their back out. They excelled at a lot of things, but particularly at doing exactly what would be called for in Abbottabad: hitting a target fast and hard, making correct split-second decisions about whether to shoot or not to shoot, and distinguishing between friend and foe, combatant and noncombatant. They usually did their work in the dark, wearing night-vision devices, but had in recent years been mixing it up with day raids, partly to vary the pattern and partly just because of the demand to move quickly on fresh intelligence—staying inside the information cycle of the enemy.

Being called in like this to begin rehearsals after just rotating home was enough to tip them off that the mission was special. When they were told that they were going after bin Laden, the men cheered.

They reassembled for a second week of rehearsals in Nevada, where the heat and altitude—about four thousand feet—were similar to Abbottabad's. Again chairman Mullen and Vickers and the others came out to watch. This time the rehearsals were designed to duplicate the conditions they would be flying in. On the real mission the helicopters would have to fly ninety minutes before arriving over Abbottabad. They would be flying very low and very fast to avoid Pakistani radar. Mission planners had to test precisely what the choppers could do at that altitude and in the anticipated air temperatures. How much of a load could the choppers carry and still perform? Originally they had thought they might be able to make it there and back without refueling, but the margins were too close. The choppers would have been coming back on fumes. So the refueling area was necessary. In Nevada they went through the entire scenario. The mock-up of the compound was much cruder. They had already practiced storming it again and again at Fort Bragg. This time the buildings were just Conex containers, and instead of stone walls around the compound there was a chain-link fence. The purpose of this rehearsal was not to duplicate the storming of the compound. The purpose here was to simulate the stresses on the choppers. It came off smoothly. The Black Hawks handled the job well.

Again, McRaven wanted Mullen and Vickers and the others to be impressed, because he wanted his own confidence in his men and the mission to be fully conveyed to the president. The best way to do that was not just to tell him about it. He understood that confidence was key if the SEALs were going to get the job.

Because the alternative, the drone strike, was tempting. It was so much less risky. The air option offered a kind of magic bullet, in the form of a small guided munition that could be fired from a tiny drone. No one involved with planning the mission would discuss its particulars, but the weapon sounded very much like a newly designed Raytheon GPS-guided missile about the length and width of a strong man's forearm. General Cartwright was its chief advocate in the White House. Designed to help reduce the collateral damage that had always been an inevitable consequence of air strikes, the missile could strike an individual or a single vehicle without damaging anything nearby. Called simply an STM (small tactical munition), it weighed just thirteen pounds, carried a five-pound warhead, and was fired from under the wing of a drone that itself was no larger than a model airplane, small enough to escape the notice of any country's air defenses. It was a "fire-and-forget" missile, which meant you could not guide it once it was released. It would find and explode on the precise coordinates it had been given. Since the Pacer tended to walk in the same place every day, Cartwright believed the missile would kill him, and likely him alone. It placed no American forces at risk. If the missile missed, or if the Pacer turned out not to be bin Laden, well, then it would just be an unexplained explosion in Abbottabad. No one need be the wiser. And if the missile did kill bin Laden, any Pakistani anger over an unauthorized U.S. drone strike would likely be offset by the embarrassment of revealing that the world's most wanted terrorist had been living safely not just in Pakistan, but only a short drive from Islamabad and less than a mile away from its national military academy.

The weapon had yet to be used in combat, although the technologies involved—drones and missiles—were hardly new. The only difference with this one was its size. Still . . . did you want to hinge such a critical opportunity on one shot, with a missile that had never been fired in anger? The drone option also robbed the strike of certainty. To his followers and to those who thought as he did, bin Laden still had tremendous influence, even though he had not been seen in years. If there was no proof he was dead, the organization could theoretically keep issuing statements and pronouncements to the faithful, raising contributions, urging and planning future attacks as if he were alive. And Obama would become the third U.S. president to have let him slip through his fingers. Arguments in favor of the drone kept coming back to these two things. What if the missile missed? And, if it killed bin Laden, how would you know for sure?

It was clear that the only way to know for sure was to send in a team of operators and bring him out, dead or alive.

But there were so many things that could go wrong. Recent history was littered with examples of how badly things could turn out. The failure of Desert One was an obvious caution. With its long insertion, desert refueling rendezvous point, and the target inside an urban area surrounded by potential enemies the situation was so similar it was eerie. The Iran disaster had shaken the military to its core, embarrassed the nation, and ended a presidency. And the long firefight that had followed the shooting down of two helicopters in Mogadishu on October 3, 1993, had so rattled the Clinton administration that it had shied away from using military force for years afterward, with some disastrous consequences such as the slaughter of hundreds of thousands in Rwanda in 1994. In Iran, the mission had been an abject public failure; in Mogadishu, the mission had actually been a success but had prompted a bloody eighteen-hour firefight that effectively pulled the plug on the American mission to Somalia. One or the other of these missions, or both, had come up at nearly every meeting to discuss options.

There was only one "ground option" scenario that wouldn't cause trouble. If bin Laden was not there, the SEALs might be able to exit without hurting anyone and without setting off any alarms. No one would be the wiser. All the other outcomes had a big downside. Even perfect success—killing or capturing bin Laden without mixing it up with Pakistani forces—would exact a price: it would certainly trigger outrage and poison relations between the two countries for the foreseeable future. The list of worse outcomes was scary: dead SEALs, dead Pakistanis, embarrassment, a propaganda triumph for bin Laden and al Qaeda, a blow to the reputation of the U.S. military and the CIA.

So confidence was the key. If the president decided to go with McRaven, it would be because the admiral's confidence was contagious.

The final meeting was held in the Situation Room on the afternoon of Thursday, April 28. Popular accounts of this decisive session have portrayed Obama facing down a wall of opposition and doubt among his top advisers. In fact, there was overwhelming support for launching the raid.

Filling the black leather chairs around the table were Obama, Vice President Joe Biden, Secretary of Defense Robert Gates, Secretary of State Hillary Clinton, Chairman of the Joint Chiefs Michael Mullen, Vice Chairman James "Hoss" Cartwright, John Brennan, Thomas Donilon, DNI James Clapper, CIA Director Leon Panetta, and Panetta's deputy, Michael Morell. McRaven did not participate. He and the SEAL team had relocated to JSOC's base in Jalalabad, to be ready to launch in two days. Throughout this series of meetings, the rule was that if you were not in town, you were not involved. Hooking up a satellite link for videoconferencing opened up the discussion to too many people. Technicians that could listen in would be involved on both ends, which compromised secrecy. Most of the president's national security team—including Ben Rhodes, who had been informed weeks earlier—started considering how to announce the mission to the world. Top staffers of the principals ringed the room on the smaller leather chairs.

All sensed that the secret had held about as long as it could. As the planning had progressed over the previous four months, the circle of knowledge had grown. There were now hundreds of people in on it. No secret survived numbers like that for long. It was inevitable that at least one of those hundreds would screw up, let something slip. Somebody was bound to confide in someone else untrustworthy, or might decide for their own reasons to leak it. If they missed the new moon this weekend, they would have to wait a month for another. So for the raid option it was time to decide.

The week had been full for the Pentagon and the CIA. The day before Obama had announced, pending congressional review, that General David Petraeus, who had been commanding allied forces in Afghanistan since the previous July, would leave the army after thirty-seven years to head the CIA, and that Panetta, who had spearheaded this effort to find bin Laden, would become the new secretary of defense, replacing Bob Gates, who had announced months earlier that he would be stepping down. Petraeus had been read in on the bin Laden secret only recently, because the beefed-up rescue force Obama demanded required air and ground forces from his command. Weeks earlier—in fact the day before McRaven's team performed its first rehearsal at Fort Bragg—the president had awarded the admiral his fourth star and promoted him to lead the Special Operations Command.

The president was juggling the usual array of responsibilities. The U.S. military was still helping with massive relief operations in Japan, enforcing a no-fly zone over Libya in cooperation with European allies, and monitoring various stages of revolution or protest in Egypt, Yemen, Syria, Bahrain, and Jordan. That week the president had unsuccessfully lobbied India to award an $11 billion contract for fighter planes to American firms. An outbreak of tornadoes in the Midwest had torn through Kentucky, Alabama, Louisiana, and Tennessee, requiring federal disaster assistance. On the day before this meeting, the president had held a press conference to deal with what he called the "silliness" over the place of his birth, releasing that "long form" birth certificate.

In the week before this session, Brennan had asked the Counterterrorism Center director, Mike Leiter, to assemble a team to perform one last "red teaming" of the intelligence on Abbottabad. So the final meeting began with Leiter's findings, which were deflating. Leiter told the president that his group could arrive at only 40 percent certainty that bin Laden was in the compound. One of those on that red team, an experienced analyst, had estimated the chances at only 10 percent, a number so far below any they had heard, and coming so late in the game, that it drew nervous laughter in the crowded room. "I think you guys are telling yourselves something you want to hear," was that analyst's opinion. Still, 40 percent, the team's estimate, was "thirty-eight percent better than we've been for ten years," said Leiter. This was hardly confidence boosting. Obama asked if the estimate was based on anything new or different. It was not. This team had looked at the same information as everyone else. The president asked Leiter to explain the disparity. Why was their confidence so much lower than, say, that of "John," the leader of the CIA's bin Laden team, whose confidence had been 95 percent all along? Leiter could not explain to the president's satisfaction, and so this new assessment was effectively dismissed. As far as Obama was concerned, the level of certainty was the same as it had been all along, fifty-fifty. So other than dampening the mood, this last red teaming had little influence on the final deliberations.

One by one, the principals around the room were asked to choose one of the three options: the raid, the missile strike, or doing nothing—and then to defend their choice. The president said that he would not make a decision himself at the meeting, but he wanted to hear everyone's final judgment. Nearly everyone present favored the raid.

The only major dissenters were Biden and Gates and, by the next morning, Gates had changed his mind.

Biden was characteristically blunt. "Mr. President, my suggestion is, don't go," he said. "We have to do more things to see if he's there."

The vice president was never shy about political calculations. He believed that if the president decided to choose either the air or the ground option, and if the effort failed in any of the many ways it could, Obama would lose his chance for a second term. Biden felt strongly about it, and never hesitated to disagree at meetings like this, something the president had encouraged him to do. In this case he even disagreed with his top adviser on such matters, Tony Blinken, who was not asked for an opinion at this meeting but who had earlier made it clear to the president that he strongly favored the raid.

Gates spoke with quiet authority against it. He favored taking the shot from the drone. He acknowledged that it was a difficult call, and that striking from the air would leave them not knowing whether they had killed bin Laden, but he had been working at the CIA as an analyst in 1980 when the Desert One mission failed. He had, in fact, been in this very Situation Room when the chopper collided with the C-130 at the staging area in the desert and turned that effort into a gigantic fireball. It was an experience he did not want to revisit. He had visibly blanched the first time he had heard that McRaven was planning a helicopter-refueling stop in a remote area outside Abbottabad, similar to the one inside Tehran in 1980. The contours of this mission looked so much like the earlier failure that it rattled him. He had more of a personal sense for what another disaster like it would mean. He also mentioned the Black Hawk Down episode. He remembered how painful the loss of life and loss of face had been for the previous presidents Carter and Clinton, and he smelled the same potential here. As defense secretary, he also had a deeper appreciation than anyone else in the room for logistics, for the importance of sustaining the huge daily flow of fuel and matériel from Pakistan necessary to the ongoing war in Afghanistan. Blowing up the always dicey relationship with Pakistan would likely short-circuit that vital artery. There was so much to lose, he said, and the intelligence indicating bin Laden's presence in the compound was still so flimsy—strictly circumstantial. Leiter's presentation had driven that home for him. A raid gone wrong would have a huge downside: loss of the SEAL team or a potential hostage situation, a complete break with Pakistan, attacks on the U.S. embassy in Islamabad . . . So he told the president that he would choose the drone. If bin Laden was the Pacer, then they stood a very good chance of killing him. If not, if they missed or they were wrong, it would be disappointing, but the cost would not be so great. That was his advice, and it hung heavily in the room. It carried the weight of long experience and Gates's own formidable reputation.

Cartwright agreed with Gates, but that was expected. He had put the drone option on the table, and after further testing he was more confident than ever that the small missile would do the job. It was the simplest and least risky way to go. The missile also won the endorsement of Leiter. He had expressed relatively low confidence that the Pacer was bin Laden but endorsed taking a killing shot at the fellow anyway.

Everyone else favored sending in the SEALs. At first it didn't seem like Clinton would. She had famously faulted Obama years earlier for asserting that he would take a shot in Pakistan unilaterally if there was a good chance of getting bin Laden, and now, as secretary of state, she would bear the brunt of the diplomatic fallout if he did. Presenting a detailed assessment of pros and cons, she outlined the likely dire consequences for the U.S.-Pakistan relationship but wound up concluding that, because it was built more on mutual dependence than friendship and trust, it would likely survive. Someone pointed out that if going after bin Laden was enough to destroy the relationship, it was probably doomed anyway. Suspense built as Clinton worked her way around to her surprising bottom line. They could not ignore a chance to get Osama bin Laden. It was too important to the country. It outweighed the risks. Send in the SEALs.

Admiral Mullen, the president's top military adviser, gave a detailed PowerPoint presentation before delivering his verdict. McRaven's rehearsals for him and the others had achieved the desired effect. Mullen said he had such high confidence in the SEAL team that he advocated launching the raid.

Brennan, Donilon, Clapper, Panetta, and Morell all agreed. Brennan had long believed in his bones that it was bin Laden hiding in the compound, and if they indeed had found him, he argued, they *had* to go after him. The CIA director felt particularly strongly about it, which was not unexpected. This had been his project all along, and the analysts who worked for him were so eager to go in that they would have felt betrayed by their boss if he hadn't supported them. The former congressman told Obama that he ought to ask himself, "What would the average American say if he knew we had the best chance of getting bin Laden since Tora Bora and we didn't take a shot?" And going in on the ground would give them the proof they needed to make the mission worthwhile, or, possibly, gave them a chance of slipping out if bin Laden was not there.

Not all of the advisers present were asked for their opinions during this meeting, but they had all made their feelings clear in the previous weeks. To a man and woman they favored the raid. And soon the man who had made the most convincing argument against the raid would reverse himself.

At the Pentagon, when Gates's undersecretaries Michael Vickers and Michèle Flournoy learned what he had recommended, they were distressed. No one knew yet what the president would decide, but they had every reason to believe that their boss's opinion would weigh heavily. They briefly debated confronting him with how they felt, wondering if they would be overstepping, whether it would anger him, and they both decided it was their duty. So they went into his office first thing Friday morning, sat with him at a conference table, and went to work on him for a full hour.

"Boss, we think you're wrong," said Flournoy.

Like most of the other principals, she explained, he had been brought into the loop fairly late. She and Vickers had spent a lot more time working through the questions about the mission than he had. They believed he didn't fully understand how well thought through McRaven's plan was. They again outlined for him the raid's plan, the backup plan, and the plan that backed up the backup plan, to demonstrate how carefully the mission had been designed. They sang McRaven's praises. They had dealt with generals and admirals who rightly saw themselves as experts in their field, and who tended to bristle when a civilian bureaucrat second-guessed them, or expressed doubts about their well-laid plans. McRaven had approached this effort utterly without ego or emotion. He had understood from the start that the significance of this mission meant that he would have a lot of people at the Pentagon and White House and CIA looking over his shoulder asking questions, looking for flaws. Flournoy admired a quality in McRaven that was not always evident in the top brass: a willingness to admit that he didn't know everything. He would sometimes respond to a good question with, "You know, I haven't thought about that but I need to. Let me get back to you about it." And he would. He was unusually open to suggestion, and had made substantial revisions to his plan based on the president's concerns and those of everyone else involved. Flournoy and Vickers had also seen how carefully McRaven picked the members of his team, choosing men coming off fresh deployments who had honed their skills night after night for months. Gates had not, as Vickers had at the rehearsals, met those men and talked to them and obtained a sense of their maturity and experience. Gates had not been as close to any of this as they had, so he did not have their level of confidence.

They also argued that he had not adequately considered the downsides of the drone strike, the alternative he advocated. They questioned the idea that this was a clean, virtually risk-free alternative. First of all, neither Flournoy nor Vickers bought Cartwright's optimism about the small missile hitting the target. The target, after all, was moving. The missile could not be guided. It had never been fired anywhere but on a testing range. You get one shot, they reminded Gates, and if you miss, that's it. Bin Laden escapes again. Imagine the criticism that would follow: *You got the chance of a lifetime and you blew it with something untried?*

At the end of the hour, Gates phoned Donilon at the White House and asked him to tell the president that he had changed his mind. Obama would not learn of Gates's change of heart until after he had made the decision—but when he did hear, it strengthened his resolve. In the end every one of the president's top advisers except Biden was in favor of taking immediate action. Two—Cartwright and Leiter—wanted to use the drone. Everyone else backed McRaven.

The Thursday meeting ended early in the evening, and with the opinions of the vice president, the secretary of defense, and the vice chairman of the Joint Chiefs still weighing heavily against those calling for the raid, the president's choice seemed anything but certain.

"You'll have my decision in the morning," Obama said.

In truth, as the president told me, he had all but made up his mind when he left the Thursday meeting. He had been thinking about it for months. The advantages of the raid were obvious and, to his way of thinking, outweighed the risks. A missile might go astray and, unlike taking a shot from a drone, the raid offered certainty. If bin Laden was there, they would know it and they would bring him out, dead or alive. Getting him without being able to prove it—worse, without *knowing* it—would forfeit a big part of the accomplishment. Here was a chance to bring closure to the great tragedy of 9/11 and strike a mortal blow to al Qaeda. Add to that Obama's trust in McRaven, and the near-unanimous support of his advisers, and the decision was clear.

There was another compelling reason to send in the SEAL team. If this had been bin Laden's hideout for years, it might hold a trove of valuable information, perhaps the kind that would enable the United States to further dismantle al Qaeda. Obama knew the logic behind F3EAD. The only way to exploit bin Laden's personal data was to send in men who could collect it.

No matter how compelling it was to attempt the raid, the risks were great for the men he ordered in, for the alliance with Pakistan, for the reputation of the U.S. military and intelligence communities, and for his own presidency.

He reviewed the process over and over again in his mind Thursday night into Friday morning. Just as had been the case ten years ago, when he was a state senator in Illinois, his habit was to stay up much later than Michelle and his girls. They had turned in at ten o'clock. He was up another three hours pacing and thinking in the Treaty Room, the upstairs room that functioned as the family's living room and also the president's private office. The room displays Henry Ulke's portrait of Ulysses S. Grant, Théobald Chartran's large painting of William McKinley signing a peace treaty with Spain, and George P. A. Healy's depiction of Abraham Lincoln conferring with his military advisers near the end of the Civil War. History bears down on you in a room like that.

"It was a matter of taking one last breath and just making sure, asking is there something that I haven't thought of?" Obama explained to me. "Is there something that we need to do?"

The questions stayed with him even as he tried to sleep that night. He believed that waiting longer would not accomplish anything, and might risk everything. They were not likely to get better intelligence, that had been clear. In the end, it boiled down to his confidence in McRaven. He had met him first in 2008 when touring Iraq with several other members of the Senate Foreign Relations Committee. David Petraeus had hosted a dinner in Baghdad and had invited the JSOC commander. He had dealt with him a lot more as president, particularly in these last four months.

"I just felt as if I'd gotten to know McRaven," Obama said. "I had gotten to know the SEALs. I had obviously been monitoring their capacity to carry out night raids consistently in Iraq and Afghanistan. We had mocked up the compound. We had experimented with it. They had run it . . . McRaven—he inspires confidence. And I had pressed him hard. And at that point my estimation was that we weren't going to be able to do it better a month or two months or three months from now. We weren't going to have better certainty about whether bin Laden was there, and so it was just a matter of pulling the trigger."

On Friday morning, before getting the phone call from Gates, before he walked out to the South Lawn to board a helicopter on a trip to the southern states to view tornado damage, he sent an e-mail to Donilon asking him to meet him in the Diplomatic Room at eight o'clock.

Donilon, McDonough, and Chief of Staff Bill Daley were waiting in the large formal room when Obama entered, wearing a dark blue windbreaker. The view from the room is one of the most dramatic in the White House, over the sloping back lawn, with the Washington Monument in the distance. They could see the waiting presidential helicopter.

"It's a go," said Obama. "We're going to do the raid. Prepare the directives."

8

The Finish

May 1–2, 2011

McRaven's men were in Jalalabad, poised. After the president's order was conveyed Friday afternoon—Afghanistan is eight and a half hours ahead of Washington—they knew the earliest they would go would be early the following evening, Saturday, April 30.

Most of the twenty-four handpicked team were members of Red Squadron of SEAL Team Six. In the more than a year that has elapsed, only one of the men has spoken publicly about it. None were interviewed by me. My account of the raid is based on interviews with the president; senior officials at CIA; sources at JSOC, the White House, and the Pentagon; on interviews with SEAL team members who did not participate directly, and on the account published by the former SEAL under the pseudonym "Mark Owen."

The SEALs were selected primarily because their commander was available, and the corresponding commander of the army's Delta Force was not. With its expanding numbers, JSOC had been divvied up three years earlier by McRaven, with Delta assigned to continue operating in Iraq and the SEALs working from Forward Operating Bases (FOBs) throughout the most contentious regions of Afghanistan. Part of the reasoning for choosing the SEAL team, according to several top Pentagon officials, was that in recent years it had successfully conducted about a dozen secret missions inside Pakistan. They were used to conducting these raids with high-level commanders looking over their shoulders, linked by live audio and video—the men called it "General TV." Sometimes their remote commanders got carried away, steering them around like figures in a video game—"Turn left! Turn right!"

The actual commander, the man they would follow into the target compound, was a short, thickly built, brown-haired naval officer in his late thirties who had chiseled features—if Hollywood were looking for someone to play the role they would be hard-pressed to improve on the original. He had become something of a legend even in these elite ranks, with ten years of experience leading them into combat. It had become so routine for him that he spoke about the job the way an experienced foreman might talk about a construction project. He had a strictly deadpan way of talking; when he cracked a joke, which didn't happen often, there was usually a delay before anyone noticed. Some of the men he commanded were older than him, but not many. Going in with them would be a Pashto translator and a highly trained dog—a Belgian Malinois named Cairo. The translator, a middle-aged man who had to learn how to rope out of a chopper for this mission, and the dog would help keep the curious away from the compound while the SEALs did their work. As they did before every mission, the men spent time readying their gear and weapons, oiling and cleaning and testing laser sights and night-vision devices, and adjusting straps on harnesses and helmets. The barracks at Jalalabad were familiar to all of them; it had been home away from home for years.

The one thing that was not often in their conversation but always in their thoughts was danger. There were small FOBs all over Afghanistan named after team members who had been killed on raids, friends of these men who had gone about their work with the same skill and care but who had been sent home in an aluminum box. Inside the FOBs there were memorials posted on walls or bulletin boards, displaying photos of the dead, and special operators were disproportionately represented. Their photos contrasted with the faces of the other fallen, the eighteen-, nineteen-, and twenty-year-old regulars who had been killed by roadside bombs or in mortar attacks or on routine patrols. The special operators were older, and in the pictures they were often bearded and dressed in local civilian attire. Either that or they appeared in official portraits wearing uniforms decked with ribbons and stripes and medals. They were war-fighting professionals. For most it was their chosen career and, unlike younger men who tended to find reasons why this or that soldier had been hit and they had not—a poor decision, a perceived weakness, a fatal lapse in quickness . . . —these men knew better. You trained and practiced and then you performed with a team made up of men every bit as good as you were, and sometimes in spite of all of this you got killed. This mission, targeting Osama bin Laden, was one nearly everyone in the force had imagined being on since 9/11. It was the raid all of these men believed would someday come, and that they had hoped would include them.

Behind this initial force were the men and choppers and planes that McRaven hoped he would not need. There were three MH-47E Chinooks, big as tractor trailers with flat rotors front and back. Also on alert were the fighters and combat-control aircraft that might be needed to fend off Pakistani fighters and ground-to-air defenses. If it came to that, command of the operation would shift from McRaven's Joint Operating Center in Jalalabad to the theater command center in Kabul, where General Petraeus presided.

Petraeus himself hadn't known about the mission until just weeks earlier, when he had been informed about it in general terms by General Cartwright and by the CENTCOM commander. His resources would not be used at all unless the mission went badly, so he had not been fully briefed by McRaven until a few days earlier. No one on his staff knew about the raid. His history with bin Laden went back a dozen years, to when Petraeus had stood on the tarmac at Pope Air Force Base as the bodies of American servicemen killed in al Qaeda's attack on the USS *Cole* were flown home. He had been in on the earlier discussions during the Clinton administration when it had decided to launch the cruise missiles at targets in the Sudan and Afghanistan. He would have a ringside seat for this raid, but if all went well he would have nothing to do but watch.

On Saturday afternoon, McRaven took a call from the president. Obama told the admiral that his confidence in him and his men could not be higher.

"Godspeed to you and your forces," Obama said. "Please pass on to them my personal thanks for their service."

He added something that went without saying.

"I will personally be following this mission very closely."

Hours later, on Saturday afternoon Washington time, Ben Rhodes sat down in his small White House office before his keyboard . . . and froze. At some point, the president was going to have to speak to the United States and the world about what had happened, or was happening, inside Pakistan. Rhodes's job would be to have draft re-marks ready for success or failure.

George Little, a CIA press officer, had just spent a few hours with the president's staff reviewing every outcome the agency could imagine. They had gone through the various press guides and public-messaging guides for each contingency—which heads of states needed to be informed and in what order, how statements should be made. They roughed them all out. There was one for a clean in-and-out, the best case. If they went in and bin Laden wasn't there and they got out without setting off any big alarms, then they planned to just deny it. It was to remain a covert operation: that is, officially it would not have happened. But what if things got messy? There were a number of those possibilities: messy with bin Laden dead, messy with bin Laden captured, messy but no bin Laden. They went through pages and pages of public-messaging options.

After all that, his head spinning with possibilities, Rhodes sat down to begin drafting something. He planned to start with the best-case scenario, and got as far as the first line, but then stopped. *I can't*, he thought. *I might jinx this*. If he wrote a speech about them getting bin Laden, and they didn't, that was going to be an awful document. If he wrote one about not getting bin Laden . . . well, his heart wasn't in it. If he had to do it, he would, but he wasn't going to do it unless he had to. So he didn't write anything. He gave up and got ready to attend the correspondents dinner.

There had been some conversation the evening before about the timing. The dinner was the major black-tie social gala of the year in Washington: televised, and attended by celebrities from Holly-wood and the sports world, and by all of the most prominent govern-ment leaders and journalists. The main attraction was always the president of the United States, who typically delivered a stand-up comedy routine poking fun at himself and the press. If Obama chose the raid, it would likely take place at the same time as the dinner. How would it look for the president to be making jokes at a podium while the men were risking their lives? And what if something went wrong and everyone had to suddenly leave the party? Every journalist in Washington would realize something major was up. Then again, if they all decided simply not to go, it would alert every news organization in the world that something big was happening.

When someone floated the idea of asking McRaven to postpone the mission for a day, Clinton had heard enough.

"We are not going to let a White House correspondents' dinner drive an operational decision," she said.

That ended it. Obama told Donilon, "Tom, if it turns out that's when we decide to go, you'll just tell them I have a stomachache and I have to bow out."

The question of what to do about the dinner became moot when McRaven's weather experts predicted fog in the Abbottabad area for Saturday night. He decided to push the mission back one day. They would launch on Sunday night.

So in this tense moment, the most suspenseful of Obama's presidency, he and his staff dressed for a formal party.

Rhodes was so nervous that at first he decided not to go, but then he changed his mind. He figured if he stayed home he would just pace and obsess. The dinner would be a distraction. But it was strange. There were maybe a dozen people among the many hundreds in attendance who shared the secret. They were all throwing themselves into the party in an effort to forget the strain for a few hours, and succeeding somewhat, except when they would see someone else who knew. When Michael Morell spotted Rhodes in the crowd he gave him a slight pained smile that made him laugh.

Obama lived up to his reputation for cool. If he was anxious about the next day's mission, he didn't show it, garnering laughs as he poked fun at the long-running dispute over his origins and his own sometimes messianic public image, offering a supposedly never-before-seen video of his live birth, which, he said, he himself had never seen. It turned out to be a clip from the Disney movie, *The Lion King*, showing the birth of the future king on the plains of Africa — the clouds part and a shaft of heavenly light beams down on the uplifted cub. "Back to square one," Obama joked. Then he took pains to explain to the "Fox TV table" that the video was a joke, a "children's cartoon," he said. "If you don't believe me, you can check with Disney, where they have the long-form version." He skewered New York real estate magnate, publicity hound, reality TV star, and sometime presidential candidate Donald Trump, who for weeks had been loudly demanding proof of Obama's citizenship. The president then gratuitously suggested that Representative Michele Bachmann, a vocal critic and Republican presidential aspirant, might have actually been born in Canada.

There was laughter.

"Yes, Michele," he said. "This is how it starts."

Great care was taken to preserve the appearance of normalcy on Sunday. President Obama left for his weekly golf outing at Andrews Air Force Base, but this time he would play only nine holes. Arrival times at the White House for all of the top staffers and cabinet members were staggered. The principals were instructed to keep their security details at a distance — a thick herd of black SUVs arriving at the gates always attracted attention. They were told not to park in their usual spaces. The West Wing tours normally booked for Sunday had been canceled, which raised the suspicion of ABC TV's George Stephanopoulos, who understood the rhythms of White House life from his years on President Clinton's staff. He got wind of the cancellations and asked Chief of Staff Bill Daley what was going on. He was told there was a "plumbing issue." The Sunday tours were popular with the executive department staffers, who had a chance to show off their access by escorting family members and friends through the White House. Out-of-town guests sometimes planned visits around such perks, so the cancellations caused some disappointment. Obama's personal secretary had planned one for that day, intending to show around the cast members of the hit movie *The Hangover*, who had come to town for the previous night's gala. Rhodes got a phone call from her that morning.

"Can I just come in as an exception with these guys?" she asked.

"No," said Rhodes. No exceptions.

The National Security Council staff convened at eight o'clock that morning. The deputies met at nine.

Halfway around the world, it was already late in the afternoon in Jalalabad. McRaven had timed the strike to hit the target in Abbottabad at one o'clock in the morning, Pakistani time, looking for the moment when things would be quietest at the compound and in Bilal Town, and when his men would have the longest stretch of darkness possible to finish up the work, fly north to Kala Dhaka for refueling, and get out of the country. That meant they would depart from the base in Afghanistan at about eleven o'clock at night, local time—the force would pick up a half hour on the clock flying east into Pakistan, so they would fly for an hour and a half and arrive at the targeted time. That meant the mission would launch at two-thirty p.m. Washington time and hit the compound at about four in the afternoon. McRaven kept an iPad in front of him throughout the night displaying multiple time zones just to help keep things straight.

So as the assault force readied, the White House pulled itself together. Some key Obama staffers were being called in and informed of the mission for the first time. Jay Carney, the president's press secretary, was on an outing with his children and didn't notice the e-mail on his phone from Rhodes until an hour after it was sent. He forwarded the note to Dan Pfeiffer, the communications director.

"Do you know what this is about?" he asked.

Pfeiffer said that he had received the same summons, and, no, he didn't know what was happening, either.

In the Situation Room and the complex of small meeting rooms around it, staffers worked on setting up the videoconferencing. Panetta, who would officially command the mission from his conference room at Langley, would be up on the big screen relaying the running commentary of McRaven, who would be at his post in Jalalabad. High over Abbottabad, much too high and too small to attract attention, was an RQ-170 Sentinel, a stealthy drone with a high-powered lens, which would provide a live video feed of the assault. In his blue uniform, Air Force General Marshall "Brad" Webb, a broad-faced man with a crew cut and a chest full of ribbons, was testing the video links to it and to Admiral McRaven in one of the small conference rooms. When Donilon learned that he planned to move himself and the feeds into the Situation Room, he put a stop to it. Donilon did not like the prospect of Obama communicating directly with McRaven and watching the mission live. It might appear that he was micromanaging the raid. Webb would have to confine these direct links to the smaller conference room.

The principals convened at noon for a final review of the plans and the president dropped in briefly, wearing his white golf shirt and blue windbreaker. Each of the principals was given the plans for four possible outcomes, and each was tasked with making certain phone calls, depending on what happened.

Anticipating a long day and night, the table in one of the smaller side conference rooms was covered and topped with a heaping Costco plate of sandwiches, chips, and baby carrots and a tub of sodas and bottled water on ice. The NSC staff spent most of the early afternoon reviewing their "playbook," a large three-ring binder developed for an even broader range of possibilities. If something goes awry, who calls whom? How much of the intelligence case should be laid out after the fact, to explain why the action was taken? If trouble developed, which countries would they contact for support? Who would be the best person to reach out to, which Pakistani leader? Who had the best personal relationship? For instance, Admiral Mullen had a very good relationship with General Kayani. Who were the right people to leverage if the men on the raid found themselves in a bad spot? Did they want to put the president on the phone with the leader of a foreign country if this went badly? Whatever happened, there would be a lot of explaining to do with Pakistan: *Here's why we took the extraordinary step of not sharing this information with you. Here's why we didn't work with you.*

Success scenarios were easier. There were many more pages devoted to failure.

The president returned at two-thirty p.m., still wearing the white golf shirt and blue windbreaker.

*　*　*

In Kabul, General Petraeus paid a surprise visit to the JSOC situational awareness room.

"Do you know what's going on?" he asked Colonel Bill Ostlund, who was JSOC's liaison there.

"Yeah, we've got nine operations going on right now and a few more that I think will happen tonight," said Ostlund. His center monitored operations being run out of task force headquarters in Jalalabad, in case problems developed that needed the attention of higher command—typically a helicopter accident or an issue involving civilian casualties. The activity he described was the normal nightly pace.

The colonel knew nothing about the bin Laden raid but had suspected for a few days that something big was in the offing. McRaven had come up from Jalalabad for a short visit and before stopping in to see the commanding general had asked the colonel when Petraeus's office had last been swept for listening devices.

"Sir, I don't know if it has ever been swept," said Ostlund, and joked about the relative openness of the conventional army's habits compared to their own. "General Petraeus will probably have his window open and an Afghani right outside the window."

McRaven laughed and told Ostlund that he wanted him to stay outside while he met with the commander. This was unusual, since Ostlund had been in on every meeting with the admiral up until that point, even the most sensitive ones with the CIA station chief and Petraeus. So he knew something especially interesting was afoot, and since Petraeus rarely stopped by his ops center, he figured tonight must be the night.

"Why don't you ask the rest of your folks to leave?" the general asked Ostlund. "And then we can talk."

As the others filed out, Petraeus said, "They don't need to come back for a while."

When the others were gone, and they were sitting alone, Petraeus asked, "So, what do you think is going on?"

Ostlund guessed that either they were going to do a raid to try to free Bowe Bergdahl, an American soldier taken captive by the Taliban almost two years earlier, or they were going after bin Laden. He wanted to add Ayman al-Zawahiri, al Qaeda's Number Two, but he couldn't remember how to pronounce the name.

"Yeah, it's the latter," said Petraeus.

They sat side by side in the large windowless room, at the head of a U-shaped table lined with now-empty computer stations, facing a wall with eight different plasma screens. They received no video feed from the bin Laden raid because the CIA was running it, but both men could monitor the live chat from JSOC headquarters, the CIA, and the White House.

Petraeus commandeered Ostlund's keyboard and began tapping out questions to the various principals. At one point he directed a question to Admiral McRaven, calling him "Bill," which alarmed Ostlund. Petraeus's comments were being conveyed on the colonel's line, and he was not used to addressing his commanders by their first names.

He asked, "Sir, could you let them know that this is coming from you?"

With a final order from Panetta—"Go in there and get bin Laden; and if he isn't in there, get the hell out!"—McRaven launched the raid.

The two Stealth Black Hawks lifted off from the airfield at Jalalabad precisely at eleven p.m. local time. They were blacked out and both carried a full, minutely calculated load. Each of the

SEALs was in full kit: desert camouflage, helmet, night-vision goggles, gloves (for fast roping), and hard knee pads (better for dropping to a knee for shooting). Each carried a booklet with photos of the people they expected to find in the compound. They were armed with various pistols and short-barreled automatic rifles outfitted with silencers. They carried only light arms because the compound was not heavily defended. While they might encounter armed men once on the ground, there would not be many. Attacking loud and fast in darkness, with finely choreographed moves, able to operate in the night as if it were day, the SEALs would have an overwhelming advantage.

About ten minutes into the flight the choppers rose above a series of rugged peaks and crossed into Pakistan. As soon as they did, the three big Chinooks lifted off from Jalalabad. One would set down just inside the border on the Afghan side. The other two would proceed to the staging area north of Abbottabad by a different route. The Black Hawks eased down into the wide Mardan Valley, flying well north of Peshawar, moving fast and hugging the terrain.

The special operators of JSOC like to see themselves as "the point of the spear," and these two helicopters racing east in darkness were unquestionably that. Here was the final thrust of an enormous effort that stretched back over nine and a half years—further if you considered the whole modern history of special ops. The post–9/11 effort to find Osama bin Laden and his small band of zealous killers had engaged two presidential administrations and many thousands of people in America's military and intelligence communities: the analysts working in shifts, the CIA officers rebuilding human spy networks, and the combined satellite and aerial and electronic surveillance efforts of an alphabetical jumble of agencies and branches, developing drones and secure live telecommunication links, creating computer software, and honing strategy and tactics. If a nation must learn how to fight each war anew, borrowing from its existing arsenal, adapting, and innovating to meet the threat, then the SEALs on these Black Hawks were, in effect, America's response to the challenge of 9/11, closing in at last on the war's ultimate target.

McRaven sat in a large rectangular windowless room with plywood walls, surrounded by manned computer stations and looking up at a wall of video monitors. One monitor would show video of the raid itself—the Sentinel feed—but there was nothing to watch there yet. Another had a graphic display showing the location of the choppers. There was some tension as the two smaller choppers crossed into Pakistan, followed about fifteen minutes later by the two Chinooks, but none of them tripped alarms at that country's air defenses. With the full array of national security assets at his disposal, McRaven was able to monitor *exactly* what the Pakistanis were doing . . . and as the minutes went by it became clear that they were doing nothing. The task force had entered Pakistani airspace before, on covert missions into the tribal areas, so they had been confident they could slip in unnoticed, but it was nevertheless a relief when it had been done. The admiral had precalculated a point where, even if the Pakistanis woke up, the mission would proceed. Soon enough they had passed even that point. Now, as the blacked-out choppers moved toward Abbottabad, there was nothing to do for about an hour but wait.

At that point, McRaven knew he would have decisions to make only if something went wrong.

Up on the big screen in the White House Situation Room, Panetta read out occasional updates on the choppers' progress. One of Obama's aides said, "Mr. President, this is going to take a while, you might not want to sit here and watch the whole thing unfold."

"No, I think I'm going to go ahead and watch," said Obama. In Chicago, nine and a half years earlier he had watched 9/11 unfold in a crowded basement room, now he would watch the final act of that drama from another.

Biden was typically restless, moving in and out of the room, and when he noticed that the live feed of McRaven and the Sentinel were up in the side room, he went in and sat down to watch there. Webb was hunched over his laptop at the head of the table.

In Jalalabad, McRaven's sergeant major was sitting alongside the admiral, communicating on a chat line with Webb and others in the command loop. He looked up.

"Hey, sir," he said. "General says the vice president just walked in."

Secretary of Defense Gates was not far behind.

McRaven knew that the drumming chop of the approaching Black Hawks would be faintly audible about two minutes before they reached the target. The helicopters were stealthy, designed to avoid being spotted by radar, and quieter than standard models, but they still created racket when they were directly overhead. Approaching the compound from the northwest, the Black Hawks were now visible in the grainy overhead feed from the Sentinel.

After that, things happened very fast.

Everyone watched with shock as the first chopper, instead of hovering over the compound to drop the SEAL team from ropes and then moving off, as planned, abruptly wheeled, clipping the compound wall with its tail and hitting the ground. This clearly wasn't good.

The Night Stalker pilot had tried to bring his Black Hawk to a hover, but the chopper wouldn't perform the maneuver. It "mushed," or began to skid uncontrollably. An after-action analysis would conclude that because the compound was encircled by stone walls, whereas the mock target in Nevada had only had a chain-link fence, the air beneath the hardworking Black Hawk warmed more rapidly than anticipated. That meant the air density was insufficient for the precisely calculated weight of the aircraft. The chopper could stay airborne only if it kept moving, so when the pilot halted its forward progress it fell.

The pilots of the 160th train for frantic moments like these. The pilot of the faltering Black Hawk moved with practiced speed. He found a plot of flat ground to execute a hard, controlled crash. It was in the compound's western corner near an animal pen. He swung the craft's tail in that direction and deliberately used it to clip the top of the western wall. This pitched the chopper forward and into the ground. The landing was hard, but upright, which was key. In those seconds the pilot's maneuver had prevented the Black Hawk from pitching over on its side, which is a disastrous way for a helicopter to crash. If its still-spinning rotors strike the ground, the body of the chopper could be thrown or violently rolled. Instead, the nose was in the dirt. The SEALs were strapped in and were on seats designed to absorb a hard landing like this. One second the craft was skidding, and the next it was still, tilted at a forty-five-degree angle, its tail rotor hung up on the top of the wall.

No one watching the small screen in the White House, viewing the scene from far overhead, could see exactly what had happened, or even tell that the chopper was pitched forward with its tail hung up on the wall. They could see only that it was down inside the compound. They knew that was not the plan.

Excruciating moments passed as McRaven sought word from the scene. Every discussion of what could go wrong on this mission had referenced the helicopter that clipped the plane and exploded in the Iranian desert in 1980, and the helicopters that had crashed in crowded Mogadishu in 1993. Here in the first seconds of the mission, they had a Black Hawk down.

Obama had been following Donilon's advice up to this point, receiving mission updates secondhand, talking with Panetta via the video hookup in the Situation Room, and letting others monitor the video feed and chat lines in the side room, but when the chopper went down he abruptly got up and crossed the hall.

Clinton, standing over the food tray in the adjacent room with Ben Rhodes, watched him go.

"Ben, do you think it's a good idea for the president to watch this?" she asked.

"He's not going to be directing anything," Rhodes said. "It's just a feed."

Sitting at the head of the small conference table, Webb stood up to surrender his seat when he noticed Obama enter. The president waved him back down.

"I'll just take this chair here," he said, sliding into the corner. "I need to watch this."

The president's entrance was noted by Webb on the chat line.

In Jalalabad, McRaven's sergeant major said, "Sir, the president just walked into the room."

Clinton followed and took one of the remaining chairs at the table. Other staffers began crowding into the small room to see what would happen next.

* * *

In Jalalabad, McRaven was understandably preoccupied. He didn't have time to worry or watch the screen, or to explain things to Washington. He quickly ascertained that no one on the chopper had been hurt. They were already preparing to assault the target house from their downed position. All of these men had long ago proved their talent for adapting quickly to setbacks. This is why they had been picked. Setbacks were commonplace. It was the rare plan that survived even the first minutes of an assault. McRaven had lost helicopters before, and he had options at his fingertips.

Watching on the screen at Langley with Panetta and the other top CIA officials and bin Laden team members, Michael Morell felt a moment of panic when the chopper went down but was immediately reassured, as was everyone watching, by McRaven's manner. The admiral did not seem ruffled or even particularly surprised.

"Mr. Director, as you can see, we have a helicopter down in the courtyard," he said to Panetta. "My men are prepared for this contingency and will deal with it."

At the White House there was still no explanation of what was going on. Obama's face was etched with worry. A White House photographer snapped a picture of the now-crowded side room that would become famous: Webb at the center in his blue uniform, head down, intently monitoring the video feed and chat line on his laptop screen, trying to figure out what had happened; Obama seated in the corner with furrowed brow; Donilon standing behind Webb with his arms crossed, flanked by Admiral Mullen and Bill Daley; Clinton with her hand to her mouth; Gates and Biden looking glum; staffers lining the walls—all fixated on the screen off-camera.

Obama was as nervous as he had ever been. He knew the stakes were huge, mostly for the men in that chopper, but also for the country, for his administration . . . for him. He had persuaded himself that he was willing to accept failure, but to be staring at it in real time on the screen . . . he would later say that these were the longest minutes of his life, with the possible exception of waiting for word from doctors when his youngest daughter was hospitalized with meningitis.

When the first chopper went down, the second Black Hawk diverted from its planned course and landed outside the compound walls in a newly planted field. The mission had called for it to hover briefly outside to drop the translator, the dog, and four SEALs, and then move directly over the three-story house to drop the rest of the team on its roof. It seemed to the viewers that the entire assault plan had gone awry.

Then, abruptly, SEALs began streaming out of both choppers, inside the compound and out. The assault was on. The downed chopper had caused only a momentary delay. To their relief, those watching in Washington concluded that whatever had happened the mission was proceeding. In his flat Texas twang, McRaven ordered one of the two Chinooks waiting on the riverbed at Kala Dhaka to move up.

The team from the crashed chopper moved quickly along the inside wall of the compound, pausing only to blow open a metal door that led to the house. The team from the chopper outside the wall blasted in through another entrance. There were flashes of light on the screen. The men were moving on the house itself now, and then were inside.

Upstairs in that house, according to accounts given by bin Laden's family, the household had been startled awake by a loud crash. One of bin Laden's adult daughters ran up from the second floor to the third and was told to go back down. Bin Laden instructed his wife Amal to leave the lights off. They would not have been able to turn them on anyway, because CIA operatives had cut off electricity to the entire neighborhood in advance of the assault—darkness favored the SEALs. The Sheik waited upstairs with Amal in the dark.

One group of SEALs entered the garage area of the guesthouse. Teams like this had hit houses that were wired to explode, and had encountered people wearing explosives. When they encountered men, they were inclined to shoot on sight. There was a single brief spray of gunfire as they approached, but it was wild and ineffective. It had most likely come from the courier Ibrahim Saeed Ahmed—Ahmed the Kuwaiti.The SEALs returned fire, killing Ahmed and wounding his wife in the shoulder.

Another part of the team moved on the main house, clearing it methodically. Abrar Ahmed, the courier's brother, was in a first-floor bedroom with his wife Bushra. Both were shot dead.

They cleared the first floor room by room, encountering no further gunfire. They passed through two large storage rooms and a kitchen. No one knew the layout of the interior. When they encountered a locked metal door in the rear sealing off a stairway to the upper floors, they slapped on a small C-4 charge, blew it off its hinges, and moved up the stairs. Bin Laden's twenty-three-year-old son, Khalid, a slender bearded man wearing a white T-shirt, was shot dead at the top. There were wailing women and children on this floor, none of whom posed a threat. The team didn't know it yet, but there was only one adult male left in the compound, and he was in the third-floor bedroom.

Originally, half the assaulting SEALs were to have come down through the balcony into the third floor, in which case bin Laden would have been encountered immediately, at about the same time the Ahmed brothers were being shot downstairs. Instead, the Sheik had about fifteen long minutes to wait in the darkness as the SEALs methodically approached. Their rifles had silencers, and if none of the victims had fired he would not have heard the blast of gunfire by Ahmed and then shouting and crying and the sound of the metal doors being blown open. He might also have heard the muted pop of the SEALs' silenced weapons. The only windows on his secure third floor looked north, out over the compound walls. The downed chopper was in the western corner of the compound and the other had landed to the south, so he could only have surmised who was coming for him. He might have thought it was a Pakistani force. The assaulters blew off the door barring the third floor and he would have heard men ascending, coming for him.

The SEAL team started up those stairs in single file, scanning different angles, searching while protecting each other. The first man up spotted a tall, bearded, swarthy man in a prayer cap wearing traditional flowing Pakistani clothes, the knee-length shirt worn over pajama-like bottoms. The lead SEAL fired at the man, who retreated quickly into the bedroom. At the top of the stairs the lead SEAL tackled two women, likely two of bin Laden's wives, fearing they were wearing explosive vests. The second SEAL up the stairs moved into the bedroom and encountered the tall man in the prayer cap, whom he recognized immediately. Bin Laden stood behind Amal, his hands on her shoulders. As she moved toward the SEAL he shot bin Laden twice in the head. The Sheik fell over backwards, face up, and the SEAL fired one more round into his head. The team members who followed pumped more rounds into bin Laden's torso, but he was already dead.

The engagement was over in seconds. In these final moments of shooting, Amal was shot in the leg. Bin Laden had a weapon on a shelf nearby, but had not picked it up. His identity was unmistakable, even with the grotesque wounds to his head. His beard was shorter and grayer than the SEALs had seen in pictures, but the face was instantly recognizable. The architect of 9/11 had become the most infamous face in the world."*

McRaven heard "for God and Country, pass Geronimo. Geronimo. Geronimo." The word "Geronimo" was part of a coded "mission execution checklist." It meant the critical milestone of the raid had been passed successfully, securing bin Laden. McRaven conveyed the report immediately to Panetta, and it began to spread waves of excitement through the CIA and White House, and in Kabul where Petraeus and Ostlund were listening in. Petraeus pumped his fist with satisfaction.

In the White House, in the corner of the small crowded conference room, Obama heard "Geronimo ID'd."

The president knew the ID was still tentative, so he didn't let himself fully believe it. To whatever extent he felt relief or excitement or satisfaction . . . he fought those feelings down. To him it meant the SEALs could now start extricating themselves, which meant they might soon be fighting their way out. There had been a chopper crash and explosions at the compound. If the United States was going to have to defend the raiders on their way out—and there were fighters ready—it meant the worst part might still be ahead. Hearing the report, the president thought, *Get the hell out of there now!*

---

* Two varying accounts of these final moments have become public since the original publication of this book. The version given here is, for reasons I explain in the afterword to this edition, the most likely one.

But after McRaven had passed that along, it occurred to him that he had not asked specifically whether bin Laden had been killed or captured.

So he asked, "Find out whether it's Geronimo EKIA [Enemy Killed In Action]."

The answer came back, "Roger, Geronimo EKIA." So McRaven passed that on to Panetta and the White House.

"Looks like we got him," said Obama, only half believing it.

The delay between these two reports would cause some confusion in later accounts, which suggested that the SEALs had first found bin Laden, chased him, and then, a few minutes later, killed him. The finding and the shooting had happened in the time it took the three SEALs to crash into his room. Eighteen minutes had elapsed since the choppers had arrived.

McRaven told Panetta: "Look, I've got a Geronimo call, but I need to tell you it's a first call. This is not a confirmation. Please keep your expectations managed a little here." He explained that the adrenaline of operators was sky high on these raids. They were looking at everything through night-vision goggles. They were professionals, but . . . "Let's not count on anything until they get back and we have some evidence." Echoing the president's thoughts, McRaven reminded Panetta, and everyone else watching, "We've still got SEALs on the ground without a ride."

The video on the screen now showed SEALs emerging from the house, herding the uninjured women and children to one corner of the compound, away from the downed chopper. Some of the men came out carrying a body bag—bin Laden's body had been dragged feet-first down the stairs, leaving a bloody trail. One of his daughters would later say that she remembered her father's head banging each step on the way down. The SEALs eventually zipped it into a nylon bag. The assaulters moved deliberately, and Obama felt they were taking too long. Everyone was waiting for the Pakistani response at this point. The president just wanted them in the air.

But the commotion at the compound had, in fact, attracted little interest in the neighborhood, or the country. The translator, wearing a Kevlar vest under his traditional long Pakistani shirt, shooed away the few residents who came out for a look. His training to fast rope was for naught, since his helicopter had instead landed outside the compound. The dog Cairo was enough to convince most to back off. The translator told them sternly in Pashto to go back to their houses, that a "security operation" was under way. People obliged. Monitoring the Pakistani defense forces carefully, McRaven saw no sign that the country's defenses had been aroused.

There was much to do yet at the compound, inside and out. Upstairs, SEALs were hastily bagging bin Laden's papers and computer, discs, flash drives, anything that might contain useful intelligence—the site's pocket litter. Bin Laden's youngest wife, Amal, wounded, was helped down the stairs and outside, haranguing the Americans in Arabic. All four of the men who had lived in the compound, along with one woman, were dead. The surviving women and children were flex-cuffed. The women assumed they were going to be taken away. Questioned by an Arabic-speaking SEAL, the women confirmed that they had killed "The Sheik." One of the children confirmed that it was Osama bin Laden.

The Chinook summoned by McRaven now landed noisily outside the compound walls. Men were working on planting explosives on the downed Black Hawk and destroying its secret avionics with a hammer. A medic from the Chinook unzipped bin Laden's body bag, took swabs of blood, and inserted needles to extract bone marrow for DNA testing. Twenty more minutes elapsed before the body bag was carried out to the Black Hawk. One of the bone marrow samples was placed on the Chinook. The intelligence haul was likewise distributed between the two choppers.

Finally, the White House audience saw the downed Black Hawk explode with the set charges. The demolition team scurried to the Chinook and the choppers lifted off, leaving behind a huge blaze, a stunned collection of cuffed women and children, and four bodies. A photo purporting to be the bloody corpse of Khalid bin Laden would turn up on the Internet in the coming days.

Even with the choppers airborne, the tension didn't lift. They first flew north to Kala Dhaka to rendezvous with the second Chinook and to refuel the Black Hawk. Twenty-five minutes later they took off for the flight back to Jalalabad. All of it without any Pakistani response. When that country's air force did scramble two F-16s into action, the raiding party was safely across the border.

The choppers landed back in Jalalabad at three a.m. local time. None of the men who went on the raid had been hurt. They had lost a helicopter but they had avoided Pakistan's defenses completely. And they had killed Osama bin Laden.

The SEALs were certain of it, but the White House and the world would demand more proof. McRaven signed off on his narration for about twenty minutes to go out and meet the men on the tarmac as they lowered the body bag from the chopper. It was unzipped, and photos were taken and transmitted immediately to Washington and Langley. The man had been dead for an hour and forty minutes, and he had taken a shot to the head, so the face was swollen and distorted.

McRaven called Langley with a question for the bin Laden team.

"How tall is this guy?" he asked.

He was told, "Between six-four and six-five."

The dead man was certainly tall, but no one had a tape measure, so one of the SEALs who was exactly six feet four lay down next to it. The body was roughly the same height.

The president had gone back upstairs while the choppers were in flight and asked to be summoned when they landed. Early Sunday evening in Washington, he surveyed the first photos with other members of the team.

When Rhodes saw the picture he recognized bin Laden immediately, even with the wound. Here was the man who had called a press conference to declare war on the United States fifteen years ago, and who had inspired a trail of blood ever since. Rhodes thought, this is either bin Laden or a six-foot, four-inch, slender, dark-skinned man with a long beard who looked exactly like him, and who had been living in hiding surrounded by bin Laden's family, protected by a known al Qaeda intimate. It was bin Laden.

When McRaven returned to his command center, Obama asked him, "What do you think?"

"Well, without DNA I can't tell you I'm a hundred percent sure," the admiral said. "But I'm pretty damn sure." He said that the men were just beginning to be debriefed, but that there was some indication from the women interviewed at the compound that they had killed the right man. He reiterated, "Mr. President, I have fairly high confidence that we have killed bin Laden here."

Still, the president was inclined to be cautious. What would be worse than to announce that you had killed the founder and leader of al Qaeda only to be proved wrong? When Panetta, Morell, and

"John," the bin Laden team leader, arrived at the White House, Morell walked the president through the details of the agency's facial analysis, which had concluded with 95 percent certainty that the dead man was bin Laden. The president asked about DNA analysis, which would be even more conclusive, but Morell told him that the earliest they would get those results would be Monday morning.

Wouldn't it be best then to wait? Why take chances? It was now early Sunday evening. From his command seat in the Situation Room, Obama asked if they should announce bin Laden's death that evening or wait for the DNA results. Would the secret hold? Everyone agreed that the secret would not hold, not with Twitter and e-mail and the Internet and cable TV, not with the miniconflagration and dead bodies at the compound in Abbottabad, with bin Laden's wives and children in Pakistani custody, and with word now spreading happily from Jalalabad to Kabul and outward. If the White House said nothing, then who knew what version of the story would come out or what kind of conspiracy theories would take root.

"It won't really be true until we say it's true," said Obama. "So I'm not worried about it leaking out. We should confirm it when we are in a position to confirm it, but not feel pressured to do so."

No matter when the White House chose to make an announcement, it had to contact Pakistan and explain. No one knew how that country would react. The raid had been a clear violation of its sovereignty, and the fact that the United States, an ally, had not sought its help or consulted with it beforehand was deeply insulting. Still, as Obama explained to me later, "It would be easier for them to manage the fallout if it was definitive that it was bin Laden, as opposed to there being ambiguity out there for two or three days, in which case the whole issue of Pakistani sovereignty would be magnified."

So Admiral Mullen called General Kayani. The Pakistani army chief by then knew, of course, that there was a downed American helicopter in Abbottabad, but in those early hours of the morning in Islamabad, no one had yet sorted out what had happened. Mullen told him that the United States had conducted a mission and had killed Osama bin Laden.

"Congratulations," said Kayani.

The conversation went downhill from there. There was going to be trouble ahead between the two countries, for sure, but the general immediately helped resolve the question over when to make the announcement.

"Look, I've got a problem," he said. "There are all these stories about American helicopters and a raid inside Pakistan, all without a good explanation. It would be very helpful if you would stand up and say what happened."

That decided the matter. They would make the statement that night. Rhodes went to work drafting the comments he had not been able to bring himself to write the day before. Other principals picked up the playbook for a successful raid, each assigned to telephone a different world leader. Obama got on the phone to inform former presidents Bush and Clinton, who had hunted bin Laden during their terms, and British Prime Minister David Cameron, whose country had been America's staunchest ally during the effort.

Jay Carney went to work assembling the White House press corps for a special announcement. He and his staff started contacting reporters, mostly by e-mail. He told them, one after another, "Look, you'll want to be here, but I can't tell you why." Most guessed that Muammar Gaddafi had been killed—one of the Libyan dictator's sons had been killed the day before. No one guessed bin Laden.

But the news did break out. Twitter users from Abbottabad had been buzzing for hours about helicopters and strange explosions. A Pakistani computer technician named Sohaib Athar filed a report just as the SEAL choppers arrived over the compound, writing "Helicopter is hovering over Abbottabad at 1 a.m. (is a rare event)." Minutes later he reported a loud bang that shook the windows where he was staying nearby. There were other reports like this, but no one knew exactly what had happened until Keith Urbahn, a former chief of staff to Bush Defense Secretary Donald Rumsfeld, tweeted: "So I'm told by a reputable person they have killed Osama bin Laden. Hot damn." Urbahn quickly followed with, "Don't know if it's true, but let's pray it is." This was an hour before Obama appeared in the East Room to make the announcement, and the news was quickly everywhere.

In the White House, Carney was alerted to ESPN's *Sunday Night Baseball* broadcast of a game between the Phillies and the Mets in Philadelphia's Citizens Bank Park. The sellout crowd was chanting, "USA! USA! USA!" It was 10:45 p.m. The game announcers interrupted to deliver the news that there were reports that bin Laden had been killed.

Still, as Obama had predicted, it would not be true until the United States confirmed it. So he sat behind his desk in the Oval Office making last-minute changes to the speech Rhodes had drafted, and then he walked over to the East Room to give it. There were already crowds across the street in Lafayette Square celebrating and chanting "USA! USA! USA!"

It was 11:35 p.m. when the president appeared on television striding up the red carpet toward a podium, and began: "Good evening. Tonight, I can report to the American people and to the world that the United States has conducted an operation that killed

Osama bin Laden, the leader of al Qaeda, and a terrorist who is responsible for the murder of thousands of innocent men, women, and children."

He spoke about the attacks on 9/11, which were, he said, "the worst attack on the American people in our history," and which were "seared into our national memory." He spoke of how long bin Laden had eluded American forces. The president felt proud of his own contribution to the effort, citing his instruction to Panetta soon after taking office to move the priority of the top al Qaeda leaders "to the front of the line." He mentioned the national effort to oust the Taliban, but did not mention Iraq. He believed part of his own contribution had been to alter the misguided priorities of President Bush.

"Then, last August, after years of painstaking work by our intelligence community, I was briefed on a possible lead to bin Laden," he said. "It was far from certain, and it took many months to run this thread to ground. I met repeatedly with my national security team as we developed more information about the possibility that we had located bin Laden hiding within a compound deep inside of Pakistan. And finally, last week, I determined that we had enough intelligence to take action, and authorized an operation to get Osama bin Laden and bring him to justice.

"Today, at my direction, the United States launched a targeted operation against that compound in Abbottabad, Pakistan. A small team of Americans carried out the operation with extraordinary courage and capability. No Americans were harmed. They took care to avoid civilian casualties. After a firefight, they killed Osama bin Laden and took custody of his body."

He noted that the threat of attacks from this group had not ended, and pledged a continued effort against them, and he emphasized once more that the United States was not at war with Islam, pointing out that President Bush had also labored to make that clear. He accused bin Laden of the very thing the Sheik had worried about, his unwanted legacy: "Bin Laden was not a Muslim leader; he was a mass murderer of Muslims. Indeed, al Qaeda has slaughtered scores of Muslims in many countries, including our own. So his demise should be welcomed by all who believe in peace and human dignity."

The president thanked "the countless intelligence and counterterrorism professionals who have worked tirelessly to achieve this outcome. The American people do not see their work, nor know their names. But tonight, they feel the satisfaction of their work and the result of their pursuit of justice.

"We give thanks for the men who carried out this operation, for they exemplify the professionalism, patriotism, and unparalleled courage of those who serve our country. And they are part of a generation that has borne the heaviest share of the burden since that September day."

The president closed by invoking the spirit of unity that the nation experienced after the 9/11 attacks, and was reexperiencing briefly that night.

"Let us remember that we can do these things not just because of wealth or power, but because of who we are: one nation, under God, indivisible, with liberty and justice for all. Thank you. May God bless you. And may God bless the United States of America."

The night was not over for the White House. In Carney's West Wing office, Michael Morell, Mike Vickers, and John Brennan held a group telephone conference with reporters. Morell, who had been with President Bush on the day of the attacks and at the center of efforts to catch bin Laden ever since, now declined to answer most of the detailed questions about the hunt, but he did offer a convoluted summary off the top of his head about finding Ahmed the Kuwaiti.

"It was multiple detainees debriefed over a number of years," he said. "And then it was a composite picture of the courier network and this particular courier that we were interested in—that led us to this compound, and that came out of a composite picture and then was developed further through other intelligence means."

Morell saluted the cooperation between CIA and the military.

"You know, this CIA-U.S. military operation was obviously a major success, and it's a sign of the tremendous partnership that has existed between the intelligence community and the military in the years since 9/11. And it is a testament that the CIA is immensely grateful to those in the military who participated in this operation . . . We understand that the fight against al Qaeda continues, and that fight continues even as we mark the death of Osama bin Laden."

It was very early in the morning when they were done. Morell left the White House at about half past midnight. He heard the large crowd across the street chanting "USA! USA! USA!" and then heard something that this lifelong agency man never thought he would hear. The crowd began chanting, "CIA! CIA! CIA!" He walked out to his car for the drive home to his family. For the last two months he had been working sixteen-hour days and he hadn't been able to tell his wife why. Just that afternoon their daughter, who he had peeked in on at the end of that long day nine years earlier, had been in the last choral concert of her high school career. When he had left at six that Sunday morning, his wife had asked if he could make it.

"I can't come," he'd told her.

"It's her last," she said.

"I just can't," he'd replied, unable to explain why. She had not been happy about it.

Earlier that evening, when the president decided to make the announcement, he had phoned her at home, the concert long over.

"Turn on the TV," he'd told her. "You'll understand why you haven't seen me in the last two months."

Now he was eager to get home.

Carney and Rhodes didn't leave the White House until after two in the morning. The press secretary had some beers in the refrigerator in his office, and they had celebrated by drinking them. They heard the chants across the street, still going at that hour, and were surprised to learn that the crowds had grown so large that White House security at first would not let them drive out. So Rhodes walked home.

It felt like New Year's Eve. There were crowds of people dancing and chanting and singing. The streets were full of honking cars. Young women were standing up in the sunroofs waving their arms and cheering. It brought back all of his memories of 9/11, watching in horror from the Brooklyn waterfront as the towers fell. Most of the people celebrating on this night were of college age, in their late teens or early twenties, likely students from nearby Georgetown or George Washington University, which meant they had been children on the day of the attacks.

Rhodes himself was now thirty-two. Al Qaeda and bin Laden had been a dark shadow over all their lives. Now the shadow was lifted. In his own way, he had been involved in that fight from the start. He was not a soldier. He had not risked his life in the battle as so many in his generation had. He was not a shooter like the brave SEALs who had executed the raid, but he had brought his own talents fully to the effort. He had redirected his life, from deciding to work for Lee Hamilton instead of writing fiction, to helping to write the 9/11 Commission Report, to going to work for Obama—working to shape and articulate his thinking about the war, about who was the right enemy, and why fighting them was not only critical to the nation's safety but just and honorable. From that day in Brooklyn, to sketching out the president's remarks that night about bin Laden's death, the killing of bin Laden formed a full circle for Rhodes. It was the story of his own young life. And that night, walking home, he felt like he had won.

9

Glitter

Spring 2011

Finding and killing Osama bin Laden was an extraordinary accomplishment. President Obama had ample reason to be proud. But whose accomplishment was it? In his speech that night, Obama credited the "countless intelligence and counterterrorism professionals" who had labored over the past decade and more, spanning three presidential administrations. He also thanked the SEALs who had risked their lives in the raid, and who had pulled it off seamlessly. He also thanked allies who had cooperated for years in hunting down and interrogating al Qaeda figures, including, even with its violated sovereignty and the insult of not having been consulted, Pakistan. But the president reserved a large share of the credit for the accomplishment for himself.

"And so, shortly after taking office, I directed Leon Panetta . . .

"I was briefed . . . I met repeatedly with my national security team as we developed . . .

"I determined . . . and authorized . . .

"Today, at my direction . . ."

And all of this was true. Obama did deserve credit for making the search for bin Laden a top priority of his administration, for cautiously laying the groundwork for a raid that avoided killing outright innocents and minimized disruption in Abbottabad, and for shouldering a big risk, not just to the men who carried out the mission, but to his own presidency and legacy. Perhaps it is only fair that having accepted the very large potential downside of a raid gone wrong, Obama should now fully reap the rewards for it having gone right.

But his White House team soon began hyping and spinning a story that really did not need to be spun. They did what political professionals exist to do; they began working the story to their own benefit.

Small falsities began to accrue around the story like splashes of glitter. It started almost immediately. Sitting on the couch in Carney's office after the president's remarks, John Brennan told reporters, "The American team engaged in a firefight . . . Osama bin Laden did resist." He went on to say that the men in the compound "certainly had used women as human shields." The next day he went further, saying that bin Laden himself had used his wife as a shield, as part of an effort to paint the al Qaeda leader as cowardly and hypocritical — "Here is Osama, living in a million-dollar compound, hiding behind women who were put in front of him as a shield. It speaks to just how false his narrative has been over the years . . . he's putting other people out there to wage jihad while he is secure in his luxury compound."

In future interviews, Obama's oft-voiced conviction that al Qaeda was the appropriate enemy and his direction to his intelligence chiefs to move finding bin Laden to the "top of the list" would be portrayed as the impetus that led to finding him, after the previous years of futility. In conversations with me, a number of top administration officials used the expression "limited bandwidth" to describe how even high priorities within administrations can be pushed aside or even forgotten—specifically, how Bush's two wars had crowded out the bin Laden hunt. Obama had made similar comments in his speeches, particularly as a candidate in 2007 and 2008, when he argued that President Bush had "taken his eye off the ball."

Early on in the planning, Obama had insisted that the SEAL team be prepared to fight its way out of Pakistan rather than defend the compound and wait for the United States to negotiate its exit. This was a risky call, made for the right reasons. The president was placing the safety of American soldiers above concerns for preserving diplomatic ties with Pakistan. Approaching the mission this way, which had not been Admiral McRaven's suggestion, might have meant leaving in its wake dead Pakistani soldiers and police and downed Pakistani fighters. Making that decision had altered the planning for the mission, requiring the addition of more backup forces and other options. Members of Obama's staff, after the fact, would point to this decision as critical to rescuing the mission after the first Black Hawk crashed. Only because the president had insisted on a beefed-up backup plan, they argued, did McRaven have the ready recourse of a Chinook loaded with a Quick Reaction Force.

In the weeks after the raid, analysis of the documents seized at the compound revealed, as CIA and administration officials presented it, that bin Laden had not been the isolated, irrelevant figure some said he had become, but, rather, had been actively steering his organization from his hiding place, hatching assassination plots against Obama and Petraeus, for example, and setting in motion further attacks on the U.S. homeland.

Then there was Vice President Biden, with his special gift for the self-aggrandizing overstatement, now in the service of his boss, who would call the raid "the most audacious plan in five hundred years." Biden said that Obama had made this gutsy call after being roundly advised not to, suggesting that only Leon Panetta had been clearly in favor of it. He said Obama had "a backbone like a ramrod."

Versions of all this appeared in accounts of the raid and its aftermath. It was not a coordinated effort, just a cumulative one. Pulling all of it together, the official glitterized version of the tale could be summarized thusly. A bold new president resorted national defense priorities to go after bin Laden. At his direction, the moribund hunt was revitalized, and a new lead to the al Qaeda leader was found and developed. It discovered bin Laden living not in a mountain cave but, rather, like a millionaire in a "luxury" compound in a polite Pakistani suburb. Steered by the president in strict secrecy, the military was emboldened and directed to alter its plan to, in effect, surrender to Pakistani authorities if discovered, and instead to prepare sufficient backup forces to confront any resistance head-on—to be ready to fight its way out. It was this advice that saved the mission, because when a Black Hawk crashed, a backup helicopter was at hand. Surrounded by advisers who either were opposed to launching the raid or expressed deep misgivings, the president overrode them to order one of the boldest military actions in human history. The brave SEALs then killed Osama bin Laden in a firefight inside the compound, despite his effort to shield himself behind his wife. Documents seized at the compound revealed that bin Laden had been a hands-on leader of the terror organization, not just a sidelined recluse.

There is some truth to this version, but only some.

Start with Obama's direction to Panetta and Mike Leiter in May 2009, summoning them to that impromptu huddle in the Oval Office. The newly elected president did make it clear that he regarded the hunt for bin Laden and Ayman al-Zawahiri as the top national security priority of his administration. But did that really change anything? One senior intelligence official told me that it did not.

"This did not represent a big change," he said. "We were already doing everything we could, and had been for years."

Obama's urgency did have an effect, he said, forcing the various bin Laden team leaders to prepare regular progress reports. He also said that having Director Panetta so actively interested "tends to focus people . . . I think that requiring regular updates pushed our guys even harder, but I doubt that was the reason for the breakthrough. The resources available didn't change at all. Our focus on AQ senior leaders never suffered from a lack of resources, certainly not the hunt."

Viewed dispassionately, it appears that the trail to Abbottabad resulted not from redirection but from a slow grind. Each of the critical "breaks," such as learning the pseudonym "Ahmed the Kuwaiti" from several sources, finding out his true identity in 2007, locating him in 2010, and tracking him to Abbottabad, came as the result of steady, patient, unremarkable effort over many years. None of the breaks was even recognized as significant until the compound started raising eyebrows. Until then, Ahmed the Kuwaiti was just one of many, many thousands of possible leads, stored in a growing catchall database. The more remarkable achievement was *connecting* these disparate facts, and even then the sum of them led only to the residence of a man suspected of once acting as a courier and aide to bin Laden. It was because the

CIA had been following every lead for nine years that the compound was found, and because its analysts had been thinking long and hard about how bin Laden might be living—without heavy security, surrounded by his wives and family, with only one or two trusted aides—that they found the configuration of the compound so compelling. So the argument that it was Obama's redirection of effort in 2009 that led to bin Laden is true only insofar as every step on the road to success turns out to have been the right one. It was a factor. Obama deserves credit for it. The larger truth is that finding bin Laden was a triumph of bureaucratic intelligence gathering and analysis, an effort that began under President Clinton and improved markedly after 9/11 under President Bush. The effort was going to continue for as long as it took. It took just under ten years. It is hard to find one man in the wide world when he is smart about not being found.

It should also be noted this effort did involve torture, or at the very least coercive interrogation methods. The first two mentions of Ahmed the Kuwaiti were made by Mohamedou Ould Slahi and Mohammed al-Qahtani in coercive interrogation sessions. The third, the misleading characterization of the Kuwaiti as retired by Khalid Sheik Mohammed, came during one of his many waterboarding sessions. Hassan Ghul verified the Kuwaiti's central role during secret interrogation sessions at an undisclosed CIA detention center. It is not known what methods were used on Ghul, but the agency did seek permission from the Justice Department to employ coercion. There is no simplistic narrative of a hard-pressed detainee coughing up a critical lead, but there is also no way of knowing if these disclosures would have come without resorting to harsh methods. In the case of Qahtani, in particular, given his long and stubborn resistance, it seems unlikely. Torture may not have been decisive, or even necessary, but it was clearly part of the story.

Efforts to characterize bin Laden as living a cushy life in a "luxury" compound were not just false—they missed a far more telling point. The compound in Abbottabad was large for the neighborhood, but it housed four adult couples and nearly twenty children. By all indications, bin Laden's lifestyle, by choice, was a far sight below an American middle-class citizen. There are prisons in the United States with better accommodations—although none allow cohabitation with three wives. Far more revealing was his need to hide from everyone, even his own family and closest neighbors. Colombian drug kingpin Pablo Escobar, the most notorious criminal of his time during the 1980s and early 1990s and a fugitive from his own country and U.S. special forces, lived and moved openly for most of that time in his home city of Medellin, where he was revered by many. There are men the United States considers terrorists living right now in regions of Pakistan and Afghanistan who are revered in their own tribes and regions, and who live openly in them. Bin Laden had no place in the world where many revered him. Al Qaeda was not a popular movement in his home country of Saudi Arabia or anywhere else in the Arab world or the Middle East. It had its adherents, enough to turn out an angry crowd when provoked by, say, the publication of a cartoon depicting the Prophet, or a public demonstration of Koran burning by a buffoonish Florida pastor, but compared to the millions of Arabs who took to the streets to demand the vote in the spring of 2011, al Qaeda was nothing more than a small and violent cult. Bin Laden's "Nation" of like-minded Muslims was pure fantasy. If he had dared show his face in Pakistan, a Muslim country, someone would have turned him in, if not because it was the right thing to do then for the $25 million reward. It is possible that someone did, since the CIA has not told the whole story and will not say whether anyone has collected the reward.

Obama's decision to beef up the assault force, to plan for the possibility that the SEAL team would have to fight its way out of the country, did not save the raid. No JSOC mission like this one would proceed without a Quick Reaction Force close by. McRaven would have brought two Chinooks into Pakistan for backup and fuel anyway. The larger force commissioned by Obama, the soldiers and aircraft that would have been summoned if there were a significant response by Pakistani forces, stayed parked in Afghanistan throughout. They were not needed.

The president's decision to equip the force with enough backup strength to fight its way out of Pakistan, if necessary, said a lot about the deteriorating state of relations with that country. As one of the principals pointed out at the April 28 decision meeting, if the ties were so weak that this raid would break them, then they were not going to last long anyway. Coming off bitter negotiations to free CIA contractor Raymond Davis, Obama clearly did not relish the idea of negotiating for the release of two dozen SEALs—or, as he put it to me, "I thought the possibilities of them being held, being subject to politics inside of Pakistan, were going to be very, very difficult." McRaven had been running occasional raids into North and South Waziristan for years, raids that were officially forbidden but privately winked at by Islamabad, so he had every reason to believe that if his men were discovered in Abbottabad and confronted, something could be worked out. In weighing the repercussions of a mission gone bad, he made the entirely reasonable decision that dead Pakistanis would be more harmful to America's interests than a team of SEALs discovered to be someplace they didn't belong. The president felt differently. As it happens, the skill of the raiding force made such considerations moot.

When Obama decided to launch the raid, he was not acting against the advice of his top-level advisers. There was near unanimity for taking action at the April 28 decision meeting, with only Biden urging the president to wait, and with Cartwright and Leiter preferring to strike bin Laden with a small missile fired from a drone. Gates preferred the drone option at the meeting but had reversed himself by the following morning. All of the other top aides and advisers, principals, deputies, and staffers, particularly those closest to the analysis and planning process, unequivocally supported the raid. And as for Biden's "five hundred year" boast, it says less about the audacity of the mission than it does about the vice president's appreciation of military history.

It is worth noting one far more daring effort, thirty-one years earlier, if only because it is rarely appreciated as such. When President Carter rolled the dice on a long-shot mission to free more than fifty American hostages in Iran, even the men who went gave themselves only a 20 percent chance of success. The consequences of its failure—eight dead, another nine months of captivity for the hostages, Carter's loss of a second term—painfully illustrate how much of a gamble it was. Nevertheless, a year after the bin Laden raid, Mitt Romney, Obama's Republican opponent in the 2012 election, would take a gratuitous slap at Carter in diminishing the significance of Obama's decision, arguing that "anyone in the Oval Office would have made the same call, even Jimmy Carter." A stronger argument could be made that Romney himself would not have ordered the raid, since he had criticized Obama in 2007 for even considering to do such a thing.

Of all the exaggerations that followed the raid, perhaps the most interesting was Brennan's initial insistence that bin Laden had been killed in a "firefight" and had used women as "shields."

The White House subsequently backed off these statements, and the most obvious explanation for them appears to be a combination of three things: genuine confusion in the first hours, a completely unnecessary desire to boost the heroism of the SEALs, and the eagerness of an old warrior to paint his longtime enemy in an unfavorable light. Brennan had been on bin Laden's case for almost fifteen years, ever since he had worked as a CIA officer in the Middle East in the 1990s, and the success of the raid was as much of a personal triumph for him as anyone. So he gloated a little, before a worldwide audience. His comments proved to be an embarrassment.

Contrary to initial reports, there was no firefight at the compound. Based on my own reporting and the published account of one of the SEALs, it appears that after an initial burst of inaccurate rounds from Saeed, all of the shooting was done by the SEALs. It is important to note that the SEALs were fired upon initially, even if only briefly and ineffectually. The gunfire confirmed that at least some occupants of the compound were armed and resisting. Having taken this fire, the team had to expect to be fired upon again until the entire compound was secured. None of the other five adults shot in the raid—four killed and two injured—were armed. The raiders were discerning. None of the children were harmed, and only one of the three women shot was killed. It is difficult to second-guess men risking their lives in the rapid takedown of a residence harboring implacable enemies who had fired on them, in the dark, but available evidence suggests that if the SEALs had wanted to take bin Laden alive, they could have.

The Sheik had been upstairs for nearly fifteen minutes as the men approached. If the house had been rigged with explosives for a final suicide blast—and the presence of children argued against it—there would have been ample time for him to detonate before he was confronted in the upstairs bedroom. Amal's wounding and the need to move her away from the fallen bin Laden apparently prompted the claims of a human shield. According to published accounts and my sources, bin Laden was killed by several shots, one to his head, which knocked him down, and the others to his chest as he lay on the floor, apparently dying. Bin Laden was not actively surrendering, but he was not actively resisting either. It is reasonable to argue, under the circumstances, that if the SEALs' first priority had been to take him alive, he would be in U.S. custody today, and Obama would have his "political capital" for the criminal prosecution of the 9/11 ringleaders.

What is more likely is that the SEALs had no intention of taking bin Laden alive, even though no one in the White House or chain of command issued such an order. Indeed, it would have taken a strong directive to capture him to forgo the chance to shoot him dead. The men who conducted the raid were veterans of many raids, hardened to violence and death. Their inclination would have been to shoot bin Laden on sight, just as they shot the other men they encountered in the compound.

It is worth imagining, however, the alternative scenario. Bin Laden at the defendant's table before a judge and jury might have been considerably less inspiring to his followers than bin Laden the martyr. He might have proved implacable in interrogation, but often the more powerful, elder figures in an illicit organization are more amenable to compromise than their underlings. If he chose to talk to his interrogators, he possessed more information than anyone about al Qaeda, its organization and finances, its personnel and methods, its history and ideology, its ongoing projects. Having him in custody would have posed legal and political challenges, but as the president

explained to me, he felt such a coup might have worked to his benefit. So as satisfying as it was for millions of Americans to learn that
the world's most notorious terrorist was dead, and that his last sight
on Earth was of a Navy SEAL leveling an automatic rifle, a live de-
mythologized bin Laden might well have been a better outcome.

The documents seized at the compound revealed bin Laden
to be a determined and hectoring correspondent, still dreaming of
mass murder in America, but also clearly isolated, frustrated, and
out of touch with his group's remaining capabilities. The currents of
history had left him behind; he just hadn't accepted it yet.

All in all, these efforts to massage the facts about the killing
of bin Laden were nothing on the order of President Bush's show-
boat landing on the aircraft carrier USS *Abraham Lincoln* in 2003,
and his speech beneath the giant MISSION ACCOMPLISHED banner,
which set a standard for presidential hotdogging that will long stand
and will no doubt embarrass Bush until his dying day. In that case
the mission—the U.S. invasion of Iraq—was still decidedly unac-
complished, and would remain so for another long and bloody eight
years. In his memoir *Decision Points*, Bush suggests that the message conveyed by that event was not the one intended, but nevertheless concludes: "It was a big mistake."

There was nothing on that scale from the Obama White
House. Nevertheless, its handling of success illustrates the folly of
straining to take credit. Harry Truman said, "It is amazing what you
can accomplish if you don't care who gets the credit." The flip side
of that observation ought to be: "It is amazing how much credit
flows to the deserving who *don't* claim it."

Obama has apparently received lasting credit from the American people. His poll numbers jumped almost 10 percentage points
after his Sunday evening announcement, and a year later had leveled

off to a point slightly higher than where they were before. Killing bin Laden did diminish the perception of Obama as inauthentic, despite the efforts of his Republican opponents. The president's popularity remained high even among those who were disappointed in his policies. It also took away any hopes they had of portraying him as a pacifist. Having ended America's military involvement in Iraq and begun the withdrawal from Afghanistan, he might have been vulnerable to charges of "softness" on national security. Killing bin Laden placed Obama's commander in chief credentials on secure footing. It boldly underscored his punishing pursuit of al Qaeda's leadership. Even as this effort spread to Yemen, the number of terror attacks attributed to al Qaeda's various franchises has declined steadily. By 2012 the United States was increasingly targeting midlevel fighters, and the overall number of U.S. drone strikes steadily fell. There is no way to know for sure, but the numbers suggest a dwindling number of targets. U.S. intelligence capabilities have not themselves diminished.

Three days after the raid, in an interview on *60 Minutes*, the president said, "It was certainly one of the most satisfying weeks not only for my presidency, but I think for the United States since I've been president. Obviously bin Laden had been not only a symbol of terrorism, but a mass murderer who had eluded justice for so long, and so many families who had been affected I think had given up hope. And for us to be able to definitively say, 'We've got the man who caused thousands of deaths here in the United States and who has been the rallying point for a violent extremist jihad around the world,' was something that I think all of us were profoundly grateful to be a part of."

Killing bin Laden was not a feat of leadership comparable to launching armies across the English Channel or staring down Nikita Khrushchev at the height of the Cold War, but it was a clear military victory in an age that produces few of them. For Americans, it supplied the right hard ending to the story of 9/11, and will likely mark the symbolic end of al Qaeda, if not the real one. The organization itself was already reeling when its founder died, as much from the unfolding revolutions in the Arab world as the constant pounding of American drones and special operators, which is why bin Laden's death, or martyrdom, did not act as a spur to recruitment. Whatever romantic appeal his cause once had, and it never had that much, has been superseded. The popular election of Islamist governments in Egypt and Tunisia may worry the West, but the ability to effect change through legitimate means has undercut the pull of violent extremism. Bin Laden himself was wrestling with this problem in the weeks before his death. The group's methods had already alienated it from even like-minded Muslims. Ayman al-Zawahiri, the group's new leader, was still at large in mid-2012, but he exhibits little of the talent to inspire or organize.

Almost a year later, the president told me, "I think, internationally, it reminded the world that the American military is head and shoulders above anybody else, and that we can do things really well that nobody else can do. I think it reminded the American people that there are at least aspects of our government that can do things really well, and that when we put our mind to something we can pull together and fulfill our commitments.

"When I went up to New York for that small ceremony after bin Laden was killed, to talk to those guys at the fire station who had lost half their unit, and to meet with the children of those who had been killed in 9/11, and the widows and the widowers, and to just understand how fully they appreciated that America hadn't forgotten about them and what happened, the feelings were profound. The mission created some difficulties for us. I think it strained our relations with Pakistan, and we already had strained relations there, and so laid bare this tension, the fact that there are still safe havens inside the country. And so managing that has been a challenge over the last year. But this is one of those times where you make a decision, you're not sure that it's going to work out and, in retrospect, you can say that it did work out."

America's troubled relationship with Pakistan badly worsened for a time, and then worsened still more after a "friendly fire" incident in November 2011 killed twenty-four Pakistani soldiers. But the relationship, which, as Hillary Clinton noted, has long been based more on mutual need than on friendship and trust, has endured. Pakistan reopened supply routes to U.S. forces in Afghanistan in July 2012, and American drone strikes in Waziristan continued.

Pakistan held bin Laden's wives, children, and grandchildren for nearly a year and then deported them to Saudi Arabia. Under interrogation by intelligence agents there and by the CIA, the women revealed that bin Laden had been living in Pakistan for seven or eight years. He had moved four times before settling into the Abbottabad compound, and had fathered four children. If accounts from Pakistani authorities are to be believed, the al Qaeda founder's domestic arrangements were less than blissful. The eldest of the three wives with him, Khairiah, especially resented the youngest wife, Amal—so much so that she was accused by Siham, the third wife at Abbottabad, of betraying their husband to the CIA. If so, I found no evidence to support it. None apparently had any useful information to disclose about al Qaeda's surviving leadership. The compound was destroyed in February 2012.

The Pakistani doctor who worked with the CIA in an effort to obtain a DNA sample from the bin Laden children, Shakil Afridi, was arrested and tried for treason. He is serving a thirty-three-year sentence. Pakistan claims the conviction was for charges unrelated to assisting the CIA, but the doctor's imprisonment was roundly condemned by the United States and American authorities continue to work for his release.

"This is the man's passion, keeping children healthy," said one senior U.S. intelligence official. "He sets up clinics throughout Pakistan to inoculate children. We offered him money to set up an inoculation clinic in Abbottabad, not a fake one, but a real inoculation clinic. The money we paid him was put back into his program. He had no idea why we were interested."

A Senate panel voted to cut $33 million in aid to Pakistan in retaliation, a million for every year of the doctor's sentence. Senator John McCain called his work for the CIA "the furthest thing from treason."

On the Friday after the raid, Obama flew to Fort Campbell, Kentucky, to meet with the SEAL team and chopper pilots. Initially, the president asked to meet with the SEALs, and McRaven suggested that if he traveled to Campbell he could also thank the Night Stalker pilots based there, whose unit had not received the same recognition as the mission's shooters.

"We can bring all the players to Fort Campbell," the admiral told Donilon, and suggested that in addition the president could then also meet with the 101st Airborne Division, which had just returned from a deployment to Afghanistan. So Obama attended four events there that day, ending it with a speech to more than two thousand soldiers.

The first event was with the SEAL team and pilots from the actual mission. They assembled in a drab classroom on the base. Obama was struck by how "ordinary" the group was. With only one or two exceptions, the men did not resemble the bulked-up heroes of Hollywood action films, but a group of fit-looking men who ranged in age from their late twenties to early forties. There were some with gray hair. Dressed differently, he thought, they could have been bankers or lawyers. It wasn't their physical skills that distinguished them, he realized, it was their hard-earned experience and wisdom.

In the front of the classroom was a model of the compound. McRaven had said they would walk the president through the mission in detail. They would tell him everything, except which of them had shot bin Laden. That secret would stay with the team. The president did not ask, and the team did not offer.

Then the helicopter pilot who had so skillfully crashed his Black Hawk inside the compound stood up to speak. He was a tall, thin man with dark hair, who appeared unused to speaking before a group, especially one that included the president of the United States. He described exactly what had happened with his chopper, and how deliberate his crash had been. He explained that once he realized it was going down he maneuvered it to catch the tail on the wall so that it would land upright.

"Was the weather a factor?" Obama asked.

"Yes," the pilot said. The air had been warmer and less dense than the mission plan had anticipated, and then he explained in detail the aerodynamics that brought the Black Hawk down.

When he was finished the SEAL team commander spoke. He was dead serious and perfectly at ease addressing the group. He began by thanking the chopper pilot. "I am here today," he said, "because of the amazing work that this guy did." He then gave a long account of exactly how their successful mission had been "ten years in the making." The capability he and the other men in the classroom represented had been honed over all those years of combat, he said. Their skills and tactics had been purchased with the lives of many men who had served with them. He mentioned the operating bases in Afghanistan that were named in honor of these men. Every one of them, along with everyone else they had served with over the years, was, in effect, a member of the team. Then he explained how the raid's success had depended on every member of the team present in the room, and gave examples. He cited the skill of the pilot setting the falling chopper down upright. He cited the middle-aged translator who was able to turn away the curious people outside the compound.

"I don't know what we would have done if all those people had just started rushing the compound," he said.

He cited others. He even mentioned Cairo, the dog.

"You had a dog?" the president asked, surprised.

"Yes, sir, we always have a dog with us," the commander said.

"Well," said Obama, "I would like to meet that dog."

"Well, Mr. President, then I would advise you to bring treats," said the commander sternly.

The men in the room laughed.

The commander then walked the president through details of the raid. When he made reference to some of the errors and controversy in the press about the details, Obama dismissed them.

"Don't worry about it," said the president. "That's just Washington, that's just media, that's just noise."

Again, the men laughed.

The commander described how going through the house and encountering bin Laden had happened quickly and without complication, from his perspective. He said he and the men had been surprised by how much potentially valuable material was upstairs, and how they had just begun rapidly stuffing it into bags. Perhaps the most complicated part of the mission, he said, had been herding the wives and children to a far corner of the compound while the downed chopper was rigged with explosives, making sure that no one was hurt when they blew it up.

When the commander finished, the president stood and thanked them. He described how, among his advisers, there had been a wide range of estimates about whether bin Laden was in the compound.

"But early on in this process I came to terms with the fact that there was always going to be a fifty-fifty case on the intelligence side," he said. "I made the decision I did because I had one hundred percent confidence in your capability." He called them "the finest small fighting force in the history of the world."

Rhodes looked around the room and thought that the claim, while extreme, might actually be true. Here was the cream of JSOC, handpicked for this mission. Given the previous ten years of constant fighting, it was not likely there had ever been such a group of experienced assaulters, at least not in modern times. The president had earlier presented McRaven with a gift, a gold-plated tape measure, because he had not had one the night he tried to measure bin Laden's body. Now he presented the team with a Presidential Unit Citation, the highest honor the nation bestows on an entire military group. He then shook every hand in the room. He was startled and moved when the team presented him with a gift, a flag they had taken on the mission and had framed, signed on the back by all the team members. He hung it in his residence on the second floor of the White House.

When I spoke with the president in the Oval Office, he reflected on how drones represented the most remarkable new tool he had in fighting al Qaeda, and how the nature of drone warfare posed unique dangers for someone in his position.

"I think creating a legal structure, processes, with oversight checks on how we use unmanned weapons is going to be a challenge for me and for my successors for some time to come—partly because that technology may evolve fairly rapidly for other countries as well, and there's a remoteness to it that makes it tempting to think that somehow we can, without any mess on our hands, solve vexing security problems."

But nearly as remarkable, he said, was the evolution of small, highly skilled teams of warriors like those SEALs.

"I think with Special Forces, the dangers [of using them too liberally] are smaller because the human element is still there. Those are still somebody's dad, somebody's husband, somebody's son. When you send them in, you know they may not come back. And for me at least, as commander in chief, I don't think about that any more casually than I do when I'm sending some green kid off to Kandahar. I think there's just a solemnity and caution that that instills in me that probably won't go away. I do think that just from a broader military strategy perspective, that we can't overstate what Special Forces can do. Special Forces are well designed to deal with very specific targets in difficult terrain and oftentimes can prevent us from making the bigger strategic mistakes of sending forces in, with big footprints and so forth. And so when you're talking about dealing with terrorist networks in failed states, or states that don't have capacity, you can see that as actually being less intrusive, less dangerous, less problematic for the country involved.

"But ultimately, none of this stuff works if we're not partnering effectively with other countries, if we're not engaging in smart diplomacy, if we're not trying to change our image in the Muslim world to reduce recruits [to extremism]. It's not an end-all, be-all. I'm sure glad we have it, though."

Taken together, these capabilities, this weapon forged to fight the latest kind of war, has all but done the job. I asked what the impact of bin Laden's death had been on al Qaeda.

"It was what we anticipated," he said. "They are without focus, without effective leadership. And when you combine that with the degradation of their operational personnel, they're on the way to strategic defeat. But again, you can't overstate the importance of these other elements of American power, because even before bin Laden was killed, we had already seen the operational capacity of al Qaeda shift to AQAP [al Qaeda in the Arabian Peninsula] and Yemen. We had already seen al Qaeda metastasize into al Qaeda in Maghreb. And so the need for vigilance and stick-to-it-ness is critical.

"And what we've also seen is the capacity of lone-wolf terrorists to do damage—not the kind of damage we saw on 9/11, but damage that is still obviously painful, and we've got to do something about. So it [killing bin Laden] didn't solve all our problems, and we didn't expect it to. But it was a big piece of business. And I'll always be grateful for both the intelligence and the military personnel who were involved in it. They deserve all the credit."

In the days after the raid, an album of photographs was delivered to the White House, a series of shots of the dead bin Laden. There would be much discussion that week about whether these photos should be made public, as proof of death, but the president had firmly decided that they would not. The decision was made easier because no one disputed the fact of bin Laden's death. America was not, the president said, going to "spike the football."

As the White House had worked that Sunday night to get the message out, stumbling on the presentation but basking in the country's exhilarated response, Admiral McRaven's men were, in the early hours of Monday morning, at work preparing for the disposal of the Sheik's body.

After much discussion and advice, it had been decided that the best option would be burial at sea. That way there would be no shrine for the martyr's misguided followers. So the body was washed, photographed from every conceivable angle, and then flown on a V-22 Osprey to the aircraft carrier USS *Carl Vinson* cruising in the North Arabian Sea.

As a formality, the State Department contacted Saudi Arabia's government and offered to deliver the body to his home country, but bin Laden was as unwanted there in death as he had been in life. Told that the alternative was burial at sea, the Saudi official said, "We like your plan."

Procedures for a simple Muslim burial were performed on the carrier. The body was wrapped in a white shroud with weights to sink it.

The last sequence of color photos in the death album were not grotesque. They were strangely moving. A navy photographer recorded the burial in full sunlight Monday morning, May 2. One frame shows the body wrapped in the weighted white shroud. The next shows it diagonal on a flat board, feet overboard. In the next frame the body is hitting the water with a small splash. In the next it is visible just below the surface, a ghostly torpedo descending. In the next shot there are only circular ripples on the blue surface. In the final frame the waters are calm.

The mortal remains of Osama bin Laden were gone for good.

Afterword

Shortly before the first printing of this book last year, one of the
Navy SEALs who participated in the raid that killed Osama bin
Laden published his own account.

The SEAL in question, who adopted a pen name curiously
similar to my own, had held several long discussions with me in the
months prior. "Mark Owen" was leaving the service after a decade,
and he knew his story was valuable. I tried to talk him into working with me, but he opted instead to hire a ghostwriter and sell the
story himself. His book, *No Easy Day*, jumped on bestseller lists and
was still there the last time I checked. His decision prompted some
grumbling in the upper ranks about a breach of security, but I doubt
he regrets his decision.

It was only a small setback for this book. Just as Owen's book
does, *The Finish* ends with an account of the critical raid, but his
is a memoir, while this book tells a much wider story. Finding bin
Laden was the hard part. It drew upon nearly every resource of our
military and intelligence community. Deciding how to respond
once the compound in Abbottabad was found posed one of the most
difficult decisions the White House has faced in modern times. The
mission itself, after all that, was blessedly uneventful. Apart from

the crash-landing of a Black Hawk as the raid began, it unfolded as planned. SEAL Team 6 invaded the compound and encountered only brief and ineffectual resistance. They methodically killed every adult male inside the target house and then flew bin Laden's body out of Pakistan without tripping any alarms. All credible accounts of the mission itself agree in nearly every particular.

But not in every particular. After Owen's book was published, I made several hasty changes to the first edition of *The Finish* in order to accommodate for several of those discrepancies. His version of the raid was slightly different than the one I had gathered from my own sources. He was the first SEAL to publicly describe it, and he had to be taken seriously. Since then, another team member told his story to Phil Bronstein of the Center for Investigative Reporting. His account, which was published in *Esquire* as "The Man Who Killed Osama bin Laden is Screwed" (February 11, 2013), told a story slightly different than Owen's. I expect there will be more to come.

In early 2012, before any of this, I had a conversation with Admiral Bill McRaven, commander of the Joint Special Operations Command for the raid. It was part of my failed effort to gain permission to interview men who took part in the mission.

"What's in it for me?" the admiral asked, and laughed. He was not looking for a payoff; he was asking what larger purpose would be served by granting me such access.

It would be better, I argued, to have one definitive account than a host of differing ones. A story of this importance was bound to come out sooner or later, I said. It might be better for everyone if it did not drift out in competing versions from various sources. People remember things differently. I have experience sorting through the inevitable disparities and conflicts between individual memories in such cases. The admiral said he could see my point but that no such problem would occur with the bin Laden raid, because "None of my guys are ever going to talk."

The difference between the two versions we have heard so far boils down to this: each SEAL claims, in so many words, to have been the man who killed bin Laden. All agree that the SEALs were delivered to Abbottabad in two stealth Black Hawks, one of which was forced to execute a very skillful controlled crash inside the compound walls. Improvising their attack on the target house, the team members killed the Ahmed brothers and one of their wives at ground level before methodically working their way upstairs, killing bin Laden's son on the second floor, and then confronting their primary target on the third.

Owen places himself second in the line of SEALs heading up that last staircase. He says the lead man fired at bin Laden as he poked his head out a bedroom door, and hit him. Owen himself encounters bin Laden supine and dying of a head wound on the bedroom floor. He says that he and another SEAL then delivered the coup de grâce, firing multiple rounds into bin Laden's torso.

The *Esquire* version agrees more with the one I originally heard. In it, not Owen but a SEAL who is identified only as "The Shooter" is second in line coming up the staircase. The first SEAL fires at bin Laden and misses. He then tackles two women out of the entrance to the bedroom, fearing they are wearing explosives. The Shooter then enters the bedroom and comes face-to-face with bin Laden, who is standing behind his youngest wife, Amal, his hands on her shoulders. The Shooter puts two bullets in bin Laden's forehead, and one more in his head after he hits the floor, killing him. This SEAL remembers other team members coming into the room after this and firing more rounds into bin Laden's body.

Both SEALs were there, and there is no reason to believe either of them is lying, but I am inclined to place more weight on the *Esquire* account for two reasons: it agrees with the story I was originally told, which was drawn from debriefings of the entire team; and, it readily accommodates Owen's own memory. He recalls finding bin Laden on the floor, shot in the head, when he entered the third floor bedroom. It seems entirely possible to me that Owen thought he was the second man in line up the stairs, when he was, in fact, the third. Given the excitement of the moment, and the speed of action involved, it is easy to understand the confusion.

Any book about a watershed historical event is bound to inspire many different treatments and accounts. By far the greatest controversy has been generated by Kathryn Bigelow and Mark Boal's feature film *Zero Dark Thirty*. In the weeks after its release, it was targeted by what looked a lot like an orchestrated campaign of unfair criticism. The charge was that the film, in depicting harsh interrogation methods, tacitly condoned torture, and falsely showed it to have played a role in finding bin Laden. The film took home its share of prizes but was hurt by the attacks.

I found the film to be remarkably accurate, as Hollywood dramatizations go. It hardly glorified torture, as its critics claimed. Rather, *Zero Dark Thirty* depicts the failure of the ugly methods employed in the early years of the hunt for bin Laden and other al Qaeda figures. And so far as the facts go, torture was part of the story, although not a key part of it, just as the film depicts. Failing to show it would have left out the actual moral compromises that were made in the years after 2001 and that form a central theme in the story.

The Hollywood label "based on a true story" works as both a boast and a disclaimer. There was a female CIA field officer who performed heroic service in the ten-year hunt for bin Laden, and her fixation on "Ahmed from Kuwait" helped steer the effort to success. In the film, she is seen butting heads with an intelligence bureaucracy that regards her fixation on Ahmed as wishful thinking. This makes for some dramatic scenes and gives Jessica Chastain a great many chances to brood with ethereal intensity. The real-life Maya may be even more beautiful than Chastain, but she was just one of many officers and analysts fixated on Ahmed in an agency that never stopped regarding him as an important lead. There are small errors and some curious storytelling shortcuts. The raid itself involved four helicopters: two Chinooks and two Black Hawks, not the three Black Hawks shown. Key planning sessions that occurred in the White House Situation Room, chaired by President Obama, are depicted as having happened at Langley with CIA Director Leon Panetta—indeed, those who have accused the current administration of rolling out the red carpet for Bigelow and Boal in the hopes of hyping its role may be surprised to find that the president, whose participation was central throughout, has been almost completely edited out. The list could go on. The same is true of any film "based on a true story," whether it is the Jerry Bruckheimer/Ridley Scott version of my book *Black Hawk Down*, Steven Spielberg's *Lincoln*, or Ben Affleck's *Argo*, which defeated both *Lincoln* and *Zero Dark Thirty* for the best picture Oscar. Hollywood's "true story" aims only to color safely inside the lines of history.

The hunt for bin Laden and other al Qaeda leaders began with efforts that were clumsy, costly, and cruel. We wrongly invaded Iraq, for instance. We stupidly embraced a regime of torture in our military prisons. Some of the steps we took were tragic and are likely to remain enduring national embarrassments. But over the years, tactics, priorities, personnel, and even administrations changed. The nation learned how to fight this new enemy intelligently. Through it all, the search for bin Laden proceeded with bureaucracy's unique talent for obduracy. This is not as sexy or dramatic as watching Jessica Chastain paling before the stink and blood of rough interrogation, a red-tressed Ahab pursuing her lead through bullets, bombs, and boneheaded bosses—but it stays within the lines.

As for the real story, the question of what role torture played is clear. The key interrogation that focused the CIA's attention on Ahmed concerned Mohammed al-Qahtani, whose relentless months-long ordeal was detailed in a particularly gruesome WikiLeaks disclosure, a case that prompted the Department of Defense to rewrite its guidelines for interrogation. Qahtani said that Ahmed was a key player in al Qaeda and one of bin Laden's prime couriers, two facts that elevated him to prime importance in the search. Those who now say that torture played no role in Qahtani's revelations argue that he offered the information *before* the rough stuff started. I do not know if this is true, but I will accept it for argument's sake. It hardly removes torture from the mix. The essential ingredient in any coercive interrogation is not the actual infliction of pain or discomfort, but *fear*. There can be little doubt that before Qahtani was actually tortured, he knew damn well that he was in trouble. In the film *Zero Dark Thirty*, Ammar, who is a fictional amalgam, gives up the name *after* his torture sessions. Does this mean that the prior pain and discomfort played no role? In either case, real or fictional, torture creates a context. It creates fear. The only way to know if Qahtani would have been cooperative without being pressured is to have conducted a torture-free interrogation, which did not happen.

The most prominent among those who faulted the film's depiction of torture were Senators Dianne Feinstein, Carl Levin, and John McCain. All three have access to classified material and are in a position to know what they are talking about. Indeed, in a letter protesting *Zero Dark Thirty* to Sony Pictures Chairman and CEO Michael Lynton, they claim to have reviewed "six million pages" of intelligence records, which may help explain why Congress has such a hard time getting anything done.

But there is lawyerly subtlety here. In the letter, they raise the rather fine point about the timing of Qahtani's mention of Ahmed as proof that torture was not involved, and they write that the CIA "did not first learn" of the courier's existence "from CIA detainees subjected to coercive interrogation techniques." True. As detailed here, the CIA first heard the name from Mohamedou Ould Slahi, a Mauritanian who was arrested in 2001 at the behest of American authorities and questioned in his home country and in Jordan. He says he was tortured. I believe him. Acting CIA Director Michael Morrell, another critic of the film's veracity, has been more careful. He does not deny that torture was part of the story, although he uses different words to describe it: "Some [information leading to bin Laden] came from detainees subjected to enhanced techniques, but there were many other sources as well," he wrote. "And, importantly, whether enhanced interrogation techniques were the only timely and effective way to obtain information from those detainees, as the film suggests, is a matter of debate that cannot and never will be definitively resolved."

I am with Morrell on this. The story of finding and killing bin Laden makes a good case neither for nor against torture. It makes a poor case for torture because neither of the original sources, Slahi and Qahtani, necessarily realized they were giving up something terribly important by naming "Ahmed from Kuwait." It is doubtful they even knew who he really was. Neither they nor their questioners could have imagined that Ahmed would end up sheltering bin

Laden in Abbottabad. Khalid Sheik Mohammed could not have known this either, but he certainly realized the man's importance. Despite repeated waterboarding, he lied about Ahmed. So much for torture producing a breakthrough. Ironically, it was Mohammed's mendacity that further piqued the agency's interest—his claim contradicted everyone else's. Under torture, he lied, but his lies *helped*. The Senate Intelligence Committee has wisely declined to hold hearings on the matter.

The truth about torture itself is not clear-cut. Those who argue that it simply does not work go well beyond saying that it is wrong. They do not even consider it a moral question. After all, if threatening or mistreating a detainee will *always* fail to produce useful intelligence, who other than a sadist would bother? I am not convinced. I think the moral question arises precisely because torture can be an effective tool in interrogation. If we as a nation ban it, we do so despite that fact. We forego the advantages of torture to claim higher moral ground. In order for that be to a virtuous choice, as opposed to a purely practical one, it means we must give up something of value—in this case, intelligence that might forestall tragedy.

That is not the choice our nation made back in 2001, when this story begins. The fear that contaminated our military prisons in subsequent years became a scandal. It would be very tidy to conclude that because it was wrong, it was also useless, that it yielded nothing of value. Neither *The Finish* nor *Zero Dark Thirty* do that, nor should you.

There are likely to be more tellings of this story. It usually takes years for a full account to emerge, for details to be unclassified, and for participants to feel comfortable talking about it. In this case, I doubt that there will be any big surprises. I think it is significant that the only other eyewitnesses to the raid, bin Laden's wives and children, who were held by Pakistani authorities until their release in 2012, did not significantly contradict the story as it was officially told. There were so many people involved in the successful decade-long pursuit of bin Laden, and so many agencies involved, that the story has emerged from a great variety of sources, from Abbottabad to the White House. And why not? Success has many fathers.

Acknowledgments
and Notes

On the theory that Osama bin Laden's command of his native language was comparable to the average English speaker's mastery of his native tongue, I have taken the liberty of here and there smoothing out the clumsy phrases in the translation of bin Laden's documents by the CIA. The official translations can be found at the Web site of West Point's Combating Terrorism Center: www.ctc.usma.edu.

It has been my practice to compile detailed source notes for my books, but in this case the number of those who did not wish to have specific information attributed to them directly, even when the source seems obvious, would have made the exercise more frustrating than helpful.

This work has been informed by two excellent articles, Nicholas Schmidle's "Getting Bin Laden" (*The New Yorker*, 8/8/2011), and (in portions of Chapter Four) Shane Harris's "Killer App" (*The Washingtonian*, 1/31/2012). Anyone who writes about Osama bin Laden is indebted to Lawrence Wright's *The Looming Tower* (Knopf, 2006), and to the superb reporting of Peter Bergen, who over the last ten years made himself the foremost journalistic authority on the man. This book was particularly informed by Bergen's oral history, *The Osama bin Laden I Know* (Free Press, 2006), and by his *Manhunt* (Crown Publishers, 2011). In the latter book, Bergen recounts some of the same scenes I have described here, but those passages in this book, like the rest of it, are based entirely on my own reporting and interviewing — in some cases with the same participants.

I would like to especially thank my son Aaron, my cousin David Keane, and their company, Wild Eyes Productions, for help interviewing. I would also like to particularly thank Ben Rhodes, Jay Carney, Dave Moniz, and Preston Golson for helping me set up interviews, and also those at the CIA and in the JSOC who agreed to be interviewed but asked not to be named.